A Question of Technique

C000135107

A Question of Technique focuses on what actually happens in the therapy room and on the technical decisions and pressures that are faced daily.

Coming from the Independent tradition in British psychoanalysis, the contributors, a range of experienced practitioners and teachers, describe how their technique has quietly changed and developed over the years, and put this process in its theoretical context.

This book will appeal to child and adolescent psychotherapists, analysts and counsellors who wish to explore more Winnicottian approaches to therapeutic work.

Monica Lanyado is a training supervisor at the British Association of Psychotherapists. She is co-editor with Ann Horne of *The Handbook of Child and Adolescent Psychotherapy* and author of *The Presence of the Therapist*.

Ann Horne trained as a child and adolescent psychotherapist in the Independent tradition at the British Association of Psychotherapists. She lectures, supervises and teaches in the UK and abroad.

"This is a welcome and much needed book, describing how child psycho-therapists engage with troubled children, young people and their families, carers and the wider community. The reader is offered a unique glimpse of child therapists at work, how and what they say to their patients in the different settings in which child therapists now work.

The contributors, most of whom trained at the British Association of Psychotherapists – either as child and adolescent therapists or, having completed their child training elsewhere, undertook additional BAP training in work with adults – have as their theoretical and technical frame of reference the Independent tradition of British psychoanalysis. The authors meticulously spell out the 'whys and wherefores' of changing, extending or adapting technique to meet the therapeutic needs of those patients who are not susceptible to more 'orthodox' interventions.

Of all the pioneers of child analysis, it is Winnicott whose voice resonates most clearly throughout the book. It will surely become essential reading for teachers and trainees of child and adolescent psychotherapy. Seasoned practitioners will find much to refresh their thinking. It has also much to offer to other professionals working in the field of mental health.

The editors are to be congratulated on bringing together such wide-ranging and illuminating papers, which put the work and thinking of child psychotherapists trained and working in the Independent tradition firmly on the map."

Lydia Tischler, Consultant Child Psychotherapist, British Association of Psychotherapists

A Question of Technique

Independent psychoanalytic approaches with children and adolescents

Edited by Monica Lanyado and Ann Horne

Independent Psychoanalytic Approaches with Children and Adolescents series

Series Editors: Ann Horne and Monica Lanyado

Routledge
Taylor & Francis Group

LONDON AND NEW YORK

First published 2006
by Routledge
27 Church Road, Hove, East Sussex BN3 2FA

Simultaneously published in the USA and Canada
by Routledge
270 Madison Avenue, New York, NY 10016

*Routledge is an imprint of the Taylor & Francis Group, an informa
business*

Typeset in Times by Garfield Morgan, Mumbles, Swansea

Paperback cover design by Sandra Heath

British Library Cataloguing in Publication Data
A catalogue record for this book is available from the British Library

Library of Congress Cataloging-in-Publication Data
A question of technique : independent psychoanalytic approaches with
   children and adolescents / edited by Monica Lanyado & Ann Horne.
      p. cm.
   Includes biographical references and index.
   ISBN 0-415-37913-X – ISBN 0-415-37915-6 (pbk.)
   1. Child analysis. 2. Adolescent analysis. 3. Child psychotherapy.
   4. Adolescent psychotherapy. I. Lanyado, Monica, 1949– II.
   Horne, Ann, 1944–

   RJ504.2.Q84 2006
                                                        2005056282

ISBN13: 978-0-415-37913-7 (hbk)
ISBN13: 978-0-415-37915-1 (pbk)

ISBN10: 0-415-37913-X (hbk)
ISBN10: 0-415-37915-6 (pbk)

Contents

Contributors

Teresa Bailey is Principal Child and Adolescent Psychotherapist employed by the South London and Maudsley NHS Trust. Trained at the British Association of Psychotherapists, she is based in the Belgrave Department of Child and Adolescent Psychiatry in King's College Hospital and in the Southwark Child and Family Service in Peckham. Her particular interests are depressed and traumatised children and adolescents and young people with chronic physical illness.

Bernard Barnett is a Fellow of the Institute of Psychoanalysis, a member and training and supervising analyst of the British Psychoanalytic Society. He is a Child and Adolescent Psychoanalyst and former Chair of the Education Committee of the Institute. He was Director of Psychology Training at the Child Guidance Training Centre, Tavistock Clinic, and Director of Psychology Training at the Tavistock Children and Parents Department. He has a special interest in Independent thinking and is currently Director of the Squiggle Foundation, which seeks to promote the work of Donald Winnicott. He has recently completed a book on the superego, theory and application in analytic practice.

Deirdre Dowling is Head Child Psychotherapist at the Cassel Hospital. She trained at the British Association of Psychotherapists. Previously she worked as a social worker, manager and trainer in child care. She has a particular interest in parent work, working with severely deprived families, and teaching and consulting to other professionals interested in applying psychoanalytic ideas to their work with families.

Iris Gibbs trained as a psychoanalytic child and adolescent psychotherapist with the British Association of Psychotherapists. She has worked for many years with children in care with the Integrated Support Programme (ISP) and more recently in the parent–infant project at the Anna Freud Centre. She lectures and runs seminars on infant development and has a special interest on the impact of race and culture on development.

Victoria Hamilton trained as a child and adolescent psychotherapist at the Tavistock Clinic, and completed her adult training at the Los Angeles

Institute of Psychoanalytic Studies. She emigrated to the US, where she worked in private practice for 20 years. A training and supervising analyst at the Institute for Contemporary Psychoanalysis in Los Angeles, she has lectured widely throughout the US and in training programmes in LA. She is author of many papers and reviews, and two books – *Narcissus and Oedipus* (1982) and *The Analyst's Preconscious* (1996). She currently lives in New York and is on the faculty of the Parent-Infant programme, Columbia University Centre for Psychoanalytic Training and Research.

Juliet Hopkins trained as a psychoanalytic child and adolescent psychotherapist at the Tavistock Clinic and worked on the staff of the Child Guidance Training Centre and the Tavistock Clinic until her recent retirement from the National Health Service. She has continued to teach at the Tavistock where she is an honorary consultant child psychotherapist. Juliet also trained as an adult psychotherapist at the British Association of Psychotherapists and works in private practice. She has published a variety of papers on themes concerned with child psychotherapy and infant development.

Ann Horne is a member of the British Association of Psychotherapists and the Scottish Institute of Human Relations (SIHR) and an Honorary Member of ČSPAP, the Czech Society for Psychoanalytic Psychotherapy. Trained as a child and adolescent psychotherapist at the BAP, she served terms of office as head of training and later of postgraduate development. A previous joint editor of the *Journal of Child Psychotherapy*, she is co-editor with Monica Lanyado of *The Handbook of Child and Adolescent Psychotherapy: Psychoanalytic Approaches* (1999). Recently retired from the Portman Clinic in London, she has a particular interest in the child's use of the body in delinquency, abusing or seemingly seeking perverse solutions.

Anne Hurry is a member of staff at the Anna Freud Centre where she is a clinical consultant and supervisor. She was the founding Chair of the Child Psychotherapy Training at the British Association of Psychotherapists where she is also a supervising and training therapist for the Adult Psychoanalytic Psychotherapy Training. She is a past editor of the *Journal of Child Psychotherapy* and has published widely on both clinical and theoretical topics. She is editor of *Psychoanalysis and Developmental Therapy* (1998).

Monica Lanyado trained at the Tavistock Clinic and was the founding Course Organising Tutor of the Child and Adolescent Psychotherapy Training at the Scottish Institute of Human Relations. She is a training supervisor at the British Association of Psychotherapists. She is a consultant to a Childhood First Therapeutic Unit and works in private practice in London. Monica is a former co-editor of the *Journal of Child*

Psychotherapy and is joint editor with Ann Horne of *The Handbook of Child and Adolescent Psychotherapy: Psychoanalytic Approaches* (1999). Her book *The Presence of the Therapist: Treating Childhood Trauma* was published in 2004.

Maria Pozzi trained at the Tavistock Clinic as a child and adolescent psychotherapist and at the British Association of Psychotherapists as an adult psychotherapist. She has special interests in treating children with autism, Asperger's syndrome and mental handicap, and in brief work with children under five. She has published and contributed papers to books on a wide variety of subjects and was the winner of the 1999 Frances Tustin Memorial Prize. Her book *Psychic Hooks and Bolts: Psychoanalytic Work with Children Under Five and their Families* was published in 2003.

Janine Sternberg trained as a child psychotherapist at the Tavistock Clinic and subsequently as an adult psychotherapist at the British Association of Psychotherapists. She is very involved with teaching and the organisation of training at the BAP. For many years she was the consultant child psychotherapist at the Tavistock Mulberry Bush Day Unit, a small unit for children with complex difficulties. She now works at the Portman Clinic. Her book *Infant Observation at the Heart of Training* (2005) addresses what capacities and skills are needed for psychotherapeutic work and how these may be enhanced by infant observation. She is currently co-editor of the *Journal of Child Psychotherapy*.

Foreword

Bernard Barnett

The psychoanalysts and psychotherapists who align themselves with the Independents (formerly entitled 'the Middle Group') of the British Psychoanalytic Society, adopt a theoretical position somewhere between the Contemporary Freudian group (formerly 'the Anna Freudians') and the followers of Melanie Klein. This tradition favours learning from experience and an attitude to clinical practice which is summed up in the phrase 'evaluate and respect ideas for their use and truth value no matter whence they come'.[1]

This theoretical stance has a number of advantages which are outlined below, but it also has some drawbacks. These arise from the absence of a unified system of thought, a definitive set of concepts and a recommended analytic technique. Independents are accused by some colleagues of not having 'a proper system', of being too eclectic (i.e. in the sense of being 'wishy-washy') and, therefore, of having no effective technical method. This results in some Independents (especially trainees) feeling themselves to be disadvantaged, and of having 'a hard life'. These colleagues may sometimes suffer anxiety and indecision and experience feelings of envy towards other groups.[2]

It is a great pleasure and privilege to be associated with the authors of *A Question of Technique: Independent Psychoanalytic Approaches with Children and Adolescents*, since they are untroubled by these feelings, or rather, if not, they have found a creative solution to them. In this book they set out to, and successfully, describe in detail some principles of 'Independent' theory and its application to child psychotherapy. Though there are many publications which relate to work with adults, those which focus on children are few in number and the present work is both timely in its content and stimulating in its style.

The therapists, who are all experienced clinicians, were originally trained in different psychoanalytic traditions, but their written contributions suggest that, following work in many different settings, they now have much in common. For example, they share above all a certain flexibility in their approach to their patients, a readiness to challenge custom and tradition and a willingness to experiment with new ideas, concepts and techniques. I found this attitude to practice both refreshing and informative.

I am aware, from my own teaching experience, how even in the best and most thorough initial child psychotherapy training programmes (with their focus on the inner world), students, when they qualify, often emerge into the real world with a feeling that, though they have been well prepared for sailing on the Hampstead ponds, they have now to face and cope with the vicissitudes and unpredictability of the Atlantic ocean. In contrast these contributions are aimed to acquaint the reader with the complexities and hazards of real-life situations.

If we can accept the peculiar paradox of an 'Independent ego ideal', which these therapists follow, it seems to me to be found in a kind of sequential learning pattern. In abstract terms this can be summed up as an empirical process in which the therapist becomes subjectively engaged in a repeated pattern of observation, reflection, evaluation, intervention, response, observation, etc. This process is not tightly bound to a single theory. What the authors succeed in doing is to flesh out this skeletal process and show how, by their intimate engagement with the patient and others *in situ*, a therapeutic process may be established.

The first and most striking feature of the contributions is the spirit of open-mindedness which is on display. In their pursuit of analytic truth, the authors are engaged in a creative interplay of the views of different theoreticians, and it is this which is the very essence of Independent psychoanalytic inquiry. Building on the great tradition of psychoanalysis established by Freud, and of child analysis by Anna Freud and Melanie Klein, they draw on the many, seminal contributions from the British Object Relations school and other sources. To this is added the more recent advances contributed by research in infant development and attachment theory. In the application of this rich body of ideas perhaps the most important quality of this open stance is a tendency not to move too quickly towards theoretical closure.

A second significant feature is the focus on 'technique' which is neatly defined by one contributor as 'finding one's own voice and style'. What is demonstrated is that in the practice of child therapy, a repertoire of 'techniques' tends to evolve in the light of experience. This means that the theoretical viewpoints originally held by the therapist come to be modified as a result of the complexity of the context in which the children and parents are referred and seen. Faced with differences of situation and circumstance, the thinking and practice tends towards greater plurality and variety. In summary, the authors' thesis is that the most effective approach to the internal world of the child requires a sensitive adaptation to specific, external forces on the part of the therapist.

Thirdly, many of these contributions emphasise that therapeutic change does not necessarily occur through transference interpretation alone. What is suggested is that it often occurs through a combination of a benign unfolding of the analytic process, influenced by the setting, silences, breaks, 'being alone in the presence of the other', etc., all of which interact with the therapist's interpretative activity. One example is given of a narcissistic adolescent patient who became caught up in a severe transference illusion. A process is described in which 'the narcissistic transference' was allowed 'to flourish long enough to begin its spontaneous dissolution'. Another therapist writes revealingly of the value of 'interpretation within the holding environment', which is used to produce 'a verbal crystallisation of shared experiences'. Perhaps most crucial from the viewpoint of many Independents is the observation that 'the interpretation that is most useful to the patient is the one the patient finds in the therapeutic process for himself'.

Interested readers who search in this book for a guide to practice will find rich pickings and much to stimulate their work and their thinking. In what follows, I shall give some examples of the richness and creativity of what is on offer.

In the discussion of their work, the authors freely introduce new concepts taken from a variety of sources. In referring, for example, to 'cognitive bias', 'selective exclusion', 'learned responsiveness' and 'the grammar of imperatives' they provide interesting food for thought which can be added to the more traditional psychoanalytic concepts.[3] At the same time it is interesting to find that some older concepts, which have in some quarters fallen into disuse, are re-established. One example is that of 'the working alliance' which is defined as 'a basic willingness of the patient to attend and become involved and which implies a sufficient degree of trust and mutual interest'.

In many of the contributions, the authors stress the value of playfulness in the therapist. They also discuss the provision of toys, the nature of the therapist's participation and the approach to interpretation, all of which are potentially controversial issues. As in other matters, they tend to favour a flexible approach, tailored to the needs of the patient and the complexities of the environment and the 'Here and Now' situation. They provide illuminating descriptions of the problems posed (e.g. the management of deprived or abused children who cannot play because their quiet activity, their 'going-on-being', is overwhelmed by physical excitement). In many of the contributions, Winnicott's work and ideas are much in evidence and are used to provide an inspiring basis for work with disturbed children. A particularly valuable discussion revolves around the concept of the therapist being 'playfully present' in the session. It is noteworthy that the value of therapeutic 'playfulness' is also discussed not only in relation to children, but also in work with supervisees. I particularly enjoyed one example of a light and playful combination of words in the suggested interpretation: 'You wouldn't want to miss me too much!'

In this book there is much concern with the skilled use of the counter-transference. We are told, for example, how in work with mothers and infants, when anxiety is at a high level and communication is mainly non-verbal, the therapist's own somatic response may provide a significant diagnostic clue as to the nature of an infant's distress. In an account of 'in-care situations', the management technique may include 'holding the counter-transference' in the professional carers. We are also shown how, in work with the parents of troubled teenagers, the therapist's experience of intense feelings of despair, de-skilling and hopelessness can be utilised to give the parents insight.

In fact, much of the rich content of these contributions concerns parents. The degree to which the therapist, when treating a child, should be directly in touch with parents and others is clearly another potential source of controversy. When working with deprived and disturbed parents, the need for a balanced attitude in the therapist between under- and over-identification is emphasised. We are given interesting and informative accounts of short-term parent–infant psychotherapy, which aims to put mothers in touch with their own distress, and which leads to beneficial effects for the infant. We are shown how the mother's unique response to the birth of her child often reveals her vulnerability, which may then become a focus for the treatment. Where 'an internal map of motherhood' is missing, the therapist strives to establish such an essential framework for the mother–infant interaction.

There are many descriptions of the treatment and problems of working with children in special settings (i.e. 'looked-after children' who are being fostered, or in the care of the local authority). The case material of these 'children in transition' provides valuable illustrations of the complexity of the split-transference situations and the skilful management of the complex transference reactions, not only coming from the child, but from the 'carers' in the network of relationships.

I turn now to consider to what extent the contributors succeed in differentiating their theoretical positions and practice from the way other therapists of a differing orientation think and work. This is not an easy question to answer. Take the issue of open-mindedness that I have emphasised above. It would probably be difficult to find a therapist who would not lay claim to being open-minded in the pursuit of her craft and the ideas that underpin it. Also much of what the authors describe as 'good practice' seems to me open to a response from a colleague of the kind: 'Well I think and work that way and I am not an Independent!'

Though I can understand such comments and even sympathise with them, I think there are significant differences among child therapists in their ways of thinking and working. However, the hidden attitude and aims of a therapist are often more subtle than obvious and in any case are not easy to put into words. It is also not a simple matter to describe what actually happens in a session, or how a complex environmental situation was actually managed. If I had to sum up in one line the viewpoint of the therapists who have written this book, it would be 'Becoming the therapist that the patient needs'. For greater clarification of this issue, I can only recommend a thorough reading of their contributions.

It will be clear from the above that I think there is much to be learnt from the approach of these authors. Their work will not only prove of great value to like-minded colleagues, but it provides in itself 'a reflective space' that can be used for contemplation by child and adolescent psychotherapists of all theoretical persuasions. Indeed, because the authors' thinking and the description of their practice has been spelt out in considerable detail, an opportunity is given to compare and contrast other approaches and orientations which originate both in and outside the United Kingdom.

Finally, I would add that, though the contributors are sometimes quite rightly at pains to clarify the important differences between child and adult therapeutic work (e.g. proxy consent, physical contact, the involvement of parents, etc.), the therapist who treats adults will nevertheless find much of relevance which is clinically helpful. Again and again, I found myself noting in the margin of the manuscript 'But that is also true of my adult patient!' In short, these articles can be read with great profit by all analysts, therapists, counsellors and all who work with patients and clients of any age.

Notes

1 E. Rayner, *The Independent Mind in British Psychoanalysis* (London: Free Association, 1990)
2 A. Limentani, *Between Freud and Klein* (London: Free Association, 1989)
3 J. Bowlby, *Loss: Sadness and Depression. Attachment and Loss*, vol. 3 (London: Hogarth and Penguin; New York: Basic Books, 1980) and A. Alvarez, 'Projective Identification as a Communication: Its Grammar in Borderline Psychotic Children', *Psychoanalytic Dialogues* 7 (6) (1997): 753–68

Acknowledgements

Amongst those to whom the authors are indebted are Charlotte Jarvis and the staff, adolescents and families of Open Door; the staff and patients at the Cassel Hospital; the children and young people from whom we learn daily; and the supervisors and teachers who allowed us to find our own way within the broad containment that is psychoanalytic understanding.

Particular thanks are due: to the editors and publishers of the *Journal of Child Psychotherapy* (tandf.co.uk) for permission to reproduce A. Horne's 'Brief communications from the edge' from volume 27, (1) (2001); to the editor and publishers of the *British Journal of Psychotherapy* for permission to reproduce V. Hamilton's 'The concept of mourning and its roots in infancy' from volume 3, (3) (1988); to the editors and publishers of the *Journal of the British Association of Psychotherapists* for the use of extracts from 'Some reflections on the differences between child and adult psychotherapy' from volume 42, (1) (2004); to the editors and publishers of *Psychoanalytic Inquiry* for permission to reproduce J. Hopkins' 'Narcissistic illusions in late adolescence'. Janine Sternberg's book *Infant Observation at the Heart of Training* was published by Karnac in 2005: her chapter in this volume develops ideas from that book and we thank Karnac for granting permission for this.

In presenting work from the BAP and friends, we would like to offer particular thanks to those Contemporary Freudians and post-Kleinians who joined with Independents to start the first UK Independent Child and Adolescent Psychotherapy training in 1982. And we thank those today, trained in other theoretical traditions, who enjoy close encounters of the psychoanalytic kind with those who might do it a little differently.

Monica Lanyado and Ann Horne

A note on confidentiality

At the very heart of any therapeutic contact is the need to protect the privacy of the client – adult or child. When working with an adult, the boundaries of privacy are usually fairly straightforward as contact between the therapist and other people in the patient's life is likely to be minimal. However, with children there is often an equally important need for the therapist to be in contact with the key adults in the child's life – parents and foster parents in particular, but also teachers, social workers, residential workers and medical staff. The multidisciplinary team plays a very important role in the child's treatment as does the work with the parents and the rest of the family. In practice, issues of confidentiality are worked out within the guidelines of the Code of Ethics of the profession for each child who is seen, as appropriate. The complexity of therapeutic work with children means that a wise and flexible balance has to be found between the child's need for confidentiality and the need to communicate helpfully with the child's parents, carers, family, and the multi-professional team.

The experience of a private and protected therapeutic space is so central to the child and adolescent psychotherapist's work that the question of how to write publicly without compromising this privacy raises many issues. As with any other profession that needs an ever-evolving theoretical and experiential base, we have to share our clinical experience with each other and outside the profession if we are not to become moribund. The problem is how best to achieve this without sacrificing our relationship with our patients. This issue is very alive within the profession, particularly as we become more 'public' and venture out of the consulting room to share our work with colleagues in the multidisciplinary team, at conferences and lectures, and in the increasing numbers of books written by child and adolescent psychotherapists.

The first consideration is how to disguise the case illustration. This can be achieved by giving no more historical or biographical information than is absolutely essential to the particular aspect of the case that is being discussed. In addition, some 'red herrings' may be added, to further disguise the case as long as they do not detract from the coherency in the process. For example, if the relationships with or positions of siblings are not a key feature of the illustration, the ages and sex of the siblings might be altered to conceal a possible identification. It is always tricky to know how much to disguise a case before it begins to sound unconvincing. This has been a matter for much discussion between editors and the individual authors and we believe we have arrived at sensible solutions in each case.

Some of the children and families discussed will have been directly approached by their therapists asking for permission to write about their treatment. Depending on the individual circumstances, they may or may not have seen the actual text and given their agreement to it. There can be a problem with this direct approach when treatment is ongoing, or where, as can often be the case, it is possible that the patient may want to return to the therapist for further help as he or she grows up. The fact that the therapist has spent so much additional time thinking and writing about the patient, indicating that in some respect the patient has a 'special' status for the therapist, can interfere with and possibly disrupt any ongoing or future therapeutic contact. This is not necessarily a problem, but it can be, and has to be carefully thought about before any patient is approached for permission to publish. In many respects, because of the possibility of disrupting or distracting from the therapeutic relationship by showing the patient and/or the family what has been written, some therapists ask for permission to use disguised material for teaching or publication at the outset of treatment. This request is made in the spirit of advancing knowledge, training and practice, so that, should it be helpful to share what has been learned from a particular treatment, permission has been given.

(M. Lanyado and A. Horne, *The Handbook of Child and Adolescent Psychotherapy: Psychoanalytic Approaches* (1999): 13–14)

1   Introduction

Monica Lanyado and Ann Horne

1

The context

Coming together to compile this book, with its focus on the Independent tradition in British psychoanalysis and psychotherapy, we have had interesting discussions with our co-authors and between ourselves. In recent years – at least publicly since the 50th anniversary conference of the Association of Child Psychotherapists (ACP) in 1999 – there has been said to have been much rapprochement between the different training and theoretical traditions. While we would agree with this – and indeed see the establishment of an Independent training in 1982 as pivotal in encouraging it – it is important to acknowledge that there are still important differences in approach amongst the training schools, approaches informed by theoretical divergence. Where we have moved on, we suspect, is in our capacity to tolerate and even enjoy discussion of these differences – an acceptance of diversity, and a new capacity to be curious about each other. This takes us a long way from the 'collisions' described by Rycroft (Pearson 2004 – and see next chapter) as masquerading as 'discussions' in the Institute of Psychoanalysis in the 1950s.

However, we have not quite reached – as was hopefully proposed at a recent British Association of Psychotherapists (BAP) conference on 'Diversity' – a position where what we all do in the consulting room is actually pretty well the same (Lemma 2005). There was much disagreement at the 1999 ACP conference about what was 'correct' and what was not. Indeed, part of the spur for compiling this book came from listening to talks at subsequent conferences of the ACP where very experienced members often rather diffidently proposed what to them felt like considerable variations in technique. We were struck by the on-going need for diffidence – perhaps stemming from a continuing counter-transference relationship to the mythical 'correct' approach – and by variation being perceived as radically different. Diverse applications of technique and method have been discussed amongst Independents since Winnicott, amongst Anna Freudians in-house over decades and available to the rest of us at least since Joe Sandler and his colleagues made Miss Freud's thinking public (Sandler, Kennedy, and Tyson 1980), and amongst post-Kleinians at the latest since *Psychotherapy with Severely Deprived Children* appeared in 1983 (Boston and Szur 1983). Indeed, colleagues at the Institute of Psychoanalysis tell us that new findings from Mrs Klein's as yet unpublished technical papers are also going to startle us about her capacity for flexibility and adaptation in the consulting room.

The 21st birthday, in 2003, of the child and adolescent psychotherapy training at the BAP – a training that locates itself in the Independent tradition of British psychoanalysis – also helped us feel it to be timely to collate a book that derived from that theoretical and technical position. This book thus seeks to address a gap in contemporary psychoanalytic writing about work with children and adolescents and is in major part a response to requests from trainees and colleagues.

We would wish therefore to engage in discussion about what actually happens in the consulting room, as opposed to what it is felt 'ought' to be happening. In this way, *A Question of Technique* describes and discusses contemporary practice and how it is evolving, the 'what we do' and the 'how' of psychoanalytically informed psychotherapy with children, young people, their families and the professional networks surrounding them. The authors of the chapters have tried to tease out these questions from their clinical work. Achieving the focus of this book has not proved easy – in part because different theoretical traditions mean different belief systems and moving from one theoretical position to another requires distancing oneself from what may well have been taught as fundamental and 'right'. From our discussions and individual clinical and theoretical findings, there has emerged an interesting book that grapples with why we do what we do and makes it available to a wider readership.

The contributors come from a mixture of original training backgrounds – Independent, Kleinian and Anna Freudian – but would now identify their theoretical orientation as Independent, the majority position in the British School, the London-based British Psychoanalytic Society. In our deliberations and writing, it emerged that what linked us in a major way was our interest in building on Winnicott's thinking, as well as drawing on the Kleinian and Anna Freudian traditions. It also became apparent that we were able to draw on Winnicottian thought and come to a range of conclusions. So in many ways this book represents a contemporary view of post-Winnicottian child psychotherapists at work. Some of the chapters reflect practice in individual work; others demonstrate the application of theory to parent work, families and networks while retaining in mind the primacy of the best interests of the child.

The content

We will give a brief tour around the contents of the book, anticipating that the reader will feel able to 'dip in' according to specific interests, as well as to read the text as a whole, to gain a comprehensive view of contemporary child psychotherapy from an Independent perspective. Our roots in the Independent Psychoanalytic tradition are reflected in Bernard Barnett's 'Foreword' to the book. A senior member of the Independent group of British psychoanalysts, and a child analyst, with many links world-wide with those interested in Winnicott's work, Barnett both reinforces and further elaborates the kind of mind-set that is thought of as 'Independent'.

The running order of the book reflects the different areas of theory, practice and technique that we wished to encompass. The first section describes how contemporary Independent thought has developed within the psychoanalytic tradition. Continuing the theme of this introductory chapter, with its engaging interview of Anne Hurry by Maria Pozzi, we move to Ann Horne's description of how the Independent group of child and adolescent psychotherapists came into being through the child and adolescent psychotherapy training founded at the British Association of Psychotherapists in 1982. From delineating the Independent identity in theoretical terms, she discusses the technical and clinical implications of these Independent views. She also describes the dangers of 'pathological idealisation' within psychoanalysis, institutionalised positions and assumptions that can stop the growth of new ideas if they seemingly contradict the views of psychoanalytic elders.

A more theoretical chapter by Janine Sternberg completes this section of the book, and takes the reader from the historical differences about technique, up to current-day live issues. Sternberg usefully reminds us of the key concerns that have influenced discussions about technique in the past, and in particular how different theoretical views lead to different ways of being and behaving in the consulting room. Importantly, she discusses the impact of contemporary research on our understanding of what takes place between therapist and patient, and the ways in which microanalysis of video material is shaping our view of how we respond in the present moment to our patients. The reader will find a masterly appraisal of a wide range of themes marking points where we have to reflect on how we intervene or respond to our patients. As an adult as well as child psychotherapist, Sternberg has very interesting contributions to make – quietly given, almost *en passant* – on commonalities and differences in working with these diverse groups. Her analysis of technique includes language, tone, intonation and silence; the use of transference and counter-transference; and a very interesting comment on 'to play or not to play', a matter taken up by Maria Pozzi and Anne Hurry in their conversation. The section on interpretations is particularly thought-provoking. In offering comment on the diverse technical practices found in our analytic work today, Sternberg opens up an extremely helpful context for the clinical material that follows in later chapters.

We decided to put most of the chapters in 'developmental order' – parent–infant work, then work with latency and adolescent patients –

partly because there are some important differences in technique according to the stage of development of the patient but also rather simply because keeping development in mind is important to an Independent. The second section of the book therefore centres on parent–infant work, a comparative newcomer to the repertoire of child and adolescent psychotherapists but now rapidly expanding.

Working directly with parents who have their babies *with them* in the room during the consultation, rather than talking to parents *about* their infants who are not present, came to prominence following Selma Fraiberg and her colleague's groundbreaking book *Clinical Studies in Infant Mental Health* (Fraiberg and Fraiberg 1980). Pioneering this work in the UK was Dilys Daws whose highly readable *Through the Night: Helping Parents and Sleepless Infants*, published in 1989, has also become a classic – not only clinically, but directly for many parents desperate for a good night's sleep (Daws 1989)! Juliet Hopkins has also played a very important part, through her clinical work and her writing, in laying the foundations in the UK of this increasingly recognised method of intervention (Hopkins 1992). Hopkins has long been very active in teaching at the BAP and was a member of the original Training Committee.

Deirdre Dowling's chapter illustrates this influence in her work with families who have been admitted to a therapeutic community as a 'last chance' effort to avoid taking their babies into the care of the local authorities. This is harrowing and deeply compassionate work as the babies are at severe risk but the parents and professionals still hope that the parents can be helped to become more adequate – otherwise they would not have agreed to admission to the unit. Dowling's opinion, as a psycho-therapist, plays a crucial part in how the assessment of the parent's ability to care for the baby is reached. Through her clinical examples, and her discussion of the theory and technique which form the framework for her work, Dowling shows how she struggles to hold the parents in mind in a way that, from experience, she knows may in turn enable them to hold their babies in mind in a more nurturing and developmentally enhancing way. This isn't always possible, despite the best of efforts by all involved, including the parents. Central to her thinking is Winnicott's concept of 'the capacity to be alone' (Winnicott 1958). She demonstrates how the appli-cation of this idea to parent–infant work is very fruitful in helping the therapist to have some clarity about what therapy might be able to achieve.

The next two chapters in this section are by Victoria Hamilton. The first of these is a paper she wrote in 1988, here republished, in which she uses clinical material from parent–infant consultations to illustrate her ideas about the importance of differentiating separateness from separation, as linked with the process of mourning, during infancy. Hamilton discusses the different meanings that the concept of 'mourning' has taken on, in its ordinary everyday usage, and in the psychoanalytic literature which usually focuses more upon the pains of separation and separateness than their more positive developmental functions. The clinical material shows how, for a mother who was in foster care from a very early age, 'separateness' as well as 'separation' from her baby is extremely distressing. The baby's symptoms – a disturbing form of rocking – are understood as being this mother and baby's 'best way' of coping with the pains of separation and separateness. Understanding the developmental gains of separateness and separation helped the symptoms to subside.

The second chapter by Hamilton is a fascinating reflection, in 2004, on the earlier paper. Now retired from clinical work, she reflects on the impact of painful losses and mourning in her own life and how this has affected the way she now thinks about separateness, separation and mourning, with particular reference to her patients in the 1988 paper. This frank account of her deepened understanding of the many different kinds of losses that people try to live with, shares with the reader something that we all know but don't often write about so openly. Our own personal lives, and what we experience in them, are bound to affect our understanding of our work and our ways of being with our patients. It is unusual to have such a personal account of this experience and we are pleased to be able to include it in this volume.

The next section of the book explores technical issues when working with latency and adolescent patients. Iris Gibbs and Monica Lanyado in their chapters address the kinds of technical problems that are encountered in the therapy of looked-after and adopted children. These severely deprived, and often severely abused and traumatised, children and young people form a large proportion of the patients that are seen today by child and adolescent psychotherapists and other therapists and counsellors. Their complex therapeutic needs, together with their anarchic and often violent or aggressive behaviour in everyday life as well as in the consulting room, have raised many 'questions of technique'.

Iris Gibbs, who came from a background of social work to child psychotherapy, is particularly well placed to think about the importance of working both directly with the child *and* with the carers and professional network around the looked-after child. She thinks of this in terms of finding an appropriate balance, for each child, between these two interdependent parts of the work. Her clinical illustrations describe some of the ideas she has found helpful in what can feel at times like 'walking a tightrope' when trying to work out boundaries of confidentiality for all concerned, in as wise a way as possible.

Often children come to therapy because their placements are at risk, and work with the foster carers becomes essential. There has been much debate about the wisdom of the child's therapist also working therapeutically with the foster carers. Gibbs illustrates her view that working in this way can be very helpful in holding the whole placement together at times of crisis. She argues that by applying psychoanalytic understanding to the child's internal world, whilst also working with the real relationships in his complicated external world, the therapist is in a uniquely effective position. Gibbs's wide-ranging chapter illustrates the flexibility of the treatment models she uses, including inviting foster-carers into the therapy room for significant periods of the therapy, with the child's consent, and working with foster carers in parallel with the child. She also describes the value of working with a child going through the process of moving from fostering to adoption.

Monica Lanyado's chapter engages with the same kind of severely deprived patient, one who is further along the road to environmental and emotional recovery. Her patient, an early adolescent girl, had been adopted when she was nine and was reasonably settled in her adoptive placement when she came for therapy, but still had many painful issues around the severe rejection she had experienced earlier in her life. The feeling of rejection was compounded by the fact that she was a hearing child born to two profoundly deaf parents and there were significant communication problems between them. The patient covered her extreme vulnerability to feeling rejected with extreme defensiveness, which interfered with her ability to form new relationships.

Lanyado describes how important it became for the therapist to be 'playfully present' for this patient, in a way that echoed Winnicott's statement that therapy occurs in the overlap of the 'areas of play' of the patient and the therapist (Winnicott 1971a). This implies a willingness from within the therapist to become playfully responsive to the patient. Lanyado suggests that the therapist's playfulness can be a powerful 'antidote' to the rigid defences that such patients have erected. There are circumstances when *not* playing, because the therapist is uncertain about whether this kind of playfulness is technically 'correct' or not, can actually close down therapeutic possibilities. The value of humour in therapy is also discussed.

Ann Horne's chapter 'Brief communications from the edge: psychotherapy with challenging adolescents' (Horne 2001) is republished here as it offers consideration of *how* one intervenes in a session with reference to one's theoretical and developmental knowledge base. In this chapter, Horne – a self-confessed unreconstituted Winnicottian – explores the technical issues of working with severely 'acting out' and anxiety-provoking patients. She describes how the therapist as 'developmental object' (Hurry 1998) links with her way of enabling primitive anxieties and body-based defensive manoeuvres to be thought about and articulated before interpretation can become possible. A session is given, beginning with the classic Middle Group question: 'Why is this patient saying this to me now?' (as quoted by Anne Hurry, this volume, p. 12). The report allows the rise and fall of the work to be followed as the anxieties rise, gain words and then thought, and lessen – but the need to maintain some anxiety and leave the therapist concerned is noted! Salutary comment is made on the impact of the disturbed adolescent on his environment and the consequent tendency of the network around him to act out, reminiscent of Winnicott's experience of his clinic's refusing him permission to continue with his delinquent, first, child analytic training patient (Winnicott 1956).

There then follows a chapter describing Independent psychoanalytic technique in the more classical setting of three-times-weekly therapy with a severely narcissistic, late-adolescent patient who used the couch. Juliet Hopkins illustrates a Winnicottian way of working with this young woman, and the value of the positive regression that took place in the 'transitional relationship' that characterised the transference. The patient used illusion and merging as defences against deep ambivalence. Hopkins decided that rather than using more challenging interpretations of these anxieties and defences in a manner that would characterise a more Kleinian approach, she would follow a Winnicottian model in which the patient's regression in therapy was understood as being an opportunity for a 'second chance' to make developmental progress.

Her patient's therapeutic regression within the transference, to the point in her early life where a developmental *impasse* had occurred due to the environmental failure of her parents' inability to see her as a whole and separate person, helped the patient to de-construct or unfreeze her paranoid and vengeful relationship to her mother in particular. Hopkins also makes clear when it was *not* therapeutically helpful to support the patient's illusions and how she distinguished between positive and negative regression in the manner described by Balint (1968). By the end of therapy, the patient was able to express extremely ambivalent feelings of love and hate towards Hopkins, and also to know that whilst it could be painful, feeling 'increasingly ordinary' was a much healthier emotional place to be.

We follow this example of more classical psychoanalytic psychotherapy with Teresa Bailey's highly practical and helpful description of her work with the parents of adolescents. Those who work with adolescents know how difficult for parents, carers and referrers it can be to get the adolescent who is 'the problem' to come to see anyone for help. The healthy adolescent's developmental push towards independence, which can often co-exist with all kinds of more painful and disturbed aspects of the young person's inner world, can leave parents and carers of young people feeling baffled and desperate about how to help them – and how to survive living with them. Bailey's chapter is a response to this *cri de coeur*.

Bailey sees her work with parents of adolescents as being rather like parent–infant work. It involves keeping in mind not only the adolescent but also the adults as parents, as a parental couple, and as people with their own adolescent histories well to the fore during their children's teenager years. She helpfully likens this to Fraiberg's ideas about parent–infant work, but with the adolescent process in mind (Fraiberg *et al.* 1980). The therapist's stance, she states, needs to allow thinking about the parent who is present, the absent parent, the parental couple and the teenager whose presence is represented powerfully in the parents' mind and filtered through to the therapist via their own anxieties and defences. She describes the way in which a transitional space can be created in the midst of all this confusion, from where it is possible to view the process together with the parents, in a manner that can lead to change. Through Bailey's clinical illustrations, it is possible to see how great this potential for change in parents and their adolescents can be, even when the therapist has never met the teenager.

The final section of the book springs from very practical concerns about what it is helpful to say to the patient, and what is the best way of setting up a flexible and therapeutically 'economic' treatment plan. It is easy to forget in these number-crunching research driven days, that our clinical observations about what helps the therapeutic process to progress, and the patient to feel better, as well as what hinders it, have always been an important research engine behind clinical, technical and theoretical advances. In this last section, therefore, is an updated version of Lanyado's 1996 paper on consultation work and brief work, and a seriously lighthearted chapter by Horne: 'Interesting things to say – and why'.

The need for clinicians to 'do something else' in Winnicott's terms, that is to be able to offer treatment packages that are responsive to the individual needs of the patient, whilst doing their best to fit within the many requirements of working in a multi-disciplinary team, is a major concern for many therapists today. Lanyado's chapter enthusiastically embraces the Winnicottian model of *Therapeutic Consultations in Child Psychiatry* (Winnicott 1971b), arguing that this provides theory, technique and many examples of the kind of brief, or time-limited work, that can help many families who are referred to therapists today.

Guidelines for working in this creative and flexible way are suggested, with reference to two case studies that illustrate different ways of helping patients who are seen either intermittently or for a limited number of sessions. As well as drawing together the kind of technical issues that have been discussed throughout this book, she reminds the reader of how significant an accumulation of 'small changes' can be in the long run. Therapeutic consultations can be seen as opportunities for these small changes to take place as a result of the potential for *therapeutic communication* to happen in every consultation that we undertake. The impact of a 'small change', as a result of a helpful consultation, can take patients into new internal terrain from which they can surprisingly often add their own new small changes. It is as if the therapist starts a process which, for many reasonably well-functioning families, if offered in time, is 'good-enough' to get them back on track.

Horne opens her chapter on 'Interesting things to say – and why' with a description of an odd and potentially embarrassing situation, not untypical of what can easily happen in our work. As a newly qualified psychotherapist, one might worry about breaking what seem to be 'analytic rules' – but *are* they rules and can flexibility of approach be the right and creative response? It is a plea for creativity in our day-to-day individual encounters with children and young people, and especially for an understanding of defences as necessary, as not deliberate attacks on the therapist but intended to protect the ego. The idea for this chapter arose from the enjoyable business of supervising trainee child psychotherapists – for the supervisor, as Horne notes, it is easy to think of what might have been said in a session: the passion of the moment is, after all, no longer a pressure. A variety of situations are delineated, and responses to the child in each explored. Our theoretical understanding of the child's position, however, is clearly what drives the choice of 'interesting thing' to say. Horne would be delighted if the reader were to read the chapter and then engage in a dialogue about it: what are *your* 'interesting things to say'?

We conclude the book with our thoughts about 'Where Independent minds meet'. We come from very different traditions, yet gain much from reflecting on the common ground of clinical practice, technique and theory that link the contributions to this volume.

This 'Introduction' closes with an interview. Maria Pozzi, who trained as a Kleinian child psychotherapist at the Tavistock Clinic and then engaged with Independent thinking in her adult psychotherapy training at the BAP, curious about what makes an Independent, interviews Anne Hurry. Anne – as Chapter 2 elaborates – was the prime mover in establishing the Independent child psychotherapy training at the BAP in 1982. In this discussion emerges much of the sense of energetic and thoughtful curiosity that we would suggest is necessary if we are to be grounded yet flexible in our application of the analytic technique to the challenges of today.

2

Maria Pozzi interviews Anne Hurry

Maria P: Thank you for agreeing to be interviewed, Anne. I'd like to begin by asking you about your move from being an Anna Freudian to the Independent Group.

Anne H: I wasn't wholly a 'Classical Freudian' when I first went to the Anna Freud Centre as a student. During my clinical psychology training at the Child Guidance Training Centre I had read my way round the library. Just what I read there was largely a matter of chance, depending on what caught my eye, but it did include Winnicott and Melanie Klein and Anna Freud too. It was Anna Freud's book *The Ego and the Mechanisms of Defence* – *not* the book on the psychoanalysis of children, which she was subsequently to disown – it was Anna Freud's book with its interest in the whole child, not just the child's fantasy world, but the manifold ways in which the child coped with both inner and outer worlds, which made me want to train at the Hampstead Clinic (now the AFC).

But I also applied to the Hampstead Clinic because I knew and respected a lot of people who were in training or had trained there. They came out to the Wembley Clinic where I worked. Rose Edgcumbe, Gita Mehra, Audrey Gavshon, Rosalie Joffé all saw patients at Wembley, and their patients changed, got better. Their work made being a psychotherapist seem to me more interesting than being a psychologist where I would see children diagnostically but often need to refer them on and so not necessarily see the processes of change thereafter.

At the Hampstead Clinic there were people with many points of view and there was always very lively discussion there. There was never just the one approach. We read Bowlby as he came out and Kohut hot from the press. But still the training meant that we were steeped in Freud, that we knew how many angels danced on the pin heads of the first, second, third and fourth anxiety theories. (Later, as a teacher, I came to the conclusion that much of Freud could usefully be replaced by the clinical material in the *Psychoanalytic Study of the Child*.)

Some different views were irreconcilable: for example, some people even believed that the incomplete myelinisation of the nervous system at birth meant that the earliest experiences did not affect the child's emotional development, yet at the same time R. Spitz's work was known and taught. Some teachers were even against pre-oedipal interpretations, whereas Agi Bene, my first supervisor, when my patient was afraid to come to the room, recommended a more Kleinian approach, and picked up his toy bear's attacks on the glue pot as an intrusive attack on the mother's breast. And an interpretation in roughly those terms gave him enough safety to come back to the room – though today we might want to think about just what elements in that interpretation were effective.

Maria P: That's very interesting to hear about all that, which I certainly had not known about.

Anne H: No, people don't. They think that at the Tavi they just sloshed around with the counter-transference, and at Hampstead we just sat around to intellectualise, which is all nonsense. But I think it's lessening on both sides – don't you think so?

Maria P: Yes, surely. At the Tavi the external world of the child is taken much more into account nowadays. We talk and interpret to children in different ways now and this includes interpreting in displacement when needed, and adapting technique in order to reach the hidden and frightened child and to draw him out. There is much cross-fertilisation amongst different schools of thought.

| | And you describe training in an institution that was already rather open-minded, despite Anna Freud's more classical input? |
| *Anne H:* | Yes, but I do not think we can describe Anna Freud's input as only classical – quite the reverse. I have already spoken of her interest in the whole child. There was also her great interest in the welfare of children in society, and her huge contribution to our knowledge about attachment and early development following her experience in the War Nurseries, her interest in the effects of the law on children – and so on and so on. |

If at times it seems that she personally had to defend every aspect of her father's theories, I think we should remember first the background of her family and the threats to psychoanalysis as the Nazis took over Austria, and secondly that she spent a good many years of her life propping up her father physically over the course of his cancer. Have you read that wonderful book about that – Elisabeth Young-Bruehl's biography? Young-Bruehl is a feminist American writer whose biography of Anna Freud shows the impact of her father upon her life; it is deeply tragic. She quotes some poetry that Anna Freud wrote in her adolescence about her longing to be free. She then quotes Freud's letters to a friend – Fliess I think – saying something like: 'I know I'm using Anna, but I need her.'

| *Maria P:* | But she allowed that rather open atmosphere, didn't she? |
| *Anne H:* | Yes she did, and she'd argue and sometimes she'd be convinced. I remember when Joe Sandler and Wally Joffé – they wrote together for quite a long time – when they convinced her that the idea that there was a limited amount of 'libido' – so that if you loved yourself more you loved the other less – that this idea simply did not make sense. They believed that healthy narcissism or self-esteem was a *sine qua non* for good object relations. I remember Joe saying vigorously, 'But, Miss Freud, "libido" is not a spoonful of jam!' |

Of course no one at Hampstead would have accepted the idea of the paranoid-schizoid phase as a phase. Rosalie Joffé tells the story of Paula Heimann who remained a staunch Kleinian until she had a grandchild and then said: 'My grandson is not paranoid!' After this Heimann began coming to the Wednesday meetings at Hampstead and was to leave the Kleinian group.

| *Maria P:* | What has led to changes in your way of thinking? |
| *Anne H:* | Well first I thought I hadn't really changed in my thinking but then I realised I have, and one of the people who has influenced me most has been Juliet Hopkins. I find her enormously insightful and helpful. Another person is Anne Alvarez, who I think led me to the concept of the developmental object with |

her thoughts about the enlivening mother – centrally important for child therapy today. Then Patrick Casement's book *On Learning from the Patient*. Plus I was lucky enough to have supervision from Pearl King, on work with adults, but it permeated everything. She is very much a here-and-now person. She taught me the classic Middle Group question: 'Why is this patient saying this to me now?'

Maria P: That's interesting, as that was also part of my Kleinian training: 'why is this being said to me now?' And that's Middle Group?

Anne H: Where I was perhaps over-influenced by the Hampstead approach was in terms of the theory of resistance, because if your primary aim is to uncover the unconscious, as it were, to produce insight which will lead to change, then the concept of resistance makes sense. But why should a child want to be insightful? It's often painful. Now that I see the work much more in terms of releasing developmental forces, resistance does not make much sense. When we talk about it we are really talking about resistance to the analyst's aims rather than to where the patient is trying to go.

Maria P: Nowadays most of our children are so developmentally undeveloped . . .

Anne H: In *Psychoanalysis and Developmental Therapy* I have written about how therapists develop a relationship with those children who are so undeveloped. It seems to me that everything we do with these children is in some way a type of developmental relating.

Maria P: Is this linked with the issue of the child relating to the analyst as a real or as a transference object, perhaps?

Anne H: Yes, and here I was enormously influenced by a Finnish analyst called Tähkä [see Laine 2004 – ed.] and by Bob Furman in the States. For many years Anna Freud thought that while the real relationship was an inevitable component of the analysis, it also inevitably interfered with the transference, and that children had a tendency to 'misuse' the analytic relationship for a 'corrective emotional experience'.

But I want to introduce another concept, which is neither the real nor the transference object, but the developmental object. I believe that patients have a self-healing capacity. It may be deeply damaged but hopefully not so much that they can't use it. You provide an appropriate relationship and they use it to grow. You become a different kind of developmental object for all your patients, just like a mother is a slightly different mother for all her children. People like Loewald would call that relationship a relationship to a 'new' object. I prefer the term 'developmental' because a new object can be anything –

somebody who steals your bicycle or bangs you on the head – a new object can be a bad object.

If you have a patient with predominantly good experience of being mothered, he may bring that to you and see you as a good mother on the basis of the transference, and that may be appropriate developmentally – or may not. But what you very often get is a patient who struggles to maintain a transference relation and avoid a developmental one, because if he sees you as dangerous to him or hating him, like people in his earlier experience – say it's a looked-after child – then it's safe, he's not going to be disappointed. So he can go on and on and on provoking rejection and of course the temptation for the analyst is to fall into that trap. But if you can get through that, then you find the ability in the patient to use you in a different sort of way, to use you to develop rather than to stultify and distort his growth and confirm that all is useless. You could see all treatments as a conflict between a call to the old pathology via the transference or the possibility of developing via the developmental relationship.

Maria P: I think of the moment of change in the patient as when the therapist reaches the end of her tolerance and despair and wants to give up both hope and trying. Then something happens – but usually in the therapist first.

Anne H: It is in the area of counter-transference where I have seen the greatest changes – changes from the original Freudian view that it was an interference, something to be recognised and then laid aside. My impression is that the Tavi was more open to the use of counter-transference and here our colleagues have influenced us. But the position of the Hampstead Clinic was less straightforward than is often thought. Some colleagues and teachers did very much use their own feelings in understanding the child via what he evoked in them. They were influenced by people like Racker, Pearl King and by Sandler's paper (1976) on role responsiveness which had a huge influence not just at the Clinic but nationally and internationally.

I perhaps should add that while Kleinian theory gave projective identification a major role in child therapy, the Hampstead Clinic had 'externalisation' whereby the child set out unconsciously to evoke those feelings in the therapist – feelings which he could not bear in himself.

Maria P: This takes me to my next question: what then is the aim of treatment in your view?

Anne H: Classically the immediate aim of treatment was to increase insight, which would lead to greater ego control and more appropriate choice of defence. The overarching aim, as defined by Anna Freud, was to restore a child to the path of normal development and I still find that a useful idea. One thing that child analysts are often not good at is letting go of their patients. It's very important not to be the fussy parent. This is also true with adults: when you restore someone to the path of normal development and together enable the patient to start growing again, it's very important that you do not just unhook them from you but that they have real people in the outside world. That's one of the difficulties, as you know, for those who come from a pathogenic environment. You need to have someone to have done the work with the family.

Maria P: Would you do that part of the work yourself?

Anne H: With the young ones, yes I infinitely prefer that.

Maria P: That brings me to the question of what you do about the child's past history.

Anne H: When I was training, there was a big controversy about using material that did not come directly from the sessions. I came to think it could be quite helpful. I'm prepared to talk about a child's real history if he seems stuck without that. Of course when we reconstruct we cannot assume that such reconstruction is correct. In fact we know nowadays that autobiographical memory itself is a constant reconstruction of a reconstruction. But people seem to like reconstruction. I rather like it; it's nice to make sense of things.

Yet really we know so little. Hansi Kennedy had a West Indian patient who had been shut up in the pigpen when his parents came to England – he had been left with his granny, who neglected him and shut him up with the animals. He was identified with a typewriter, a machine. I remember that there came a point when Hansi linked his underlying neediness with the early starvation and Anna Freud said: 'What's the point of telling him that? He's starving now, he was starving then; is that supposed to help him to feel better?' She had a point. You can reconstruct with someone who needs to know 'Why am I in this state?' but for some vulnerable children that is not what they need to know – at least not at that point – and an ill-timed reconstruction can serve to confirm their worst fears.

Maria P: Thinking now of mistakes the analyst makes . . . how do you deal with real mistakes?

Anne H: Kids watch out for the analyst's response to his own mistakes and can see if he feels it's OK to make mistakes. An interesting question is whether you think that the child has provoked the mistake in which case you may take that up. It may well be that the child has provoked a necessary failure. Or it may just be that you have made the mistake for your own reasons. Both can be true.

On the whole analysts today behave in a less omniscient fashion than some of them used to do. Most of us don't interpret as if we were telling the patient what he 'really' means. We offer the patient possibilities, which he then takes, tries out, sniffs at, accepts, uses, rejects, etc. We don't expect him to say: 'Aha! Yes!' The trial nature of our interpretations cuts out a whole range of mistakes.

Many mistakes come from counter-transference muddles. At times I have prolonged a session by a few minutes or cut it short. Then I would see the patient's response and interpret his feeling trapped or rejected or whatever.

Maria P: What about the child's play: would you play with the child? Interpret in displacement at times?

Anne H: Of course. As to the question as to when one interprets the play, that is something that varies from child to child and varies for each individual child according to the stage he has reached. Juliet Hopkins's article about Paddy, the case that Winnicott supervised, illustrates this beautifully (Hopkins 1996). She had this little boy who had no evident attachment; he had two parents as far as I remember, but he wandered off, got himself lost, a completely avoidant sort of attachment. He had no language, was not clean or dry. What Juliet did first of all was to reflect what he was doing and then very gradually, with no interpretations as such, just mirroring; the boy came to enjoy their sameness. He began to have a little bit of language; they both had blue jerseys and both had buttons; they played all the baby games and he developed more and more language and she said to Winnicott: 'But should I not interpret now?' and he kept saying: 'No'. Then the child moved on to the stage where he wasn't focusing on sameness. He was focusing on differences, saying: 'I'm having these cars, you're having those cars'. Separation began to be painful and then she began with very safe interpretations. (You know when separation becomes an issue, what children play is peek-a-boo or hide and seek, and they are wonderful games for adults too.) Juliet started to interpret his pleasure and wish to be found – rather than his fear of loss.

What we have neglected a bit is how much more difficult child analysis is than adult analysis, and some of the difficulty has to do with your question about playing: do you take part in the play or do you observe it? I think you do what the child is indicating. I know there are supposed to be some therapists who sit at their desks and don't move. But I think that that can provide a child with a pretty weird way of relating. You have to provide an opportunity to interact in a different way and not a chance to interact in the pathological way the patient is used to.

Maria P: A last question: would you always play with a child?

Anne H: No, well, it depends. There's the question of play that you don't feel right about. The child who brings strings of soldiers and puts them above a slow-burning fire . . . Now, that I can just about stand and I reckon that that's all right. The child is showing his very sadistic fantasies and he needs to be able to convey these in some way. But what happens when he asks you to do it and what happens when he imagines he's doing it to you or asks you to be a sadistic doctor. At such times I will say: 'That doesn't feel right to me, I'm not going to do that,' or 'No, I don't want to do that, I don't want to pretend to hurt you.'

Maria P: Many thanks, Anne, for sharing so much with me and creating such an ease and intimacy in your home. It has been a most valuable exchange, almost like a good supervision. I have enjoyed it thoroughly and learned so much, both about you and your thinking but also for me and my own work. It has been a privilege – thank you.

References

Balint, M. (1968) *The Basic Fault: Therapeutic Aspects of Regression.* London: Tavistock

Boston, M. and Szur, R. (1983) *Psychotherapy with Severely Deprived Children.* London: Routledge & Kegan Paul

Casement, P. (1985) *On Learning from the Patient.* London and New York: Tavistock Publications

Daws, D. (1989) *Through the Night: Helping Parents and Sleepless Infants.* London: Free Association Books

Fraiberg, S. with Fraiberg, L. (eds.) (1980) *Clinical Studies in Infant Mental Health: The First Year of Life.* London and New York: Tavistock Publications

Fraiberg, S., Adelson, A. and Shapiro, V. (1980) 'Ghosts in the nursery'. In S. Fraiberg and L. Fraiberg (eds.), *Clinical Studies in Infant Mental Health: The First Year of Life.* London and New York: Tavistock Publications

Freud, A. (1966) *The Ego and the Mechanisms of Defence.* London: Hogarth Press

Hopkins, J. (1992) 'Parent–infant psychotherapy' *Journal of Child Psychotherapy* 18: 5–17

Hopkins, J. (1996) 'From baby games to let's pretend: the achievement of playing' *Journal of the British Association of Psychotherapists* 1(31), Part 2: 20–7

Horne, A. (2001) 'Brief communications from the edge: psychotherapy with challenging adolescents' *Journal of Child Psychotherapy* 27 (1): 3–18

Hurry, A. (1998) *Psychoanalysis and Developmental Therapy.* London: Karnac

Laine, A. (2004) *Power of Understanding: Essays in Honour of Veikko Tähkä.* London: Karnac

Lemma, A. (2005) 'Diversity in psychoanalysis'. Unpublished paper given at the BAP Conference, 4 March 2005

Pearson, J. (ed.) (2004) *Analyst of the Imagination: The Life and Work of Charles Rycroft*. London: Karnac

Sandler, J. (1976) 'Countertransference and role-responsiveness' *International Review of Psycho-Analysis* 3(1): 43–7

Sandler, J., Kennedy, H. and Tyson, R. (1980) *The Technique of Child Psycho-analysis: Discussions with Anna Freud*. London: Hogarth Press

Young-Bruehl, E. (1989) *Anna Freud: A Biography*. London: Macmillan

Winnicott, D. W. (1956) 'The anti-social tendency'. In Winnicott (1958) *Collected Papers: Through Paediatrics to Psychoanalysis*. London: Hogarth Press, 1975

Winnicott, D. W. (1958) 'The capacity to be alone' in Winicott (1965), *The Maturational Processes and the Facilitating Environment*. London: Hogarth Press

Winnicott, D. W. (1971a) *Playing and Reality*. Harmondsworth: Penguin, 1980

Winnicott, D. W. (1971b) *Therapeutic Consultations in Child Psychiatry*. New York: Basic Books

2 The Independent position in psychoanalytic psychotherapy with children and adolescents

Roots and implications

Ann Horne

> It was to be part of the contribution of what became known as the British School of object-relations theorists, to translate psychoanalysis from a theory of sexual desire into a theory of emotional nurture.
>
> (Phillips 1988: 10)

> An independence of mind is absolutely necessary if Freud's work is not to be permitted to stagnate.
>
> (Lomas 2004: 92)

The split in 1944 within the British Psychoanalytic Society, highlighted by the 'controversial discussions' (King and Steiner 1991), did not simply result in the formation of the 'A' Group (Kleinians) and the 'B' Group (identified with Vienna and Anna Freud) within the society; the majority of members adopted a very British position and became the 'Middle Group', later (from 1973) the Independents. I call it a very British position as it is a feature of many British institutions that, in the face of dispute, a compromise is reached – we do not seem to be creatures of extremes. It must be the climate. British social policy, for example, has frequently been described as 'muddling through' – not dogmatic or extreme in political stance, but reaching, on a good day, the best available compromise. The Independents are thus part (and the majority part) of 'the British School' in psychoanalysis – importantly to be differentiated from the term 'English School' which was applied early on by colleagues in Europe and the USA to the followers of Mrs Klein after her arrival in the United Kingdom in 1926.

It is more than simply a compromise, however – to rest with this proposition would be a great over-simplification. The thrust of the early Independents was a determination to preserve precisely that: independence of mind. As Rayner puts it, 'The key to an understanding of the Independents is their avowed openness to learning from any psychoanalytical theories' (Rayner 1991: 4). Rayner, following Gillespie, locates this British tradition within the political and philosophical liberalism of the seventeenth and eighteenth centuries, a profound influence on British intellectual life:

> Here is empiricism, and pragmatism, in practice. Love of it brings a natural leaning towards experiment and trial and error. When using this mode of learning, the experience of error is often as valuable as correctness. We will find this philosophy in the Independents' approach to psychoanalysis as a therapy as well as a theory.
>
> (Rayner 1991: 8)

Such an approach, in contrast to the European tradition of deductive rationalism, leads empiricists to 'place greater emphasis on the senses . . . and experiment to frame ideas' (Jones 2004, paraphrasing Grayling 1995).

Most commentators would see this style of empiricism and curiosity as evident in the British Psychoanalytic Society (BP-AS) prior to the controversial discussions. At a physical distance from Europe, it was perhaps easier to think freely, away from the immediacy of the transference to Freud and Vienna. Thus Mrs Klein was invited by the BP-AS to give six lectures to the Society in 1925 and, a year after the death of Abraham, feeling less supported in Berlin, she returned permanently to London. The arrival of the Freud family from Vienna in 1938 heightened the tensions that had already caused rumblings on the continent.

Although ardently a non-political grouping without a leader, the Independents have often been associated with Winnicott whose ideas have been very influential. While frequently assumed to be leader of the Middle Group, in fact he always declined to be seen as such and worked unavailingly for reconciliation between the A and B groups.

BECOMING AN INDEPENDENT

Statements about empiricism and curiosity can be open to misconstruction and may be treated as if one is somehow arguing for an eclecticism that omits rigour or rigorous theoretical underpinning. The taunt of 'eclecticism' tends to be used by those who would cling to narrower identifications and supposed orthodoxies. Yet such 'orthodoxy' brings its own dilemmas.

The greatest issue facing psychoanalysis in Britain today, paradoxically, is not the assumed threats from other psychological approaches or even the slowness in establishing an evidence-base. It lies for many of us in the incapacity of the profession to analyse its own tendency to idealisation. That most independent of Independents, Charles Rycroft, in an early paper explored ideas of 'pathological idealisation' and 'normal idealisation' (Rycroft 1955) linking these to Winnicott's concepts of illusion and disillusion in the development of the infant (Winnicott 1945) and here describing the process in the 'healthy child':

Though this illusion will require an eventual disillusion, the disillusion-ment will be confined to its belief in its omnipotent control of reality, not to reality itself. The healthy child's hero-worship of its parents and its belief in their omnipotence is to be seen as a process of idealisation which tides it over this period of disillusion until such time as it can rely on its own powers and discovers itself as an individual, potent but not omnipotent.

(Rycroft 1968: 39)

It is, perhaps, with a wry smile that we read Rycroft's own account of the reception accorded this paper when read at the BP-AS in 1954:

I entered the analytical movement without appreciating the passionate intensity, the absolute certainty, with which many analysts held their views. Too many did not have opinions that were open to discussion and possible modification but, instead, had unalterable convictions – including the conviction that anyone who disagreed with them had not had a sufficiently deep analysis. As a result the so-called scientific meetings were all too often not discussions but collisions. I once read a paper to the Society about a woman who had dreamed that the moon fell out of the sky into a dustbin (Rycroft 1955). During the discussion Melanie Klein expressed her regret that I had not had a sufficiently deep analysis; at the time I took this as an insult to Dr Payne [Dr Sylvia Payne, Rycroft's analyst]. I heard later that some of the audience had construed my paper as a conscious, deliberate allegory about Klein; it wasn't, but it's a pleasing idea.

(Rycroft 1993 reprinted in Pearson 2004: 244)

Idealisation tends, all too speedily, to be followed by institutionalisation – perhaps a variation on Rycroft's 'pathological idealisation', which has no reference point in an external reality that knows to foster disillusionment but depends upon ideal internal objects. Such a process often brings an accompanying reluctance to question the ideas and tenets of one's theor-etical forebears and carries with it an assumption that what one is taught are 'set' and 'right' techniques and principles. The danger of this process possibly lies more with those whom Winnicott called 'the proselytizers' (Casement 2002: xxiv) rather than the original figures themselves, as the story of Winnicott's tolerable relationship with Mrs Klein, until close to her death, demonstrates. Understandable as such rigidity might have been in the years close to Freud's death, and it must be considered a major factor in the 'controversial discussions', it is disappointing that, 60 years on, we may sustain the polarised theoretical positions of the 1940s. Kohon reminds us that, in the world of British psychoanalysis:

> Although there has been peaceful co-existence between the three groups, they have remained separate. . . . it is in theoretical work that the separations are – for some analysts – tightly maintained: they would never be found quoting from colleagues of any of the rival groups.
>
> (Kohon 1986: 45)

Whereas Rayner points to a growing sense that this 'necessary expedient' of the three groups is no longer useful, he too comments that 'there is frequent acrimony about group-ideological matters' (Rayner 1991: 21).

Anne Hayman (2001) tenaciously pursues a similar theme when she notes, for example, that Bion's 'eschewing memory and desire' (Bion 1970) is predated by Freud's 'evenly suspended attention', as Freud develops it in 1912, and that Annie Reich (1951) describes 'confusing incomprehensible disconnected presentations [which] suddenly make sense and become a *Gestalt* [whole]' anticipating Bion's (1967) 'selected fact'. Roazen raises a related point, that 'history-writing is inherently a subversive activity: students of history necessarily undermine generally received wisdom. . . . A typical lack of respect for historical sequences has, I think, bedevilled the writing about psychoanalysis to an exceptional extent' (Roazen 2004: 43). As theories develop and ideas are encountered and shared in this process, it may be difficult to tease out just who first thought of what. We cannot in that respect omit what Adam Phillips has called Winnicott's 'infamous statement' (Phillips 2000: 91):

> I shall not first give an historical survey and show the development of my ideas from the theories of others, because my mind doesn't work that way. What happens is that I gather this and that, here and there, settle down to clinical experience, form my own theories, and then, last of all, interest myself to see where I stole what. Perhaps this is as good a method as any.
>
> (Winnicott 1945: 145)

Today, however, in the service of clarity and theoretical rigour, and perhaps as an aid to integration and mutual respect, one would hope for generosity in the trans-ideological acknowledgement of sources.

I am reminded of the Association of Child Psychotherapists (ACP) conference in 2000 when, asked what has most aided the 'crossing of borders' between training schools of different theoretical orientations, a senior Kleinian psychoanalyst proposed in all seriousness that it was the acceptance by all groups of the Kleinian concept of projective identification. One might – from an Independent point of view, of course – offer that the saving of psychoanalysis in 1944 in Britain was the refusal of the majority of the members of the British Psychoanalytic Society to follow any charismatic leader or omnipotent theory, and so sanity lay in the formation of the Middle, later Independent, Group.

A NEW CHILD AND ADOLESCENT PSYCHOTHERAPY
TRAINING

The arrival of an Independent training in child and adolescent psychotherapy grew from a situation that was not unlike the controversial discussions – a situation of increasing polarity and lack of communication,
perhaps the controversial discussions without the discussion.

Although established in the aftermath of the disputes within the BP-AS
in the 1940s, the early atmosphere of the Kleinian child psychotherapy
training at the Tavistock was one wherein Bick in the 1950s could readily
invite Winnicott to teach the Child Psychotherapy trainees. Juliet Hopkins
also describes the possibility of some leeway within prevailing convention:

> [In 1961] I was fortunate to have Winnicott as the supervisor of one of
> my training cases. As far as I know, no other student child psycho-
> therapist ever shared this good fortune, since doctrinal differences
> dictated that students should be supervised only by the orthodox.
> However, the Tavistock Clinic training, though Kleinian in orientation,
> allowed some latitude to its few 'middle group' students like myself to
> select our own supervisors.
>
> (Hopkins 1996: 20)

This 'latitude' – tenuous enough in 1961 – appears to have encountered a
period of sudden frost by the late 1960s. Khar comments:

> The Kleinian bitterness towards Winnicott and his burgeoning inde-
> pendence reached such proportions that during the late 1960s certain
> tutors on the Child Psychotherapy course at the Tavistock Clinic . . .
> expressly forbade their students to attend Winnicott's public lectures,
> even though Melanie Klein had died some years previously. Mrs
> Frances Tustin (personal communication, 22 February 1994), a
> renowned child psychotherapist, . . . confessed that 'I in my training
> was brought up not to read Winnicott'. Another of those trainees, now
> a seasoned professional, laughed as she recalled how she visited
> Winnicott in secret, as though he epitomised some dreadful subversive
> underground movement.
>
> (Khar 1996: 77)

By the late 1970s there were three training schools in the UK. The
Lowenfeld Institute of Child Psychology had closed in 1978:

> Although economic reasons finally led to the closure of the ICP as a
> clinic, the search for comparability across trainings was felt to have
> been an influence as the ACP and its Training Council consolidated
> around a more purely psychoanalytic approach than the holistic

Lowenfeld one was felt to be. It is somewhat ironic today that many admired senior members of the profession are ICP graduates and some of the most stimulating and creative writing on children and psycho-analysis comes from that stable.

(Lanyado and Horne 1999: 8–9)

Within this brief account there lies a sense that the ICP had failed, some-how, to be 'orthodox'. Of the three remaining schools, one was Jungian (the SAP where training began in 1974); the others – the Hampstead Clinic (to be renamed the Anna Freud Centre after Miss Freud's death) and the Tavistock Clinic – centred on the thinking and teaching of each of the two women around whom the controversial discussions had stormed.

There was little communication between these two major centres. Rather, it was felt that further entrenchment had occurred. At the Hampstead Clinic there was additionally grave concern about funding and the future of the institution: dependent on American financial goodwill and applicants from outside Britain presenting for training, the staff felt that both sources seemed to be drying up. The solution to finding a transitional (independent) position 'between Anna and Melanie' and perhaps keeping alive the teach-ing and theory of Miss Freud was the brainchild of Anne Hurry, a Hampstead staff member who had also trained in Adult Psychotherapy at the British Association of Psychotherapists (BAP) where the new training was to be located. She carefully chose her planning committee to comprise Hampstead-trained and Tavistock-trained child psychotherapists, all sym-pathetic to Independent thought, and the new BAP child training had its first intake of trainees in 1982. The flyer for the training announces:

A new training in Child Psychotherapy
The British Association of Psychotherapists has trained adult psycho-therapists since 1951. This new venture has been planned in response to the national shortage of child psychotherapists, and the need to provide a training which represents the thinking of the classical and inde-pendent groups in British psycho-analysis.

(from BAP archive, 1981)

The Training Committee demonstrated this range of experience, comprising Anne Hurry, Charlotte Balkanyi, Irmi Elkan, Wallace Hamilton, Juliet Hopkins, Rosalie Joffé, Dolly Lush, Eileen Orford, Pat Radford, Margret Tonnesmann and Peter Wilson. As Dolly Lush (a Tavistock staff member until her retirement) described, 'Anne Hurry asked if I would lend my name to it, that's all that was needed.' This was said as she retired from the BAP Child Training Committee after 20 years of stalwart service. The training was 21 years old in September 2003 – it has come of age and with a strong identity.

Trainees may be in analysis with analysts of all three sections of the Institute of Psychoanalysis and supervisors are equally Anna Freudian, Independent or Kleinian. Similarly seminar leaders are from all three orientations: it seems particularly important to have a specialist Freudian teach Freud, Oedipus and latency, and to have a Kleinian specialist teach, for example, Klein and Bion.

A by-product of this training has been a greater integration across the profession as, in teaching and supervision, ideas have been shared across theoretical divides. Anne Alvarez, who had resigned her post at the Tavistock, was later to return there and find her work rightly valued. In the interim years, however, she was an engaging and stimulating teacher at the BAP. Lively discussions took place, especially around technique, and her paper 'Beyond the unpleasure principle' (Alvarez 1988), she has said, owed a small measure to her BAP trainees. Recent trainees in supervision with her report that she still says, 'But you Independents know this! This is easy for you!' – usually about technical issues.

Where does it leave us as child psychotherapists? One has fantasies – even in the Middle Group – of what happens in other trainings. One can speculate as to the containment offered by trainings that take one theoretical perspective – a consistency and nurturing that is at times enviable. Such trainees may be viewed as young plants that are growing in a greenhouse, protected from the winds of controversy and theoretical conflict. Being in the middle of an Independent training can occasionally feel like being planted out, where frosts might still come, and told, 'Grow, damn you! Grow!' To experience all weathers, however, is somehow also 'very British' – and it is essential in character formation!

ESTABLISHING AN IDENTITY

With the seminal contributions of Kohon (1986) and Rayner (1991), we see a new consolidation of the Independent Group within the British Society, clarification of the principal theoretical positions and a group defining itself by what it is as well as by what it is not, gathering the commonalities of theoretical thought but not denying the breadth of theoretical positions possible. There had long been a flourishing of ideas (Brierley, Bowlby, Balint, Milner, Rycroft, Winnicott amongst the earlier independent minds; Bollas, Coltart, Casement, Klauber, King, Khan, Rayner, Sutherland, Wright more recently – and those only a few) and much of more recent writing develops perceptions stimulated by 'the genius of British analysis', Winnicott (Rycroft, quoted in Roazen 2002: 23). It is not surprising therefore, in this volume of Independent writings from child and adolescent psychotherapy, to find Winnicott to be a common thread.

What, then, would we say are the major theoretical and technical issues for those of us who once lay 'between Freud and Klein' (Limentani

1989)? Rayner (1991) provides us with a great deal of information here and what follows is indebted to him for his erudition and clarity. He notes, initially, that the fundamentals remain the same: basic classical theory and technique – the unconscious, defence and resistance, interpretation and the transference, and metapsychology – are taken as given. To this, he notes, most Independents would add from Mrs Klein and her followers the concept of projective identification and the use of 'the mechanisms of denial, projection and introjection creating splits for defensive purposes in the personality' (Rayner 1991: 22). Equally, Anna Freud's contributions of the analysis of the ego and the defences, and her concept of developmental lines, have become part of the repertoire of Independents.

It is interesting that, in the detail of theory, the Independents appear to have taken time particularly to position themselves in relation to Kleinian theory – possibly from valuing Klein as the co-progenitor of object relations theory (Brierley's (1937) seminal paper on affects placing her equally here). Yet Fairbairn holds a key role and, for the child psychotherapist, his emphasis on the importance of environment and real experience – taken up by Winnicott – has a necessary impact on how we understand and engage with our young patients. Most 'Independents do not widely subscribe to Klein's theory of neonatal development, either in her dating or in the means by which one position is said to succeed the other' (Rayner 1991: 23). (Anne Hurry, in the previous chapter in this volume, cites Paula Heimann's revised thoughts on the paranoid-schizoid position.) For Fairbairn and Winnicott, when paranoid-schizoid features appear, these are a *reaction* to trauma and to interactions with or impingements by the environment and not a necessary developmental stage – although both value the concept greatly in thinking about pathology. Similar importance is accorded to the environment when contemplating the origins of psychopathology: Klein saw these as rooted in conflict, originally between the life and death instincts. Independents see the roots in the early experience of interaction with the environment – 'real external object-relations' out of which phantasy then arises: hence 'phantasy is an 'inference' or 'interpretation' . . . Imagination or phantasy thus probably arises out of the interplay between infant and environment and has no meaning as an innate faculty' (Rayner 1991: 24). From such a perspective it becomes easier to see the progression to Khan's later concept of cumulative trauma and the further impact of the real environment (Khan 1963). Indeed, to the child psychotherapist working today, infantile trauma, loss, perversion and distortion of reality, neglect and abuse are such a feature of the histories of the children whom we see that we could no longer – in any tradition – only perceive innate conflict.

Some Independents do subscribe to the death instinct theory very much in the form that Klein took it from Freud. But Gillespie's view [1971],

both about the idea of the instinct itself and with regard to its consequence that aggressiveness could then be seen as an original sin of a
sort, would probably be subscribed to by the majority.

(Rayner 1991: 109)

This is a fundamental difference – for Mrs Klein destructiveness is innate
and so intra-psychic. Darwinian to the last, most Independents, and
certainly Independent child psychotherapists, view aggression as necessary
for survival, part of the self-protective function of the organism. Aggressiveness thus has a central position in Independent thought, with the
emphasis on its role in normal development. In this we are, perhaps, closer
to Anna Freud. Both Winnicott and Fairbairn perceive pathological
aggression as *reactive*: this may be to the actual, assumed or phantasised
impingement of the environment. Winnicott adds the point that muscular
aggression (which the mother has to survive) is the beginning of motility
and a sense of assertiveness and potency – essential for healthy development (Winnicott 1950–55: 204). In her revision of her initial conceptualisa-
tion of the life and death instincts, based on clinical experience that she
found challenged her earlier position, Heimann explored the possibility of
two types of aggression – that (as Winnicott) in the service of survival and
agency, and another expressed in sadism and cruelty. This latter, interestingly, she saw as derived from failures in the care offered by the environment (Heimann 1964). A similar view was expressed by Suttie (whose
influence on the object relations tradition was profound, if at times rather
unacknowledged) who based it on his very early formulation of attachment
theory (Suttie 1935).

The fundamental axis of the Independent position may well be that
originally articulated by Suttie and Fairbairn, that the human being is
object seeking rather than, as in drive theory, pleasure seeking (Suttie 1935;
Fairbairn 1941, 1946): 'the orientation of the infant to others is there from
the very beginning because the infant has adaptive genic roots for his
biological survival' (Sutherland 1989). This differs from Klein in that the
object is not simply a means towards pleasure: 'pleasure is not the end goal
of the impulse, but a means to its real end – relations with another'
(Greenberg and Mitchell 1983: 154).

Finally, the place of creativity and ideas around transitional space,
transitional objects and transformational space in Independent thought
more than merit attention. The third area of the mind – between internal
and external, between me and not-me, where play and thought and psychoanalysis can happen – is after all one of the most readily recognised
contributions of Winnicott and one developed and enhanced by several
later theorists, principally Bollas (e.g Bollas 1987). The influence of work in
these two areas has relevance for the therapist in establishing the setting of
the room, the nature of the interaction, and indeed in understanding the
purpose of the analytic encounter.

BRIEF IMPLICATIONS OF INDEPENDENT THEORY FOR TECHNIQUE IN WORK WITH CHILDREN

Perceiving the child as 'object-seeking' – rather than seeking relations in the service of undoing displeasure – takes us immediately into the arena of the external as well as internal world. With Fairbairn, Ferenczi and Winnicott, we find the importance of the role of real but flawed object relations, objects who have failed to meet the creativity of the child – or who have imposed their own perversion on the child-treated-as-object. How these 'mis-steps in the dance' become replayed in the child's pathology and in the transference relationship becomes the focus of work. However, in order *not* to replicate the mis-shapen dance that the child expects and replays in his object relationships, one has to keep in mind Winnicott's injunction that psychoanalysis offers a further intimacy, like the early infant–mother relationship, in which the curiosity of the child – and the 'true self' – may be called forth. One is therefore always seeking space in which the child's defences and affect are held in mind, yet curiosity becomes possible. To be careful about 'shame' and 'humiliation' (and the vulnerability of the ego ideal) need not mean avoiding anxiety or avoiding interpretation; it does mean actively taking great care about timing. In this, the Independent motif matters – that the interpretation that is most useful to the patient is the one the patient finds, in the therapeutic process, for himself.

Aggression

To perceive aggression as fundamental for development, healthy narcissism and a sense of agency does have serious implications for treatment. The Kleinian concept of innate destructiveness and hate, based on developments away from Freud's theory of the death instinct, leads to the need to analyse these impulses and their impact on the internal world. Following Winnicott, the Independent working with the child who is prone to attack would see the need to indicate the importance and necessity of the defence and articulate this – it is, after all, life or death – and the immaturity of the ego that can only resort to such early, primitive manoeuvres must be borne in mind. Often the therapist therefore begins by condoning the aggressive defence as necessary; the subsequent lessening of anxiety may then afford a space for thought (rather than action) and enable mutual curiosity to be engaged. A similar stance is helpful when faced with the child whose main defensive preoccupation is activity.

The working alliance and the setting

It would seem axiomatic that the therapist encounters a measure of 'ego' in the patient for engagement in therapy, and that one would seek to connect with this in a treatment alliance. It is not, however, uncommon to encounter censure of the concept of the working alliance, as if to foster it is indicative somehow of indulgence or gratification of the patient. It seems, at times, as if it gets confused with the idea of the positive transference and can be taken to imply an over-cultivation of this. The two are separate, if overlapping:

> In practice, the state of the transference always has repercussions on the treatment alliance, and the alliance is not completely autonomous and independent of the transference, even though a conceptual distinction is made between treatment alliance and transference.
>
> (Sandler, Kennedy and Tyson 1980: 48)

Sternberg explores such differences in the next chapter. For many Independent therapists, however, simple matters like the therapy room being quietly but overtly a place that is welcoming to children would be of importance and would be seen as part of the process of establishing a treatment/working alliance. Although each child has a protected box of toys and play materials, it is unusual for an Independent only to have the box in an otherwise fairly bare room. Perhaps this is not unconnected to the conviction that paranoid-schizoid manifestation is reactive to external impingement and not an innate, initial 'given', hence not a state that a child might be *expected* to regress to. The model of early mother–infant interaction that Winnicott would have us keep in mind as the model for therapeutic work means that we present an environment not overwhelming in its possibilities but definitely offering a curious and engaged 'other'.

The process

With the pronouncement that 'there is no such thing as a baby' (Winnicott 1947a) the important recognition that the process of therapy is an interplay of two minds, of the patient's transference and the therapist's countertransference, has led to interesting developments in how the countertransference is monitored (Casement 1985) and used (Winnicott 1947b). The constant reminder that this is a process done in the transitional space between two people, not a procedure applied by one to the other, requires a continuous capacity to monitor oneself as therapist and to seek room in the therapeutic session for observing this interaction. This is particularly important with active children and technical inventions like 'thinking time' (see Chapter 13) arise from this realisation.

One would also include the general tendency not to go immediately for the manifest content (anxiety) below the defences but rather to wait for the individual psychological structure to emerge before going for deep interpretation. Again, this varies according to the needs of patient and therapeutic situation, but it would seem therefore that pace and timing are fundamental principles, as outlined in Chapter 9. Moving, too, from a developmental to an analytic stance and being able to go between the two would take us closer to Anna Freud's teaching in terms of technique, as would keeping the developmental position and tasks in mind. There is a certain freedom generated by the recognition that, with children, one seeks to do sufficient work to enable them to regain the natural developmental thrust – and 'developmental track' – that then takes them forward once more. No ideal personality structure is in mind, simply a spectrum of possibilities on which the child hopefully takes up a more appropriately defended and more optimistic position.

Several contributors to this volume feature 'play' and 'playfulness'. These are developed at greater length in Chapters 8 and 13, not simply because they are such Winnicottian concepts but because they take us into the area of *how* the therapist is with the patient. This is also not unadjacent to Paula Heimann's concept of the 'naturalness' of the analyst and questions of 'neutrality', sterility, emotional responsiveness and alert attention all feature strongly in Independent writing over many years, from Balint to Bollas. Perhaps Balint can sum it up, as long ago as 1939:

> The objective task demands that a patient analysed in any of the many individual ways shall learn to know his own unconscious mind and not that of his analyst. The subjective task demands that analysing shall not be too heavy an emotional burden, that the individual variety of technique shall procure sufficient emotional outlet for the analyst. A sound and adequate technique must therefore be doubly individual.
>
> (Balint 1939: 206–7)

Counter-transference

There will be a great deal in common amongst the different theoretical schools when counter-transference is considered. However, there is a perception that counter-transference has often seemed to centre, for Kleinian analysts, on the patients' projective identifications. This is undoubtedly part of the process but not its entirety. Both Winnicott and Anna Freud would argue forcefully that a certain amount of ego development is necessary before projection and projective identification is possible (remember Anna Freud's rueful comment, 'First you have to build the house before you can throw anybody out of it!'). This would take us into the arena of developmental therapy (Hurry 1998). Additionally, the Independent would be more inclined to Heimann's revision of her major work 'On counter-transference' (1950), a revision published in 1960, and developed in 1964 and 1969. There we find not only the position that the counter-transference is more than the projections of the patient, being created by *both* analyst and patient, but also the understanding that projective identification is in fact the analyst's counter-transference at work, but a little late. The balance of perception is important: active intrusion by the patient or a failure of discernment as to the nature of the transference by the analyst. Each will call forth a different technical response.

A DIVERSION INTO PARENT–INFANT OBSERVATION

Esther Bick made a major contribution to the training of psychoanalysts and psychotherapists when she developed her method of observing infants (Bick 1964). Despite the commonality of observational skills and the commonality of paying acute attention to infant development, however, there is a subtle yet important distinction in these titles – Bick's 'Notes on infant observation . . .' and the heading 'Parent–infant observation' perhaps demonstrate where the Independent would add an important emphasis. This is the infant in his/her environment. 'There is no such thing as a baby' after all (Winnicott 1947a). In observing, therefore, one is perhaps hesitant about leaping to assumptions as to the internal phantasy world of the infant, reluctant to impose a prism of theoretical knowledge, but rather always considering what is happening in the space between parent or carer and infant. The following vignettes show something of the process:

> Lisa, age 6 months, lay close to her mother's breast and gazed into her eyes as the nipple of the bottle played with her mouth. Enjoying this, she smiled at her mother and accepted the bottle. As she sucked, her right hand came up to the bottle and began to explore the feel of her mother's fingers on it. She stroked these, rather dreamily, seemingly enjoying the touch. Her mother stroked her fingers with one of her own. Lisa stopped sucking and held her mother's gaze. 'She's enjoying her feed,' said her mother. 'Isn't she?' – to Lisa. Lisa gurgled contentedly and resumed sucking. There was no urgency, simply seeming contentment.

This feeding sequence occurred once Lisa had learned to crawl. Before this her mother fed her from the bottle, the baby perched distantly at the end of her knee. Lisa had to become evidently separate – crawling and mobile – before such an intimate feeding as in this observation could take place. Lisa responds at once with sensual enjoyment, very attuned to her mother's stroking finger. It is 'parent–infant' observation. One may fantasise about the internal possibilities for Lisa – omnipotence, gratitude – but one could certainly see an infant alert and responsive to her environment and ready to be receptive to change – i.e. object seeking. This was also evident in a less comfortable situation:

Lisa at the age of three months was being bottle-fed by her young 17-year-old aunt who was simultaneously conversing with another relative. Lisa's mother was elsewhere. The bottle was being held at an angle that did not allow Lisa to suck the milk. She gazed for quite a time at her aunt's face, as if trying to engage her with her gaze. A few noises of protest followed. The bottle moved about, sometimes allowing her to feed, sometimes not. Finally Lisa stretched her legs right out, bent up her knees, arched her back, straightened her left leg, twisted her right leg beneath her left and stretched out her arms, as if trying to find a balance that allowed her to control the flow of the liquid. She gobbled it down, not her usual feeding pattern.

In this observation one can see the role of normal development and the impact of an unavailable environment. When faced with mild 'unpleasure' – or lack of attunement – or care that is not 'good enough' – the baby tries gaze, then vocalisation, to alert the object's attention. These failing, she reverts to dependency on the body ego – a regression to body-based mechanisms for containing anxiety. Without a developmental construct, one cannot understand the process. And without a knowledge base that has the infant as an object-seeking entity from the beginning, we could not make sense of Lisa's regression to the body – there is no such thing as a baby, and if there is we can see how pathology might follow.

CONCLUSIONS

There is an established tradition for the psychotherapist training in an Independent school – although the words 'Independent' and 'school' when conjoined might well be perceived as an oxymoron. While valuing Freud, Klein and Anna Freud, the trainee child psychotherapist can take pride in a subsequent body of critical and creative theoretical and technical writing. The role of object relatedness, the importance of the environment and of trauma, the relevance of development and the real-life experience, and the concepts of transitional and transformational space give rise to originality in technique and in one's response to the child patient: it is less the pursuit of a theory than an engagement with a person. To paraphrase Anne Hurry's quote from Pearl King in the previous chapter, we constantly ask: 'Why is this child communicating in this way with me now?' The next chapter looks in depth at technical approaches and differences. Behind those, perhaps, lies the other great Winnicottian question, as valid for therapist as for developing child, 'Now, what can I do with this object?'

References

Alvarez, A. (1988) 'Beyond the unpleasure principle: some preconditions for thinking through play' *Journal of Child Psychotherapy* 14(2): 1–13

Balint, M. and Balint, A. (1939) 'On transference and counter-transference'. In M. Balint (1965), *Primary Love and Psycho-Analytic Technique*. London: Tavistock

Bick, E. (1964) 'Notes on infant observation in psychoanalytic training' *International Journal of Psychoanalysis* 45(4): 558–66

Bion, W. R. (1967) *Second Thoughts*. London: Karnac

Bion, W. R. (1970) *Attention and Interpretation*. London: Karnac

Bollas, C. (1987) *The Shadow of the Object: Psychoanalysis of the Unthought Known*. London: Free Association Books

Brierley, M. (1937) 'Affects in theory and practice' *International Journal of Psychoanalysis* 18: 256–63

Casement, P. (1985) *On Learning from the Patient*. London: Tavistock

Casement, P. (2002) Foreword. In B. Kahr (ed.), *The Legacy of Winnicott: Essays on Infant and Child Mental Health*. London: Karnac

Fairbairn, W. R. D. (1941) 'A revised psychopathology of the psychoses and psycho-neuroses' *International Journal of Psychoanalysis* 22: 250–79

Fairbairn, W. R. D. (1946) 'Object relations and dynamic structure' *International Journal of Psychoanalysis* 27: 30–7

Freud, S. (1912) 'Recommendations to physicians practising psychoanalysis.' *Standard Edition*, 12. London: Hogarth Press

Gillespie, W. H. (1971) 'Aggression and instinct theory' *International Journal of Psychoanalysis* 52: 155–60

Grayling, A. C. (1995) 'The empiricists'. In Grayling, *Philosophy: A Guide through the Subject*. Oxford: Oxford University Press

Greenberg, J. R. and Mitchell, S. A. (1983) *Object Relations in Psychoanalytic Theory*. Cambridge, MA and London: Harvard University Press

Hayman, A. (2001) 'What do our terms mean?' In R. Steiner and J. Johns (eds.), *Within Time and Beyond Time: A Festschrift for Pearl King*. London: Karnac

Heimann, P. (1950) 'On counter-transference' *International Journal of Psychoanalysis* 31: 1–2

Heimann, P. (1964/1969) 'Evolutionary leaps and the origin of cruelty'. In M. Tonnesmann (ed.), *About Children and Children-No-Longer: Collected Papers 1942–80*. London: Tavistock/Routledge 1989

Hopkins, J. (1996) 'From baby games to let's pretend' *Journal of the British Association of Psychotherapists* 1(31), Part 2: 20–7

Hurry, A. (ed.) (1998) *Psychoanalysis and Developmental Therapy*. London: Karnac

Jones, E. (2004) 'Charles Rycroft and the historical perspective'. In J. Pearson (ed.), *Analyst of the Imagination: The Life and Work of Charles Rycroft*. London: Karnac

Khan, M. M. R. (1963) 'The concept of cumulative trauma'. In Khan, *The Privacy of the Self: Papers on Psychoanalytic Theory and Technique*. London: Hogarth Press, 1974

Khar, B. (1996) *D. W. Winnicott: A Biographical Portrait*. London: Karnac

King, P. and Steiner, R. (eds.) (1991) *The Freud–Klein Controversies, 1941–45*. London: Routledge

Kohon, G. (ed.) (1986) *The British School of Psychoanalysis: The Independent Tradition*. London: Free Association Books

Lanyado, M. and Horne, A. (1999) *The Handbook of Child and Adolescent Psychotherapy: Psychoanalytic Approaches*. London and New York: Routledge

Limentani, A. (1989) *Between Freud and Klein: The Psychoanalytic Quest for Knowledge and Truth*. London: Free Association Books

Lomas, P. (2004) 'The question of independence in psychotherapy'. In J. Pearson (ed.), *Analyst of the Imagination: The Life and Work of Charles Rycroft*. London: Karnac

Pearson, J. (ed.) (2004) *Analyst of the Imagination: The Life and Work of Charles Rycroft*. London: Karnac

Phillips, A. (1988) *Winnicott*. London: Fontana Press

Phillips, A. (2000) 'Winnicott's Hamlet'. In Phillips, *Promises, Promises: Essays on Literature and Psychoanalysis*. London: Faber & Faber

Rayner, E. (1991) *The Independent Mind in British Psychoanalysis*. London: Free Association Books

Reich, A. (1951) 'On counter-transference' *International Journal of Psycho-Analysis* 32: 25–31

Roazen, P. (2002) 'A meeting with Donald Winnicott in 1965'. In B. Kahr (ed.), *The Legacy of Winnicott: Essays on Infant and Child Mental Health*. London: Karnac

Roazen, P. (2004) Charles Rycroft and ablation. In J. Pearson (ed.), *Analyst of the Imagination: The Life and Work of Charles Rycroft*. London: Karnac

Rycroft, C. (1955) 'On idealisation, illusion and catastrophic disillusion' *International Journal of Psychoanalysis* 36(1): 81–7

Rycroft, C. (1968) *Imagination and Reality*. New York: International Universities Press

Rycroft, C. (1993) 'Reminiscences of a survivor: psychoanalysis 1937–1993'. Graduation Address given at Regent's College, London published as Chapter 15, 'The Last Word' in J. Pearson (ed.) (2004) *Analyst of the Imagination: The Life and Work of Charles Rycroft*. London: Karnac

Sandler, J., Kennedy, H. and Tyson, R. L. (1980) *The Technique of Child Psychoanalysis: Discussions with Anna Freud*. London: Hogarth Press

Sutherland, J. D. (1989) *Fairbairn's Journey into the Interior*. London: Free Association Books. Extract published as 'Fairbairn's achievement' in J. S. Grotstein and D. B. Rinsley (eds.), *Fairbairn and the Origins of Object Relations*. London: Free Association Books 1994

Suttie, I. D. (1935) *The Origins of Love and Hate*. London: Free Association Books, 1988

Winnicott, D. W. (1945) 'Primitive emotional development'. In Winnicott (1958), *Collected Papers: Through Paediatrics to Psychoanalysis*. London: Tavistock Publications

Winnicott, D. W. (1947a) 'Further thoughts on babies as persons'. In Winnicott (1964), *The Child, the Family and the Outside World*. Harmondsworth: Penguin

Winnicott, D. W. (1947b) 'Hate in the counter-transference'. In Winnicott, *Collected Papers*

Winnicott, D. W. (1950–55) 'Aggression in relation to emotional development'. In Winnicott, *Collected Papers*

3 Not simply 'doing'

Thoughts from the literature on technique

Janine Sternberg

This chapter considers 'technique' as the skills or activities that the therapist carries out within a psychoanalytic session. These are profoundly influenced by the therapist's understanding of psychoanalytic theory and her[1] manner of putting it into practice. These theoretical ideas have to be *put into practice*. Additionally, what the practitioner believes to be the purpose of psychoanalytic psychotherapy will influence her ideas about how it ought to be conducted.

Throughout, I cite writers who have written about technique. Only a small proportion are child psychotherapists. This volume seeks to redress this. In general, writing about technique *per se* is not common. Most psychoanalytic practitioners write about their clinical work as it illuminates theory, but often only refer to the technical aspects in passing, and child psychotherapists seem even less inclined than their adult psychotherapist colleagues to do so. While much of what I address is equally applicable to psychotherapy with both children and adults, the later part of this chapter concentrates on differences in technique needed for child work.

IN THE BEGINNING

The natural starting point when considering technique is Freud's six papers (1911, 1912a, 1912b, 1913, 1914, 1915), which give some picture of his early views on the subject. For example he advocated the use of the couch, so that the patient could not see and be influenced by the therapist's expression. He elucidated the fundamental rule of free association and the value of evenly suspended attention on the therapist's part. He emphasised the usefulness of the setting, the regularity of time, and warned the therapist against rushing to give global interpretations, stating instead the importance of waiting until the patient was receptive to the interpretation. He also wrote of being opaque to the patient, using the famous images of both mirror and surgeon, and proposed a model of analysis that had rather an intellectual emphasis in contrast to the more experiential one that is probably current today. However, he also made it clear (1912b) that he had found a technique that suited *him*, and that the work might be carried out differently by someone else.

In 1913 he reiterated that his recommendations did not have to be accepted unconditionally by future practitioners. This issue of creating one's own technique, different from Freud's, has hardly been addressed 'head on'. Today it is generally recognised that the therapist's psycho-analytic orientation will affect her technique, although some studies have suggested that this may not be as powerful an influence as might be believed. Hamilton, examining how group orientation influenced individual thinkers, found interrelationships between specific theoretical influences and technical practices, but also found considerable individuality of response (Hamilton 1996). Practitioners have an 'official' public statement about what they do, together with a preconscious model which is not the same, although there is of course some – greater or lesser – overlap. This volume presents its own blend, arising from the influence of Independent theory and its implication for practice, imbued with teaching and super-vision from the range of theoretical traditions, permitting the finding of one's own voice and style.

It has been long been acknowledged that there is no standard therapeutic technique, that although there are shared assumptions there is no common behaviour. Glover sent out 29 questionnaires asking practising psycho-analysts to evaluate certain statements about psychoanalytic theory and technique and to agree or disagree with these (Glover 1954). He received 24 replies. There was unanimous agreement on only 6 of 63 points, and of these only one (the importance of analysing the transference) could be considered as fundamental. There was considerable disagreement about interpretations, specifically their length and timing. While we must take account of the historical context in which Glover carried this out – only ten years after the Controversial Discussions – and the partisan anti-Kleinian points he hoped to make, the diversity must be taken seriously. This is especially true when we remember, as Strupp points out, that the ques-tionnaire related only to what analysts *said* they did, not what they *actually* did in sessions, so that the divergence was likely to be even greater (Strupp 1973).

Discussion of 'divergence' in current practice is often confined to com-munication within the privacy of the supervisor–supervisee relationship. A further aim of this volume is to open up discussion about variations. Indeed, diversity of practice is not only about what practitioners say they do and actually do, but also about the ever evolving dynamic between the founders, the subsequent 'tradition' and contemporary practice of psycho-therapy and psychoanalysis.

I would like to make a very flat and bald statement as a starting point for thinking about 'technique' more closely. From the beginning of any treat-ment, the therapist creates a setting within which the work can take place. Once there the therapist pays close attention to all that the patient does and the atmosphere created within the session. What is noticed and experienced through the workings of the transference–counter-transference relationship is then thought about by the therapist. A theoretical framework may help in understanding or ordering this material. At a moment the therapist judges to be right, she will say something to the patient, perhaps simply a question or a clarification or perhaps an 'interpretation'. I shall return to what constitutes an interpretation and different types of interpretation later. From the patient's response, the therapist can receive further information, which she then uses to evaluate what the patient has done with what has been said. Different emphasis can be put on how interactive the process is then perceived as being.

THE THERAPIST'S ABILITY TO LISTEN ATTENTIVELY AND WITH AN OPEN MIND

In the consulting room the therapist must observe the patient carefully, taking note of all she sees and experiences, before then evaluating it. With adult patients this noticing will take the form of watching minute gestures as well as listening carefully to verbal communication, and noting and thinking about non-verbal communication. Symington, for example, writes of patients for whom it can *seem* as if an interpretation has had no impact, but where the alert therapist can detect the flicker of an eyelid. He states that many patients *cannot* express their emotional states in words (Symington 1996).

With child patients there is also much to notice both in the child patient and about what is happening within the therapist. Children who play actively give the therapist much to observe, both in the content of their play and the way they set about it. And a child patient who is unable to play also needs the therapist to be closely attentive. As well as using her counter-transference to evaluate what the patient is experiencing, the child and adolescent psychotherapist must, as far as possible, see any tiny movements, similar to the way she will have observed an infant as part of her training. She must try to think about the sequence of the activity, to see what it might mean. At times a child and adolescent psychotherapist will facilitate the play, either taking up a role as requested or, for example, cutting or sticking if required to do so and the request feels appropriate.

As well as noticing all non-verbal activity, the therapist must have a very particular way of listening. This includes close attention to detail and listening at a more meta-level. Rayner writes that the analyst must be sensitive to the intonational, syntactical and linguistic habits of others, and hear the meanings 'between and behind words' (Rayner 1990). Allied to this is Schlesinger's suggestion that the therapist must unlearn the ways he has learned to listen conversationally (Schlesinger 1994). He points out that in conversational mode we often listen 'too closely' and lapse into identification with the speaker. We assume the speaker means to make sense and with social listening we fill in the elisions and ignore pauses. This is useless in analysis. This surely connects with Freud's idea of free-floating attention. The therapist listens, holds on to what she has heard and notes how she then feels. Although using a more hermeneutic and interactional model would dispute the separation between these activities, pointing out how each influences the other in a circular way, for the moment I think it is useful to try to think about what is coming *in* to the therapist and how it needs to be held and processed inside, before we move on to how it is then used to further the therapeutic process.

TOLERATING THE COUNTER-TRANSFERENCE

I am assuming in the reader a certain familiarity with the basic concepts of transference and counter-transference, and also with the history of how the concepts have been treated in analytic circles. Since Heimann's seminal paper, clinicians have realised that 'the analyst's emotional response to his patient within the analytic situation represents one of the most important tools for his work. The analyst's counter-transference is an instrument of research into the patient's unconscious' (Heimann 1950: 74). The analyst needs to have 'a freely roused emotional sensibility so as to perceive and follow closely her patient's emotional movements and unconscious phantasies' (Heimann 1950: 75). So we can see that the therapist must not be defended too strongly against these experiences, allowing herself to feel them but not be so overwhelmed by them as to be unable to think about why she is experiencing them.

Today therapists are more interested in exploring their counter-transference reactions to and potential enactments about patients' infantile aspects while still, where possible, avoiding acting on them. Kernberg writes of how the therapist must tolerate the patient's need to regress, in particular his aggression, without withdrawing, submitting, retaliating or acting out in the counter-transference (Kernberg 1993), while much earlier Winnicott had written of the necessity of 'expecting acting-out in the transference and . . . give it positive value' (Winnicott 1963: 210). In the therapeutic relationship because of the imbalance of power it is possible for the therapist, consciously or unconsciously, to manipulate the patient. Schafer refers to the many subtle ways of becoming an enforcer or a bully (Schafer 1983), thus playing into the view, described by Parsons and Derman, in which the child believes that the world is composed of controller and controlled, a situation not open to negotiation or give and take (Parsons and Dermen 1999: 344). With increasing interest in the interactive nature of the analytic relationship there is acknowledgement in the literature of what happens *between* a patient and therapist. The therapist must have an awareness of how the patient is using him. All too often a child will act as if the therapist could not possibly remember what had happened in the previous session, thus treating her as an adult who has no memory of or interest in the ongoing life of the child. This need to repeat on the patient's part can push the therapist into being what the patient finds familiar (Sandler 1981). Schafer warns of the need to avoid analytic work being unconsciously subverted into a repetition of that which must be analysed. In order to do this the therapist must be able to create space to think about his feelings.

Provided that we are able to study counter-transference reactions in a non-defensive way, we will learn a great deal not only about our own reactions but also about how the patient's mind works. Kernberg says that counter-transference is 'the total emotional reaction of the analyst to the patient', but then specifies that the analyst has to differentiate the origin of any particular reaction and explore it in order to incorporate this understanding in interpretative formulations without denying it or acting out in the counter-transference (Kernberg 1993). This ability to tolerate counter-transference feelings is important. These feelings are often intense. King pointed out how difficult it can be for the analyst to experience and think about what he is feeling on account of the strength of what is being aroused in or projected into him (King 1978). The therapist can feel paralysed by the rage or despair engendered in her when a child projects feelings which are experienced as too awful to think about. Carpy writes of some 'inevitable partial acting out of the counter-transference' and suggests the patient is helped by witnessing the analyst's struggles (Carpy 1989: 292).

At the same time as she identified the usefulness of counter-transference experiences, Heimann also specified that while the analyst must be receptive he must not act on the feelings but use them to understand and help formulate interpretations. This injunction against acting may be easier said than done. Renik (1993) suggests that awareness of counter-transference is always retrospective, that micro-activity within the therapist and in relation to the patient has taken place and has been noticed, although hopefully a gross enactment has been avoided. Again we see the importance of a reflective space within which the therapist must hold on to feelings and think. Ogden has enlarged this concept in a most interesting way to include the need to examine the content of the therapist's reverie around the patient (Ogden 1999).

THE REFLECTIVE SPACE

The idea of the reflective space both for patient and therapist is at the heart of effective therapy. Apart from the physical characteristics of the setting, what constitutes this reflective space? In thinking about this analytic attitude we may be helped by the idea of *where* the therapist is located in relation to the patient. Anna Freud described it as equidistant from the id, ego and super-ego (Freud 1976) while Rayner states, 'It is a primary necessity for the analyst to centre himself upon a distance from the patient that is optimal for objectivity' (Rayner 1990: 246). He goes on to say that an intermediate space between analyst and patient is necessary so that there is commonality, but they are nevertheless separate. It is in this intermediate space that the serious 'play' of analysis must occur, an idea expressed by Winnicott (Winnicott 1971). Winnicott's view on the importance of the transitional space within which the serious work, the play, of analysis takes place has been immensely influential to therapists in the Independent tradition, as is evident in many of the contributions to this volume. His often elliptical way of expressing ideas (also a characteristic of Bion's writings) allows them to be significant to his readers even when they do not fully grasp his meaning.

We have addressed' noticing' and 'feeling', and can now, briefly, think about 'thinking'. The therapist has to be able to sustain a space in her mind in which the whole maelstrom of feelings evoked in a therapeutic session can be allowed to settle and then be sorted out. An important part of thinking is the theoretical framework that underpins understanding. For Symington (1996), the therapist needs to know theory and know how to apply it, and he gives the analogy of a workman knowing which tool to use for which job; while Schafer connects this use of theory with experience to write of what he calls 'anticipation' (Schafer 1983). He employs the analogy of a tennis player, involved in a game that is each time new and fresh, using his experience of previous games and his understanding of how certain strokes operate to save himself from running all over the court.

To carry out the cognitive aspects of this complex process of holding on to feelings the therapist needs a certain detachment, an ability to think, evaluate, remember and anticipate. In this way the capacity to become temporarily and partially detached is a prerequisite of analytic work – but we must emphasise its temporary nature. We have already seen how vital it is not to be detached, but to be intimately involved in order to have the necessary counter-transference experiences.

This ability to hold on to ideas and feelings, often uncomfortable ones, is an essential therapeutic tool. Bion says that tolerating periods of not understanding is essential and unavoidable (Bion 1962). It may be that at times some of us are unable to tolerate ambiguities. We may grab at 'understanding' and make interpretations in order to deny the anxiety aroused in us. Symington points out that theoretical positions can be used to *seem* to understand, and so avoid the waiting process (Symington 1983). The same defensive use of 'knowing' is addressed by Parsons, when he states 'our understanding can only develop if we are not anxious to hold on to it' (Parsons 1986: 487). We need to differentiate between holding on to something with a deadly grip, which we all do at times, but which we know to be unhelpful, and making space for something to lodge until the right time comes for meaning and perhaps interpretation to emerge from it. An ability to wait in a state of alert interest, as a mother waits for her baby to re-engage after glancing away, rather than in acute anxiety, is essential but it is often hard to maintain when in the presence of keen distress.

With child patients we may find ourselves doing, or tempted to do, something reassuring to evade the terrible pain. Occasionally, unfortunately, with violent patients we may even find ourselves unable to pause, provoking further aggression as a way of then being busy with managing it. We have seen that sometimes the therapist *does* something because she cannot bear to do otherwise, but an important therapeutic skill lies in finding when is the right time to do something, and it is hard to exercise this judgement under pressure. Freud himself said: 'One must be careful not to give a patient the solution of a symptom or the translation of a wish until he is already so close to it that he has only one short step more to make in order to get hold of the explanation for himself' (Freud 1913: 140). We all know that understanding which we feel we have discovered is much more precious than that which we have been 'given', however impressed we are by the wisdom of the donor. As therapists we should not allow ourselves the gratification of showing off – imposing – our 'wisdom'.

DIFFERENT FORMS OF COMMUNICATION IN THERAPY

Before looking closely at interpretation, it is necessary to say something about communication as a whole. The way the therapist talks to the patient is important. Tone of voice, cadence and intonation can convey something genuine to the patient in a way words may not. It is important not to address the patient in a controlling, alienating way as an object being scrutinised from on high. The therapist's view of what is going on can be offered in quite a provisional way and interpretations made in a way that does not strip the patient of his own ability to think. Therapists often use key words and phrases from the patient's own associations. This is especially pertinent in child psychotherapy where the adults' natural role as parent or teacher may predispose both partners in the therapy to assume that the therapist holds all the knowledge. The use of appropriate language is something child and adolescent psychotherapists are very sensitive to, having to be aware of the chronological age and development of their patients. Although it is important to find a shared language, we may also have to tread carefully in thinking about how to talk with a patient about obscenities that he has used. To use them back may feel attacking, provocative or exciting, yet to 'bowdlerise' the language used may make the child feel alienated and distant.

Although interpretation is a pivotal part of verbal communication we must also consider the therapist's use of aspects of verbal communication that are not strictly interpretative. These would include the therapist asking questions and seeking clarification. This may be in the service of a future interpretation, gathering in sufficient evidence or perhaps checking out that something has been accurately understood, but it may also be sufficient in itself. The therapist attempts to provide clarification and understanding by offering observations and descriptions of what she sees in the behaviour, thoughts and feelings of her patients. These observations and descriptions are not interpretations, although they may, coming from a different viewpoint, present something new and previously unthought to the patient. Of course these questions and clarifications deal with manifest content, and although they can be used to get to deeper levels there is a risk that they can prevent the material from deepening and avoid unconscious phantasies.

Indeed, silence can be an appropriate tool for the therapist, privileging unconscious to unconscious communication. There are many different qualities of silence, but the therapist's silence during a child's play may actually increase the child's sense of being attuned to and thought about, as well as facilitate his ability to continue to play and so continue to work something out internally for himself (Lanyado 2004: 15–37).

Often children object to the therapist talking to them as they play. For some this is because it interrupts the sense of being immersed in play: they cannot 'live' it *and* stand outside it to answer questions about it simultaneously. Of course interpretation may also describe something that is painful to hear, so bringing the wish to reject it. The therapist must judge when and how to speak, following her attuned responsiveness to the child as well as her theoretical framework to evaluate what might be helpful. When a child has just used the animals to play out a scenario in which the baby animals have been snatched away by the tiger while the mother cow grazes serenely unaware, the therapist may well have many comments in mind. She might want to prioritise the un-noticing mother, the dangers of the world or the fears of the babies, choosing which of these to emphasise according to her knowledge of the child and his life history. However, any or all of them could disturb the flow of the play and push the child into a defensive retreat.

SOME THOUGHTS ABOUT INTERPRETATION

Interpretation, at its simplest, is the therapist conveying to the patient her understanding of what is happening at that moment in therapy, referring to unconscious processes and perhaps linking to the patient's present and/or past experiences and his relationship with the therapist: as Freud said, 'making the unconscious conscious'. Roth describes it as trying to introduce the patient to aspects of himself and his internal object relations that he does not consciously experience or know about (Roth 2001). However, Pine points out that the patient needs to have the capacity to realise that while the therapist is pointing out unpleasant inner or life history realities she is *not* doing so to condemn, humiliate, provoke or ultimately abandon the patient. He says that an interpretation needs 'soil on which it can fall and take root' (Pine 1985). Not all patients have this capacity; some may need to defend against feeling overwhelmed, flooded or disorganised by the interpretation. He notes that although interpretation is a powerful tool for bringing about change it is clear from clinical experience that there is no one-to-one correspondence between insight and change. This is somewhat different from a view held in the 1950s, when drive theory was dominant, when insight was thought to be the main mutative factor bringing about intra-psychic change. Today the interest in the therapist as a new or a developmental object privileges the relationship with the therapist, having the view that it is the patient's experience of new ways of relating that leads to change (Hurry 1998; Lanyado 2004; Loewald 1960; Stern *et al.* 1998; Stern 2004).

Roth has produced a most interesting paper in which she describes how the same material could produce different levels of interpretation (Roth 2001). The therapist could 'go for' interpreting the material on a historical level (level 1), at a level about the transference (level 2), about the transference in the here and now (level 3) or as an awareness of the analyst's internal difficulties which lead to an internal relationship which is in fact being enacted within the session at that time (level 4). She says the therapist has to decide where it is useful to intervene, and although we may focus our attention on one aspect of the patient's communication we must, in our minds, hold on to and be aware of the other aspects as well. We should again note the need to hold on to a number of thoughts or ideas simultaneously as an important therapeutic skill.

Things may move very fast in a therapy session, but especially in intensive therapy there is the opportunity to return to themes and issues that have only glancingly been recognised in a session at another time. Roth describes the understanding of the here-and-now transference relationship as the 'epicentre' of the emotional meaning of analysis, and says that the therapist must keep his mind located at this level at all times, 'it is where we always live within the session', but that it is not always possible or desirable to interpret at levels 3 and 4. The therapist and patient need to 'roam a bit over the wide territory' that other material provides. Indeed there is repeated emphasis on the point of interpretation, and specifically transference interpretation, *not* being to do with intellectual understanding of what is being said. A successful interpretation brings the patient and analyst together emotionally.

Pine distinguishes between an empathic statement, which describes and explains but does not link, and an interpretation (Pine 1985). Interpretation promotes *understanding*, whereas the empathic statement promotes a feeling of *being understood*. As infants we need the experience of being understood to begin the development of our own understanding. Fonagy's very inter-esting work on mentalisation outlines how vital the experience of the mother's containing mind is for the infant (Fonagy 2001). However, in and of itself it is only the first stage in a developmental process. The infant, and in this setting the patient, has to build on the experience of being understood to begin to think about and in time understand himself. The view that psychoanalysis depends on the repetition of some aspects of the mother–infant relationship, such as attunement, holding in mind and containment, is looked at in greater detail below and is an important aspect of Independent Group thinking. Late twentieth century sneers at the stereotype of the unending dependency of the patient on the therapist do not take account of the fact that the therapist should be aiming for the patient to reach a time when he can take over a number of functions the therapist has previously carried out for him, and notice, think and link for himself. With child patients the child psychotherapist has the additional advantage of the maturational and developmental thrust, which can carry this process forward once the therapist has given the child patient the experience that had previously been absent or unable to be used.

Suggestions about how and when to interpret are relatively rare. Bollas suggests that the therapist should take care that not all interpretations focus on the analyst–patient relationship, because he views these as eroding the patient's self-analytic capacity (Bollas 1989). Stewart considered the classic view that transference interpretations should be avoided in the early stages of treatment because they interfere with the development of transference neurosis (Stewart 1987). He contrasted this with the view, usually attributed to Kleinians, that they should be offered from the beginning. Different types of patients call on different aspects of technique. If the therapist clearly expects too much of the patient he wounds him, but if he expects too little he appears to be 'Pollyannaish'. In this he holds the Independent position that transference interpretation remains 'fundamental for psychic change' (Rayner 1990: 188) while not expecting only this form of inter-pretation from the start.

This has some similarities to Alvarez's (1997) work on the grammar of interpretations. She 'distinguishes between the grammar of wishes in neurotic patients and the grammar of imperative needs in borderline patients'. Describing how her thinking on this issue has changed, she considers her previous way of working with a patient as at times 'posi-tively harmful'. Her realisation that what she had previously thought of as omnipotent and paranoid defences were desperate attempts to *overcome* and *recover from* states of despair and terror is crucial. She carefully explains how this viewpoint then calls upon the therapist to interpret in a different way:

> Where there is little ego to start with, and perhaps a cruel depriving superego, the interpretive grammar of wishes may carry all too cruel

implications; rather than help the child to think about deprivation, it actually succeeds in depriving him or her further.

(Alvarez 1997: 766)

and:

Interpretations of anxiety or loss to an already despairing child can weaken him or her. Other grammars, the grammar of imperatives, may enable the child's ego to grow stronger.

(Alvarez 1997: 732)

Interestingly this way of thinking, from a leading Kleinian child psychotherapist, has much in common with ideas familiar to both Anna Freudians and Independents.

As we will see in this volume, it is not uncommon for child psychotherapists in the Independent tradition to 'interpret in the displacement', a technique pioneered by Anna Freud. The therapist may, for example, comment on the actions in a child's play: so, following an earlier example, talk of how the baby animals might have felt when experiencing the mother as careless of their safety, but not overtly link it with how the patient had experienced similar things when in the care of an alcoholic mother. The therapist's decision to interpret in this way is influenced by thoughts about what is bearable for the child to take in, and how the patient deeply knows and appreciates his similarity to the lamb without having to have it spelled out. The interpretation in the displacement acts as a spur to thinking, offered in a way that *can* be received, bringing the child to a position of engagement, basic trust and thought, when a more overt interpretation could lead to a pulling down of the emotional shutters.

Stern *et al.* applied a developmental perspective to clinical work, and used the concepts of declarative knowledge and procedural knowledge to come up with their idea of a 'now moment' and 'moments-of-meeting' (Stern *et al.* 1998). The actions that make up a 'now moment' are *not* routine or habitual, but somehow show an aspect of the therapist's individuality, her personal signature. They warn that 'an interpretation can close out a now moment by "explaining" it further or elaborating or generalizing it' (1998: 914). A 'moment of meeting' cannot be realised with a transference interpretation. Other aspects of the relationship must be accessed, and transference and counter-transference features are at a minimum in a moment of meeting, as 'the personhood of the interactants, relatively denuded of role trappings, is brought into play'. This emphasis on 'personhood', authenticity, the real person of the therapist as well as of the patient, links with the concept of the present relationship as addressed below. Moments-of-meeting leave in their wake an open space in which a new equilibrium is formed. From moments-of-meeting something new is created in the relationship, which alters the intersubjective environment. The therapist's use of herself is absolutely essential within this model. There are many examples of this in this volume.

THE IMPLICATIONS OF RESEARCH FROM DEVELOPMENTAL PSYCHOLOGY, ATTACHMENT THEORY AND NEUROSCIENCE, AND THE THERAPIST'S USE OF SELF

In the past the terms 'treatment alliance' or 'the therapeutic alliance' were thought of as separate from psychoanalytic technique *per se*. The analyst's non-interpretative interventions and spontaneous human reactions were viewed by some as important, but still on the fringes of the session, necessary for, but separate from the 'proper' work of the session. Views, especially as exemplified in this book, have changed about this. Therapists working in the Independent tradition have an interest in the present relationship that takes place between the therapist and the patient. There is an increasing view that the present relationship, which will inevitably contain certain aspects of the transference but which is not exclusively a transference relationship, is very important (Holmes 1998; Crockatt *et al.* 2001; Lanyado 2004). Indeed Parsons and, more recently, Anastasopoulos and Papanicolaou make clear the view that the work of the therapist is intimately linked to his personality, that is who we are and what we do within the session are the same (Anastasopoulos and Papanicolaou 2004, Parsons 1984). The therapist shows to the patient a non-intrusive but active interest. This can be a very new experience for a child who is not accustomed to having his actions noticed and thought about. Interestingly Strupp in the early 1970s also saw the relationship as the important dimension (Strupp 1973). Greenberg and Mitchell point out that factors which are seen by Classic Freudians as prerequisites to the interpretative function are seen as curative in the relational model (Greenberg and Mitchell 1983).

In more recent times many therapists have adopted an interactionalist point of view. Influenced by infancy studies many therapists, most notably Emde, have noted the 'to and fro' of interactions between the patient and therapist within the session (Emde 1988). In this model the therapist has to be affectively in tune with the patient *and* be able to show it. The way of showing it undoubtedly demands skills of timing and sensitively judging what is the appropriate amount and degree – skills Brazelton and Cramer highlight when taking the reader minutely through the microseconds of a suspense game ('peek-a-boo' or 'round and round the garden') between mother and baby (Brazelton and Cramer 1991). In this model, knowledge of infant research and experience of infant observation are seen to be an essential part of the therapist's tools. Familiarity with the interactions between mothers and their infants can increase the clinician's sensitivity to aspects of the contact between patient and therapist.

Awareness of the work that has been done by Stern and others on the matching of contours both within vocalisations and across different modalities can help increase the practitioner's careful responsiveness to the patient (Stern 1985). Pine also suggests that understanding child development and the parent–child relationship is important (Pine 1985). He is very interested in the ways in which child psychotherapy has some inevitable overlap with parental function as regards the growth process, and this same issue is addressed in Hurry's book where she emphasises the *new* relationship that happens in therapy (Hurry 1998). This way of thinking has been somewhat out of favour as it brings to mind what were felt to be the excesses of Franz Alexander's 'corrective emotional experience' or, from a different perspective, Kohut's ideas about repairing deficit (Alexander 1946; Kohut 1959). However, as outlined by Hurry, the function of the new *developmental* object is not about making up deficits in a gratifying way but about providing a relational framework so that these representations and processes can unfold in a relational context. It could be thought of as the relationship within which experiences of mentalisability can arise.

Indeed, it is fair to say that the view of the neutral analyst, the surgeon to the mind of the patient, is not a model currently much used. The interactive nature of the process is acknowledged, and this view is much influenced by infant research. From research into infants' capacities we have become aware of just how much the neonate can do and we have also become aware of how much he does in the presence of and through the mediation of another. Mentalisation occurs through the experience of the mind of the other. Fonagy, bringing together psychoanalytic ideas and Attachment Theory, suggests that the infant's need to be in close proximity to the adult is not today to protect him from the ravening wolves, but in order to help him introject and learn from the experience of the whole process of learning to think (Fonagy 2001). It is not difficult to extrapolate this model into the consulting room. The patient learns to experience acute emotions in the presence of another, the therapist, whose capacity to bear them and think about them gradually enables the patient to introject the possibility of doing the same. This brings to mind both Winnicott's idea of the functions of the 'good-enough' mother and that of being 'alone in the presence of another'. The therapist who is able to bear staying with the unbearable feelings creates both a space within which it becomes safe to think and a model of that capacity which can be developed over time.

ISSUES OF TRANSFERENCE AND COUNTER-TRANSFERENCE IN WORK WITH CHILDREN AND ADOLESCENTS

When considering technique it is important to note areas in which work with children calls for different skills and capacities from those needed for adult work. Of course children express themselves far less through language than adults do. Especially over recent years we have become more alert to the *unspoken* parts of the dialogue between patient and therapist, but still with adults we expect much of the emphasis in the work to be on what is said – and not said. With children, especially younger children, there is additionally a different form of communication – that of play. Child psychotherapists are accustomed to the idea that children in therapy are not going to sit and talk about what they perceive to be their difficulties – or if they do what will be offered is likely to be pseudo-adult, all on a conscious level and not having much bearing on the difficulties experienced.

Bick states that the counter-transference with children is often more difficult to bear and to process than with adult patients (Bick 1961). She sees children as evoking in their therapists parental feelings which make it hard for the therapist to bear the experience of the child's pain. She understands this as due both to the unconscious conflicts that arise in relation to the child's parents, which I will look at briefly, and to the nature of the child's material. For her the intensity of the child's dependence, and the primitive nature of his phantasies, tend to arouse the analyst's own unconscious anxieties. She thinks it is difficult to contain the violent and concrete projections. She also states that the child's material is more difficult to understand since it is primitive in its sources and mode of expression. Because of this the child analyst has to depend more on her unconscious to provide her with clues to the meaning of a child's play and non-verbal communication. While other theoretical schools might argue that this reliance on the therapist's unconscious is a double-edged sword which carries with it the risk of imposing one's own 'madness' on the child, we can see an emphasis on the child psychotherapist's need to have free access to counter-transference feelings.

While counter-transference issues may be more painful with a child patient, transference needs thinking about in a different way too. According to Anna Freud:

> Children have a continuing dependent relationship with the parents in the present. This complicates the task of distinguishing between a fixed pattern of behaviour used with parents and adults in general and the specific revival of a past experience within the context of the treatment situation.
>
> (Sandler, Kennedy and Tyson 1980: 81)

She suggests that the therapist should interpret the transference from the mother of the present before referring to the past and should not take everything as referring to the therapist. Contemporary practice is more flexible, but the importance of remembering the child's current family setting remains. It may be that the face-to-face contact with the therapist allows the child, when not too dominated by phantasies, to see and respond to some of the realities of the therapist. This face-to-face contact may also allow clues and cues to be picked up on more readily. However, perhaps due to the level of deprivation, trauma and abuse found in the children many child and adolescent psychotherapists currently see, I would argue that the capacity for distortion of the object is, at least, as great in children as in adults.

Rustin writes of her separate once-weekly work with two boys:

> As a starting point I had to get a grasp of the internal psychic pain that underlay their grossly distorted development. Since neither of them could talk to me about themselves (in fact they were a million miles away from that sort of use of a therapist), this meant I had to experience in the counter-transference, in my own emotions within sessions and in my thinking about them between sessions, the intolerable feelings which their way of life seemed designed to hold at bay.
>
> (Rustin 2001: 274)

It seems to me that one could convincingly argue that this situation of intolerable psychic pain, defended against by the patient and necessarily experienced by the therapist, is more common in work with children, who very probably have not chosen to come to treatment, than with adults who, albeit very ambivalently, have committed themselves to engage in treatment.

Work by graduates of the Anna Freud Centre has emphasised the analyst as 'developmental object', one whom the child can relate to in a new way (Hurry 1998). It could be argued that children who have lacked the experience of an interested maternal object first need the experience of someone who can notice and respond to their needs, before they can progress to experiencing loss and deficit in a way which is ultimately enhancing rather than overwhelmingly threatening. Alvarez has cogently made the case for formulating interpretations with this in mind (Alvarez 1997). Anne Hurry has stated that both modes are integrally important. At times the emphasis may be more on one than the other, as it is dependent on the needs of the patient and where they are in their development (Hurry 1998: 71–2).

THE USE OF PLAY AS COMMUNICATION

Not surprisingly, the significance of playing in psychoanalytic psychotherapy is complex, and an issue in which major theoretical differences appear between the Independents, Kleinians and Anna Freudians. These differences, which are probably less acute today than they were fifty years ago, still have importance because of underlying assumptions about early mental life and the task of psychoanalytic psychotherapy. Of course within each school there exists a range of beliefs and practices, according to the personalities and experiences of each practitioner.

Play is at the centre of child psychotherapy, but what sort of play and how it is understood will vary between theoretical groups as well as from practitioner to practitioner. Child psychotherapists provide specific limited play material, designed primarily to be used as an aid to symbolic expression, as by playing freely the child will display unconscious phantasies and conflicts of various sorts. The amount the therapist actively engages in the child's play, as opposed to watching it but not participating, will vary according to the therapist's theoretical stance.

All child psychotherapists would emphasise the importance of finding a way to the child and his internal conflicts. While Kleinians would be more inclined only to provide toys which could serve the production of fantasy, the Anna Freudians would consider it useful to play games such as chess with a well-defended latency child who, they think, might find other approaches intolerable, using the game to approach relevant issues such as those to do with competitiveness or the wish to overthrow the parental figures. The play material on offer may differ according to the age of the child. Child psychotherapists who have an Independent orientation are likely to have Winnicott's ideas about play in mind. He sees the ability to play freely and imaginatively as a crucial indicator of the child's emotional health. So as well as seeking to understand the unconscious meaning of the play, Winnicott sees the process of the changes in a child's ability to play as an important indicator of the child's progress in therapy. Creating a facilitating environment, or to use another of his key concepts in this area a 'transitional space', in the internal and external therapeutic setting in which the child can grow emotionally, as evidenced by these changes in play, is a central part of the therapeutic process. These ideas are evident in the case material in this volume and discussed in more detail in Chapters 8 and 13.

Joseph, a leading Kleinian, introduces another perspective. She says that she is always looking for the meaning of play and would only play as long as she saw it as productive (Joseph 1998). She writes that she would throw a ball back and forth and then see what happened after she spoke, and interpret according to that. If the child continues the activity as a game in order not to think about the interpretation then the therapist must understand this, interpret and probably stop the activity. Both Kleinians and Freudians are agreed that it is not the play material itself but what is done with it that is important. In line with her general 'using whatever one gets' approach, Joseph makes it clear that for her asking a child to tidy up or even keep their pictures in a folder smacks of an educational purpose inimical to proper analysis. She states that she never asks a child to do anything but waits to see what the child chooses to do and interprets according to what she sees. Other therapists might see the tidying up of toys that may be done at the end of a session (rather than after the child has left), as a helpful process, acting, as Anna Freud put it, as an opportunity of 'sealing over the regressed fantasy material that has emerged in the session', giving the child a protected way to return to the outside world (Sandler, Kennedy and Tyson 1980).

Child psychotherapists have had to be careful not to assume automatically that all playing is necessarily symbolic and expressive of underlying phantasies. From recent work with children on the autistic spectrum we have become painfully aware of the meaninglessness of certain play, and even with very different children play can be used in a repetitive, mind-numbing, defensive way. Perhaps this is in some way similar to the 'chuntering' that Joseph writes of with adult patients, which could at first sight appear to be productive but is really serving a defensive purpose (Joseph 1985). Winnicott's statement that 'if a child is able to enjoy playing, both alone and with other children, there is no very serious trouble afoot' has to come with the proviso that we have to be able to see the difference between distinct types of play (Winnicott 1964). The ability to observe closely and to be alert and responsive to the counter-transference aroused within us from what we are seeing and experiencing is surely crucial here.

It is in the area of interpreting that we can perhaps see the other major technical difference between child and adult work. Issues to do with timing, the tone of voice used and the impact of the interpretation are as vital with children as they are with adults. However, especially when one considers the technique used by the Anna Freudians and the Independents, there are other aspects of interpretation that are important. The way children use toys allows them a certain degree of displacement or externalisation of self and object relationships and of the interaction between them. Although therapists working with adults are used to *their* patients telling of events happening to other people or dreams in which the patient himself does not manifestly appear, most would link those aspects they saw as referring to the patient directly to him and not leave them displaced.

There is of course a danger of colluding with the child's defences rather than analysing them, but many child therapists nevertheless feel that such a 'parallel approach' may make it possible to begin to address difficult areas. Klein advocates the opposite by emphasising the importance of addressing the deepest anxieties in the most direct and straightforward way possible (Klein 1955). Contemporary post-Kleinians, perhaps through extensive experience with more deprived child patients, are more likely to be aware of times when addressing anxieties too early or directly can send the child into unbearable and disorganising levels of panic and accordingly they approach interpretations in a way that holds central the child's ability to hear and use them.

MANAGEMENT ISSUES

Work with children differs from that with adults with regard to the problems that cluster around the issue of the 'external' of the consulting room.

Although an adult patient may try in various subtle ways to stamp his presence on a consulting room, he is not likely to be able to do this, or at least not in ways that would then be subsequently disturbing to the next patient. However, child patients may frequently do things in the therapy room that mark walls or break furniture, which then impinges on the next patient. In clinic settings children also have to get to and from the waiting room to the therapy room. While this may be true for adults seen in institutional settings, adults are more able to grasp quickly the concept that the session begins once within the consulting room. Young children may feel that the session begins as the therapist appears, and may say or do on the way to the therapy room things that place the therapist in a dilemma. While ideally interpretations should be confined to the privacy of the consulting room, something may need to be done or said at that moment. What this will be will obviously depend on what the child is doing, but the need to address both the activity, whatever it is, and the underlying communication it contains *simultaneously* can call upon particular skills which may be less in evidence for a therapist working with adults, who may have more space to address the underlying communication with less sense of need to alter the activity *immediately*.

We also need to be aware of the way that, as Joseph warns, particularly in work with children, the therapist is liable to be drawn into some kind of acting in (Joseph 1998). In describing the question of bringing new equipment, for example paper, into the therapy room Joseph states that the analyst is frequently manipulated into situations where whatever she does she is in the wrong and the patient has grounds for complaint. While similar issues may arise with an adult patient around requests to change session times or holidays, they are much less acute in that setting. Indeed, Daws gives an example of how work with a child was able to flourish once she changed his session time, respecting his view of an external reality that made the original time offered particularly awkward (Daws 1986). Child and adolescent psychotherapists need to be aware that certain times of leaving or returning to school may be so problematic for the child that the benefits of therapy are severely undermined by the family, peer or school problems caused. Similarly, while in work with adults the regularity of sessions and a culture of not altering them are likely to be paramount, those who work with children have to evaluate in their own minds the merits of a child going on a school outing or taking part in a school performance over and above the benefits of the therapy session. Yet even if the 'external' event is deemed by all to be the better choice, the child's sense of being deprived of his session and resentful about this will still need to be addressed.

Unlike the adult therapist, the child psychotherapist may also have physical contact with the patient at times other than when restraining, helping their younger patients carry out certain physical tasks, which would be unthinkable and inappropriate with adult patients. Young children may at times react to the therapist as if she were a parental figure, expecting to be lifted down from a window sill or helped to put shoes and socks back on at the end of a session. A child's wish to clamber on the therapist's knee or give her a hug may feel seductive, appeasing or manipulative, or may feel an expression of warmth and affection that the young child has not yet found another way of expressing.

Child psychotherapists, perhaps more so currently than in the past, are concerned with the question of how to manage aggressive behaviour within the consulting room. Although some adult analysts write of occasional acts of violence from patient to therapist, usually such behaviour would lead to the termination of treatment (Bateman 1998). Clearly an attack from a fully grown adult (in the case described, the flaunting of a knife) would pose considerably more danger than one from a child; nevertheless many child psychotherapists accept a level of physical attack from their patients that would be simply unimaginable in ongoing adult psychotherapeutic work. The child's tendency to enact is facilitated by regression and the disinhibition that may occur in analysis. This level of aggression may be a result of the freedom of the analytic setting, which is described by Sandler *et al.* as mobilising anxieties and at the same time allowing for the relaxation of some of the restrictions that are normally placed on impulses (Sandler, Kennedy and Tyson 1980).

A child may well act or live out his impulses, that is attack a therapist whose interpretations he experiences as attacking him, rather than be able to express this feeling in a more symbolic way. Parsons and Dermen state that 'an interpretation which reaches the patient's vulnerability runs the risk of being experienced as a puncturing of his protective barrier and may provoke a violent reaction in the room' (Parsons and Dermen 1999: 337). The very freedom of the setting may have allowed for behaviour which the child would not allow himself in other settings. Sooner or later in a child analysis the therapist will be called upon to set limits. It is likely to be an important and necessary part of the therapeutic work that a child will test any limits to assess the therapist's tolerance for and acceptance of him. While the therapist must interpret what the child is trying to do, she must also stop the child when necessary. This is different from adult work when fantasies or thoughts are being expressed verbally. As Sandler *et al.* comment, 'In adult analysis there are no limits to free association, whereas in child analysis there are limits to action' (Sandler, Kennedy and Tyson 1980). Indeed, without limits being set, thought will never be possible.

Here Anna Freud and Klein are in accord. They both see the need to keep the child safe and to prevent him from feeling too anxious or guilty about his behaviour. Klein states that she does not allow attacks on the analyst because they stir up excessive guilt and persecutory anxiety, but that she expects and welcomes aggressive phantasies and verbal attacks which she views as helping avoid actual attacks (Klein 1955). She writes of preventing physical attacks by interpreting in time the motives for the aggression. I note her statement 'interpret in time' and wonder if perhaps the most skilled clinicians can do this, but for less gifted practitioners the consequences of their limitations are more obviously (and physically!) painful than similar limitations in adult therapists would be. Joseph is adamant that the child psychotherapist must provide a setting in which the child is able, with few limitations, to express his aggression and actual destructiveness (Joseph 1998). If the therapist is worrying about protecting the room or herself she can all too easily get caught up in action and then is unable to observe the child and think about him. In such situations the analyst can become like the child, 'violent, difficult and out of control', and the child has been able to force his desperate violent self into the analyst, who somehow has become a suitable receptacle for it. Winnicott emphasises the need for a resilient and enduring environment that allows psycho-analysis to take place, knowing that acting out in the transference will be an inevitable part of the process (Winnicott 1963).

It is essential for the therapist to be able to go on thinking, and not just defending or retaliating. Again we see the importance of maintaining the reflective space. While this is essential for any therapist, the additional strain that is imposed when the violence is physical is immense. Parsons and Dermen point out that 'the therapist working with violent youngsters has the difficult task of combining two contradictory perspectives: provision of safety, and understanding that her efforts to reach the patient will inevit-ably represent a danger situation for him' (Parsons and Dermen 1999: 336–7). Child psychotherapists need to process their reactions very fast and hold on tight to their own feelings until they have had the opportunity to do so. When reading descriptions of clinical work it may seem that some authors – amazing to recount – seem to find it easy to make effective inter-pretations while physically restraining a child, but the need for the capacity to observe, process and be involved simultaneously is surely very great.

WORK WITH THE PARENTS OF PATIENTS – SOME TECHNICAL ISSUES

The reality of a child's parents has an impact in many different ways upon child analytic treatment. Contact with the child's family is considered, to some extent, necessary, although the frequency and nature of this contact is a matter for debate. It is not possible, and I would argue not desirable, to avoid contact with parents, and especially with younger child patients the parents must be seen to be sure that they provide the continuing emotional and practical support that is needed for the child to continue in treatment. This work also enables the parents to be as receptive and responsive as possible to changes in their child as therapy progresses. Moreover there may be many circumstances in which, without changes in the child's family, the treatment for the child can only be partially successful. While an adult can remove himself from a particular situation once he has understood why it is appealing or feels necessary, a young child has relatively little control over his environment.

When the family needs help with its pathology an additional professional may well be brought in for this work, especially in Child and Adolescent Mental Health Services, but sometimes it is the child psychotherapist who will have contact with families or with others, such as teachers or social workers, who are concerned with the child. Obviously difficulties may arise about confidentiality when there is such contact. Child psychotherapists may also find themselves more actively involved in trying to influence the external world of the child by attending Social Services Review meetings or liaising with concerned professionals. Although traditionally some of this has been done by other colleagues, there may be times when it is the child's therapist herself who engages in this work, as Iris Gibbs describes in Chapter 7. She may feel herself best able to represent to others things that are important to the child. This poses problems about confidentiality and the therapist needs to be very aware of the need for a level of confidentiality. It can lead to tension between the need to communicate and the need for privacy. The child psychotherapist's awareness of the child's helplessness in the situation may lead to identification with that helplessness, or an omnipotent 'busyness', neither of which is helpful. Bick suggests that the child psychotherapist inevitably experiences unconscious conflicts in relation to the child's parents, and tends either to identify with the child against the parents or with the parents against the child (Bick 1961). The mature CPT manages not to fall into this trap and, indeed, to make use of such countertransference feelings in reflecting about the child.

Frequently therapists may experience rivalry with parents, or a desire to be a better parent to the child, and such feelings need to be recognised and well managed. Dowling, in this volume, discusses this with regard to parent–infant psychotherapy where the infant is 'at risk' and the parent/s and child have been admitted to an in-patient unit for treatment. Bailey, in Chapter 11, describes and discusses the technical issues and countertransference feelings involved in her work with the parents of adolescents when the adolescent refuses to accept direct help.

'CONSENT' AND HOW TO TACKLE THE NEGATIVE TRANSFERENCE

The question of how much, if at all, a child consents to having therapy may be very different for adult and child patients. With adults the problem is much simpler: if the treatment alliance sinks below a specific level, the patient stops treatment. If the patient continues to attend, the analyst tries to find out what brings him, but with the child all this is obscured by the fact that he is not necessarily coming of his own volition. Indeed parents are encouraged to bring the child at times when he does not want to come.

Anna Freud understands this commonly accepted necessity as being because the child is more likely than an adult to break the treatment alliance because the mature part of the person which holds a patient in analysis during phases of negative transference and resistance is less developed in the child. The situation is complicated when the therapist lacks an alliance with the family, which would enable them to help, or even make, the child attend. Anna Freud bluntly suggests that if for one week children only came to therapy if they really wanted to 'without any pressure from anybody else I don't say there would be none, but you'd be surprised by how few there would be' (Sandler, Kennedy and Tyson 1980: 18–19). However, the implications of what to do about this situation vary according to theoretical school. The Kleinians see it as necessary to interpret the deepest anxieties and for the patient to experience the relief that follows: that relief then leads to a wish to engage in analytic work. Sandler *et al.* think more in terms of a treatment alliance (Sandler, Kennedy and Tyson 1980). This may include at times doing things which gratify the child in order to keep a level of cooperation.

Anna Freud points out that many analyses of children are terminated with the expectation that in a year or two the child will come back if more therapy is needed, but emphasises that this hardly ever happens (Sandler, Kennedy and Tyson 1980). She states that relatively few analyses of children are terminated according to plan, most being interrupted by external circumstances. It seemed to me that this view of interrupted analyses may take insufficient account of the forces of development and the consequent fact that a child analysis need not take the length of time an adult one does, a view shared by Fabricius and Green (Fabricius and Green 1995). Anna Freud warns that a child's *manifest* wish to stop treatment may disguise all sorts of feelings, especially anxieties about abandonment and rejection. While the wish for termination may well follow a wish to avoid the pain that treatment inevitably brings, we also have to consider that, on balance, it may be healthier for the child no longer to wish to come to therapy but instead to use his time and energies in activities with his peers.

CONCLUDING REMARKS

These differences between child and adult also have implications for certain other aspects of technique. Children do not free associate or talk in the way adults do. Their play and other behaviour in the therapy room have to be looked on as an equivalent to free association. Being in touch with one's own feelings, without necessarily reasoning about and verbalising the causes of those feelings, might be nearer to a child's analytic experience than to an adult's. The experience of feeling differently, without necessarily understanding why, may be more common in therapeutic work with adults than has been previously acknowledged. Certainly the current emphasis on micro-interactions might well suggest that most patients are going to remain consciously unaware of the myriad of minute interactions which have transformed their internal world views.

The developmental object as described by Hurry is a valuable idea that is implied in the approach of many of the practitioners in this book (Hurry 1998). It is important to differentiate between this, where the therapist is someone with an analytic stance, and the good teacher or 'kind auntie' attitude that we can sometimes experience ourselves drifting into with certain patients. The level of external deprivation many current child patients experience also stirs up 'rescue fantasies' in their therapists. Therapists working with adults rarely want to take their patients home with them! Awareness of the complexity of family life as seen in infant observation (as well as often experienced personally) can help the child psychotherapist avoid this position by keeping in mind a more balanced attitude to parents who may themselves be very damaged and deprived. Awareness of resilience and the ordinary developmental thrust can also act as an aid in helping stem the child psychotherapist's arrogance about the importance and efficacy of her work.

In the clinical material that follows, the reader will come across the therapist, in a variety of settings, encountering transference and countertransference processes that make her reflect anew on *how* she understands and tackles the work: technique is always both answer and question.

Note

1 For convenience I have referred to the therapist as 'she' and the patient as 'he', except when I am citing the work of other authors where I use the terms that they use.

References

Alexander, F. and French, T. M. (1946) *Psychoanalytic Therapy: Principles and Applications.* New York: Ronald Press

Alvarez, A. (1997) 'Projective identification as a communication: its grammar in borderline psychotic children' *Psychoanalytic Dialogues* 7(6): 753–68

Anastasopoulos, D. and Papanicolaou, E. (eds.) (2004) *The Therapist at Work: Personal Factors Affecting the Analytic Process.* London: Karnac

Bateman, A. (1998) 'Thick- and thin-skinned organisations and enactment in borderline and narcissistic disorders' *International Journal of Psycho-Analysis* 19: 13–25

Bick, E. (1961) 'Child analysis today'. In M. Harris Williams (ed.), *Collected Papers of Martha Harris and Esther Bick.* Strath Tay, UK: Clunie 1987

Bion, W. (1962) *Learning from Experience.* London: Heinemann

Bollas, C. (1989) *Forces of Destiny.* London: Free Association Books

Brazelton, T. B. and Cramer, B. (1991) *The Earliest Relationship*. London: Karnac

Carpy, D. (1989) 'Tolerating the countertransference: a mutative process' *International Journal of Psychoanalysis* 70: 287–94

Crockatt, G., Davies, M., Green, V. and Wilson, P. (2001) 'Commentaries on "The symbolism of the story of Lot and his wife"' *Journal of Child Psychotherapy* 27(1): 35–46

Daws, D. (1986) 'Consent in child psychotherapy: the conflicts for child patients, parents and professionals' *Journal of Child Psychotherapy* 12(1): 103–11

Emde, R. (1988) 'Development terminable and interminable: innate and motivational factors from infancy' *International Journal of Psychoanalysis* 69: 23–42

Fabricius, J. and Green, V. (1995) 'Termination: a child-led process?' *Psychoanalytic Study of the Child* 50: 205–26

Fonagy, P. (2001) *Attachment Theory and Psychoanalysis*. New York: Other Press

Freud, A. (1976) 'Changes in psychoanalytic practice and experience' *International Journal of Psychoanalysis* 57: 257–61

Freud, S. (1911) 'The handling of dream interpretation in psychoanalysis'. *Standard Edition*, 12. London: Hogarth Press, pp.89–96

Freud, S. (1912a) 'The dynamics of transference'. *Standard Edition*, 12. London: Hogarth Press, pp.97–108

Freud, S. (1912b) 'Recommendations to physicians practising psychoanalysis'. *Standard Edition*, 12. London: Hogarth Press, pp.109–20

Freud, S. (1913) 'Further recommendations on the technique of psychoanalysis I: on beginning a treatment'. *Standard Edition*, 12. London: Hogarth Press, pp.121–44

Freud, S. (1914) 'Further recommendations on the technique of psychoanalysis II: recollecting, repeating and working through'. *Standard Edition*, 12. London: Hogarth Press, pp.145–56

Freud, S. (1915) 'Observations on transference love'. *Standard Edition*, 12. London: Hogarth Press, pp.158–71

Glover, E. (1954) 'Therapeutic criteria of psychoanalysis' *International Journal of Psycho-Analysis* 35: 95–101

Greenberg, J. R. and Mitchell, S. A. (1983) *Object Relations in Psychoanalytic Theory*. Cambridge, MA and London: Harvard University Press

Hamilton, V. (1996) *The Analyst's Preconscious*. Hillsdale, NJ: The Analytic Press

Heimann, P. (1950) 'On countertransference' *International Journal of Psychoanalysis* 31. Reprinted in M. Tonnesmann (ed.), *About Children and Children-No-Longer: Collected Papers of Paula Heimann*. London and New York: Tavistock/ Routledge, 1989

Holmes, J. (1998) 'The changing aims of psychoanalysis' *International Journal of Psychoanalysis* 79: 227–38

Hurry, A. (ed.) (1998) *Psychoanalysis and Developmental Therapy*. London: Karnac

Joseph, B. (1985) 'Transference: the total situation' *International Journal of Psycho-analysis* 66: 447–54

Joseph, B. (1998) 'Thinking about a playroom' *Journal of Child Psychotherapy* 24(3): 359–66

Kernberg, O. (1993) 'Nature and agents of structural intra-psychic change'. In M. Horowitz, O. Kernberg and E. M. Weinshel (eds.), *Psychic Structure and Psychic Change. Essays in Honor of Robert S. Wallerstein M.D.* Madison, CT: International Universities Press

King, P. (1978) 'Affective responses of the analyst to the patient's communication' *International Journal of Psychoanalysis* 59: 329–34

Klein, M. (1955) 'The psycho-analytic play technique: its history and significance'. In *The Writings of Melanie Klein Vol. 3.* London: Hogarth

Kohut, H. (1959) 'Introspection, empathy, and psychoanalysis: an examination of the relationship between mode of observation and theory' *Journal of the American Psychological Association* 7: 459–83

Lanyado, M. (2004) *The Presence of the Therapist: Treating Childhood Trauma.* Hove, UK: Brunner-Routledge

Loewald, H. W. (1960) 'On the therapeutic action of psychoanalysis' *International Journal of Psychoanalysis* 41: 16–33

Ogden, T. H. (1999) *Reverie and Interpretation. Sensing Something Human.* London: Karnac

Parsons, M. (1986) 'Suddenly finding it really matters' *International Journal of Psychoanalysis* 67: 475–88

Parsons, M. and Dermen, S. (1999) 'The violent child and adolescent'. In M. Lanyado and A. Horne (eds.), *The Handbook of Child and Adolescent Psychotherapy: Psychoanalytic Approaches.* London: Routledge

Parsons, M. (1984) 'Psychoanalysis as a vocation and martial art' *International Review of Psychoanalysis* 11: 453–62

Pine, F. (1985) *Developmental Theory and Clinical Process.* New Haven, CT and London: Yale University Press

Rayner, E. (1990) *The Independent Mind in British Psychoanalysis.* London: Free Association Books

Renik, O. (1993) 'Countertransference enactment and the psychoanalytic process'. In M. Horowitz, O. Kernberg and E. M. Weinshel (eds.), *Psychic Structure and Psychic Change: Essays in Honor of Robert S. Wallerstein M.D.* Madison, CT: International Universities Press

Roth, P. (2001) 'Mapping the landscape: levels of transference interpretation' *International Journal of Psychoanalysis* 82(3): 533–43

Rustin, M. (2001) 'The therapist with her back against the wall' *Journal of Child Psychotherapy* 27(3): 273–84

Sandler, J. (1981) 'Character traits and object relationships' *Psychoanalytic Quarterly* 50: 694–708

Sandler, J., Kennedy, H. and Tyson, R. L. (1980) *The Technique of Child Psychoanalysis: Discussions with Anna Freud.* London: Hogarth Press. Reprinted London: Karnac Books, 1990

Schafer, R. (1983) *The Analytic Attitude.* London: Hogarth

Schlesinger, H. (1994) 'How the analyst listens: the pre-stages of interpretation' *International Journal of Psychoanalysis* 75: 31–7

Stern, D. (1985) *The Interpersonal World of the Infant.* New York: Basic Books

Stern, D. (2004) *The Present Moment in Psychotherapy and Everyday Life.* London and New York: Norton

Stern, D., Sander, L., Louis, W., Nahum, J. P., Harrison, A. M., Lyons-Ruth, K., Morgan, A. C., Bruschweiler-Stern, N. and Tronick, E. Z. (1998) 'Non-interpretive mechanisms in psychoanalytic therapy: the "something more" than interpretation' *International Journal of Psychoanalysis* 79: 903–21

Stewart, H. (1987) 'Varieties of transference' *International Journal of Psycho-Analysis* 68: 197–206

Strupp, H. (1973) *Psychotherapy: Clinical, Research and Theoretical Issues.* New York: Jason Aronson

Symington, N. (1983) 'The analyst's act of freedom as agent of therapeutic change' *International Review of Psycho-Analysis* 10: 283–92

Symington, N. (1996) *The Making of a Psychotherapist.* London: Karnac

Winnicott, D. W. (1963) 'Psychotherapy of character disorders'. In Winnicott (1965), *The Maturational Processes and the Facilitating Environment.* London: Karnac, 1990

Winnicott, D. W. (1964) 'What do we mean by a normal child?' In Winnicott, *The Child, the Family and the Outside World.* Harmondsworth, UK: Penguin, 1987

Winnicott, D. W. (1971) 'Playing: creative activity and the search for the self'. In Winnicott, *Playing and Reality.* London: Tavistock. Reprinted Harmondsworth, UK: Penguin Educational, 1980

Part I
Parent–infant work

4 'The capacity to be alone'

Rediscovering Winnicott and his relevance to parent–infant psychotherapy

Deirdre Dowling

> It is only when alone, (i.e. in the presence of someone else) that the infant can discover his personal life.
>
> (Winnicott 1958: 38)

In 'The capacity to be alone' (1958) Winnicott shows that an adult's emotional independence develops from the experience of the infant feeling secure enough to be alone and imaginatively explore the world, because a parent is reliably present. Winnicott describes the infant's development from the baby, undefended and vulnerable, protected by the mother, to the emergence of the individual with a sense of his identity. He emphasises that the role of the mother is to be emotionally available to the infant. Simply being 'together but alone' is something that most mothers can offer their children and we take for granted, but it is an achievement that demands maturity. As a child psychotherapist working with parents and infants at high risk, I find Winnicott's analysis of the developing relationship between mother and infant helpful. He shows the changing dynamic as the baby separates from mother emotionally and how this relationship can break down under stress.

The parents I see as inpatients in a therapeutic hospital have severe emotional difficulties due to early abuse and deprivation. They find the demands of parenting overwhelming, and are often unable to separate their own feelings from those of their children. I am often at an *impasse* in therapeutic work wondering how to intervene in a fraught relationship between mother and infant when ordinary interventions fail. I wonder what I'm failing to observe or understand that could help the mother discover in herself capacities to respond to the child. Winnicott's ideas suggest that the mother, like baby, needs the experience of feeling emotionally held but separate before she could give this to her infant. There needs to be a reflective space between mother and therapist where she feels safe to explore ideas, before she can explore her relationship with her infant and develop empathy for his needs. In this chapter, I will discuss how I attempt to develop this reflective capacity with parents who at first cannot respond to interpretative help, and how I adapt my technique to facilitate their relationship to their infant until this stage is reached. Following Winnicott, I use the model of the developing infant to explore these ideas in relation to clinical work.

THEORETICAL DISCUSSION

Winnicott suggests that an adult's capacity to enjoy being alone is linked to the infant's early experience of being alone in the relaxed presence of his mother. He describes how the infant is able to play and withdraw into his inner world when 'the mother or mother substitute is . . . reliably present even if represented for the moment by a cot or a pram' (Winnicott 1958). I imagine a mother chatting to a friend or cooking, always keeping an eye on her infant, being available when needed. Winnicott analyses the building blocks of an infant's development, showing at each stage how dependent the infant is on 'good-enough' care from the mother:

> First there is the word I, implying much emotional growth. The individual is established as a unit. Next come the words I am . . .
> In the beginnings of 'I am' the individual is . . . undefended . . . vulnerable . . .
> . . . the individual can only achieve the 'I am' stage because there is an environment which is protective, . . . the mother preoccupied with her infant and orientated to the infant's requirements through her identification with her own infant.
>
> (Winnicott 1958: 33)

'I am alone', the next stage, involves:

> an appreciation on the part of the infant of the mother's continued existence . . . of a reliable mother whose reliability makes it possible for the infant to be alone and so enjoy being alone for a limited period.

Finally the development towards independence:

> Gradually, the ego-supportive environment is introjected and built into the individual's personality, so that there comes about a capacity actually to be alone. Even so theoretically, there is always someone present, someone who is equated . . . with the mother.
>
> (Winnicott 1958: 36)

If these experiences have been 'good enough', the adult will value being alone, because his inner life is fruitful and adds to his sense of self, giving life meaning. Winnicott then talks about the deprived or abused child who cannot play because these quiet moments are always interrupted by physical excitement. These children have not been protected from their environment so that there are safe, quiet times when the id instinctual impulses were sublimated in play. Winnicott also talked about signs of parenting failure in infants who lack the continuity of experience of 'going on being' because the mother has not been able to offer adequate ego protection from internal anxieties and external intrusion (Winnicott 1962). He believed the infant's experience would be of fragmentation and that this could lead to the restlessness and inability to concentrate we see in older children.

At the other end of the spectrum are those children who have developed a caretaker self, a defence of self-holding (Winnicott 1962: 58). These children have learned to distance themselves from confusing and painful feelings. Their anger and distress is often missed by adults as they do not draw attention to their deprivation with difficult behaviour. It is often similarly defended adults who are most thrown by parenthood, as the new infant's cries and neediness put them in touch again with their unmet need and it can feel unbearable. However, if this dynamic can be understood, parents with therapeutic help may be able to use this experience reparatively to overcome their deprivation through identification with their infant.

Winnicott identifies the capacities that underlie good parenting: to be preoccupied, to identify, to be protective and reliable. These skills can feel unattainable to mothers who have not had adequate mothering themselves or compensatory experiences to help them feel secure. To be 'maternally preoccupied' the mother has to tolerate powerful feelings communicated by her infant: anger, frustration, need and distress. If these feelings are unbearable, the mother can either defend herself and remain cut off or project her anger onto the baby who then becomes a persecuting figure. The infant may then withdraw from the parent to protect himself from the intensity of these feelings. Winnicott emphasised the unthinkable anxiety of the infant who feels left alone (Winnicott 1962: 57).

When the baby takes in unbearable feelings from the parent, the experience can be traumatic. I see infants who go to sleep when the parent is angry or upset, become physically sick, avoid the parent's gaze or hold back from physical contact. This response can feel like rejection to the parent and can magnify feelings of failure and loss of control. Unless this dynamic can be recognised, there is a danger that the parent will retaliate. Psychotherapy can have a crucial role here, the therapist observing and thinking with the parent about the baby, while providing a supportive setting for their relationship to unfold and develop safely.

A safe setting for this work with parents in severe difficulties is essential, so before exploring different approaches to parent–infant psychotherapy, I will describe the model developed in the therapeutic community where I work. Alongside parent–infant psychotherapy, parents receive individual adult psychoanalytic psychotherapy, couple and family therapy, and psychosocial nursing. The parents are supported by the nurses in developing the skills of daily life by taking responsibility for the practical and emotional issues that arise for their families and others.

The infants we see are at severe risk, because they or siblings have suffered neglect or abuse or the family is in severe breakdown due to a parent's mental illness. Many families are sent on a statutory order for inpatient assessment. This gives the parents a last chance to develop a reliable and empathic relationship with their infants to prevent their removal for adoption or placement with relatives. The parents when they first arrive are often angry and distrustful, 'doing time' at the hospital so they can keep their infants. The challenge to those involved in treatment is to make the setting relevant to the parents so they can begin to make sense of why their care has broken down.

The residential community provides a structure to support the parents' ego capacities when they feel shattered and deskilled. Many are single parents or couples who have been isolated or caught up in pathological relationships. Therapeutic community living gives them a chance to try out relationships and manage the conflicts in a less destructive way. In the therapeutic work, the linking of inner and outer experience provides the intense emotional holding for parents.

Observations from daily life: bedtimes, meals, and leisure activities, are shared among staff and parents so that, like fitting together pieces of the jigsaw, we can begin to make sense of the families' fragmented experience. A nurse at lunch with a family will see how food has become the focus for tension between a mother with eating difficulties and her daughter, or problems around separation will show up when the infant is left in the nursery. Gradually, patterns emerge which enable parents to learn from their own experience, and from supporting others struggling with difficulties like their own.

It can be difficult for children coming to the hospital. Many are returning to their parents after a period of separation and have lost their close bond with them. Children in foster care return to their foster home at weekends in the early phase of treatment, so they have a stable base while their future is unsure, but this means they have to adjust to moving between two homes. Other infants have never been removed but are anxious and insecure, sensitive to the precarious functioning of their parents. Faced with an unresponsive parent, an infant may develop a pattern of avoidant or withdrawn behaviour, which will exacerbate an already poor relationship with their parent. Often, it is the warmth and life of the community that offers the additional nurturing the baby needs to go through this difficult phase. However, we observe the children carefully, monitoring their physical and emotional well-being to ensure that they are protected from too much stress. If we consider a child is too distressed, or his development is being impaired, then we make the painful decision to end the placement, and ask social services to place the child with foster parents.

Inpatient assessment usually lasts six to eight weeks. It will show if the parents can be helped by this therapeutic approach. If families make progress, a plan is made for continued treatment and a gradual rehabilitation home. The whole programme can last up to a year. Currently, we are developing shorter treatments for those who can continue this work with their local services, but for some families only intense integrated therapy over a longer period can secure the change needed.

PARENT–INFANT PSYCHOTHERAPY: A HOLDING RELATIONSHIP

The assumption that becoming a mother or a father offers an opportunity to resolve earlier deprivation and trauma underlies parent–infant psychotherapy. As Selma Fraiberg and colleagues beautifully describe in their paper 'Ghosts in the nursery', the experience of parenthood revives early experiences of being parented (Fraiberg *et al.* 1980). Disowned 'ghosts' or memories of childhood can be resolved and integrated into the adult's experience if the revived feelings can be accepted and understood. The danger is that parents who have suffered abuse will re-enact their past history in the present relationship with their infant unless they are in touch with the suffering they faced as a child and use this understanding to protect their own infant. The psychic changes of pregnancy, birth and meeting the needs of an infant all place great demands on the parents but can bring a new maturity. These same pressures can overwhelm parents with insufficient emotional resources, who often cannot tolerate the absolute dependence and neediness of the new infant.

The literature on parent–infant psychotherapy shows how clinicians have tried to find an effective way to intervene in early parent–infant relationships when there is the potential for rapid change. Selma Fraiberg and her infant mental health team in America offered both practical support and insight-orientated therapy to vulnerable parents in the community. Hopkins argued for developing this work in a British context. She emphasised the value of short-term input when parents are in touch with their distress and can use the therapeutic encounter to recognise the feelings that are troubling them (Hopkins, 1992). Miller described the development of short-term Under 5s work at the Tavistock Clinic (Miller 1992). She stressed the value of the therapist as a third person to the mother–infant couple, one who can speak to the baby's needs while supporting the mother. Ideas and observations springing from the encounter between mother and infant can inform the experience of their relationship. Daws describes her work in a GP clinic (Daws 1999) offering time to parents facing the anxieties of parenthood, difficulties in sleeping, eating and separation. She shows that problems posed by parents often represent deeper emotional conflicts, yet the current crisis can often be resolved in a few meetings. The parents recognise links with their past and find different ways of looking at their difficulty with the baby. Recently, video recordings of parents with their infants have been used to help identify difficulties through observation. We have found they offer an effective way of working that parents appreciate, as videos give direct visual feedback that can make more sense than explanations.

When seeing a family in distress, we have to assess the appropriate level of intervention, dependent on the risk to the infant, the level of disturbance in the parents, and their motivation to use help. Short-term parent–infant psychotherapy can be of use to parents who have some ability to reflect, to care for themselves and their infants, and a willingness to accept help. The therapist can support those functions temporarily overwhelmed by the newness of parenthood. The experience of having a therapist alongside, observing and thinking about the baby's experience can often help a mother discover what is preventing her meeting her baby's needs. This implies a basic trust in the therapeutic process.

However, working with parents with severe emotional difficulties requires a technique adapted to their particular needs, and the treatment often needs to be longer term. The basic trust is lacking and the parents may experience the therapist as critical and unhelpful. The first task is to build a therapeutic alliance so that the parents can allow themselves to be helped with disturbing feelings and the demands of the baby. Otherwise thinking becomes difficult and can be replaced by impulsive behaviour. At these times, I take a protective stance to keep the baby safe, closely monitoring the parent's relationship both to the baby and to me. I have to manage the tension between the baby's urgent need for an appropriate response and the danger the parent will reject an intervention made too early. Often the anxiety about the baby is carried by the therapist, rather than the parent who cannot tolerate such difficult feelings and projects them on to those around.

Winnicott's idea of the therapeutic relationship as a 'holding relationship' aptly describes this work, drawing the parallel between the infant's need for emotional holding and the emotionally vulnerable parent (Winnicott 1960: 49). The parent needs a secure relationship, usually over many months, which supports her available ego capacities while recognising the vulnerability and anxiety created by the primitive feelings evoked in the relationship to the infant. The presence of the infant in the room acts as a lively catalyst, the baby often letting us know points of tension or new small developments that need to be thought about. When I assess an infant at risk, I anticipate the mother's feelings of persecution and fear of criticism, putting them into words. Usually, the mother has to know that her feelings and needs have been recognised before she can respond to her baby. Gradually, I would hope the mother can begin to reflect on her own experience and that of her infant and become more attuned to his needs, but the pace of change may be slow. As the therapy develops, I work towards the time when the mother and I can think together and she can become more confident in her intuitive responses to her child. I find that the support of the professional team is vital when dealing with such anxiety-provoking situations, as we share anxieties and help each other process the powerful feelings and projections that emerge.

This work can be managed in an out-patient or day-patient setting when the parents have sufficient capacity to manage their disturbing feelings themselves and not put the infant at risk. However, often an intensive in-patient setting is required particularly when therapeutic work is offered as part of the assessment. It offers emotional containment to the parents and protection to the infant, whose care can be closely monitored.

I will now describe my therapeutic work with some mothers and infants I have seen in an in-patient setting, looking at the challenges faced at each developmental stage in this treatment.

BECOMING A PARENT

Pregnancy is a time of preparation for the arrival of a new infant, as the mother both physically and emotionally adapts to the changes within herself. Winnicott used the phrase 'primary maternal preoccupation' (1963: 85) to describe the special state of the mother's mind when she is 'given over to' the care of her baby, who at first seems like part of herself. She can adapt to the baby's needs because she is so identified with him, but this leaves her vulnerable, needing the support of those close to her.

This adaptation may not be possible for some mothers if this vulnerability and dependency is too frightening, and there is no emotional support available. Then the reality of becoming a mother can be denied, or equally worrying, motherhood is idealised as a perfect state. The mother is left unprepared for the reality of birth, which can be felt as a trauma, and the baby may be rejected because his birth brings such persecuting feelings. When the concerns about the risk to the baby are high, it is often a professional network that takes on the holding role, either in the community or in a residential setting. Here I saw two new mothers whose histories raised concern about how they would respond to the baby's birth. It was hoped that by early intervention we could support the mother's relationship to her new baby:

Anne was an adolescent mother, who had a very troubled life in care. She had for many years retreated into silence when under stress. There were concerns that caring for a new infant would overwhelm her capacities, and she would become silent again or, feeling words were not necessary, she would remain in silent commune with her baby.

However, this did not happen. From the beginning, Anne was able to talk to her baby, though quietly. She also talked to those around her, wanting to share her achievement in becoming a mother. She responded warmly and capably to the vulnerability of her tiny infant, as if creating a cocoon around them both. Her difficulties began when the infant was nearing 6 months and was beginning to separate, as I describe later.

In contrast, Barbara was an older mother, with a lifetime of difficulties but outwardly more coping. She had come to the hospital before the birth, which was to take place at the local maternity hospital. Barbara seemed shocked by the birth of her infant whose cries and uncertainties about feeding threw her into a panic. The hospital staff members were very concerned when I visited the mother and baby, the latter only a few days old:

When I arrived, both mother and infant were distressed and crying. Barbara could not comfort the baby or see the baby's eyes looking at her with longing for contact. She talked, letting me know how frightened she was dealing with this baby whose demands she felt she could not meet. I felt the birth was a shock she had not prepared for emotionally, and the baby's vulnerability terrified her. She was desperate for me to recognise her distress and how awful she had found the first few days. As she calmed, so did the baby. I could see the baby watching her mother through the sides of the plastic cot where she had placed her, as if seeking contact with her mother. With encouragement, the mother was able to take the baby in her arms and look at her with some warmth, enjoying the close contact, maybe for the first time.

For these two mothers, the birth of a baby carried a different meaning, although each worried me, carrying the threat of breakdown. Anne could identify with an infant as vulnerable as herself and 'fuse' into an empathic relationship with the baby, responding to every need. Being a mother made her feel grown up for the first time. It was this aspect I tried to support, encouraging each sign that she was thinking about her baby's needs, while also showing an interest in her well-being. I felt that both mother and baby needed my 'maternal preoccupation' if the baby was to stay safe. I feared that any sign of discontent from the infant could threaten Anne's fragile sense of self. I could not share these concerns with her as I thought it would undermine her newfound confidence. We found it hard to assess how much she was relying on our support to manage, and whether this was masking an underlying precarious emotional state, which could easily fragment under stress.

In contrast Barbara found her baby's vulnerability and neediness threatening. It evoked a fear of dependency which she had never faced. Her childhood deprivation meant she had no internal map of motherhood to follow. It was like a foreign language she would have to discover, painfully step by step. I had to learn that it was not just this mother's resistance to caring that was getting in the way, or a fear of failure, but an inability to make contact with her baby in the simplest way, looking, holding, being there. I needed to hold her anxiety and anger at feeling so helpless in these early days, until she felt safer in this new relationship with her baby. The close support of her nurse and adult therapist were vital too in providing a feeling of containment.

I am aware that when I am assessing new mothers, like these, and their infants, I am at my most alert, observing and being receptive to the quality of the relationship between the baby and the mother. In my consulting room, I put out the baby rug and soft toys, even if the infant is too young to use them, to make the room welcoming but also, I think, to prepare myself for the task ahead. It is as if I am moving into a different register where the communication will be mostly non-verbal, and the anxiety high, particularly when the parent–infant relationship is precarious. I rely on my counter-transference to tell me what is wrong, using my observation of the infant and the mother's response to guide me to the meaning of this crisis. I often pick up the warning signals in a bodily way. I get a tightening in my stomach or a dry mouth if I am very worried. I think this reflects the level of bodily communication between a baby and his mother. It must parallel the experience of the infant who responds to tensions in his close bodily relationship with his mother with physical signs of distress, like sickness or fever.

EARLY PARENTHOOD: THE BEGINNING OF SEPARATION

Looking after an infant exposes the mother to new feelings that can be frightening and overwhelming if she does not have the emotional resources to integrate them. These fears can reinforce the defences of a mother who is struggling to hold herself together, and increase her need to distance herself from the baby. This emotional distancing can leave the baby feeling unheld and abandoned. In clinical practice, I sometimes see a baby like this, who will stare at me earnestly, responding eloquently to any warmth or liveliness from me, as if searching for emotional contact. Then I worry that the baby's emotional needs are not being met by the parents and that without other responsive adults around, the baby will be left feeling lost and uncared for.

In 'The theory of the parent–infant relationship', Winnicott describes how the ordinary experiences of physical care give the baby a feeling of being loved (Winnicott 1960). The mother provides support to the baby's emerging ego by responding sensitively to the anxiety and vulnerability of the infant. This reminds me of the ongoing conversation a mother has with her baby, talking about the bath or the next feed, not expecting to be understood, but knowing there is a communication between them that is meaningful and calming. Such conversation is rare with parents under severe stress, or those so deprived that it is not part of their own early memories. I will often encourage parents to talk in this way to help engage the baby, although they may feel painfully shy and self-conscious at first, and I may suggest words they can use. Trying to think and feel what a baby is experiencing with the parents can be the first step towards their becoming more empathic with their baby. As one father said to me, 'It is like realising he is a little person.' The parents are usually rewarded by a grateful response from the baby who enjoys being the centre of attention. It is very different for a baby when everyday events like feeding and nappy changing are charged with tension and become traumatic. Then the baby might turn away to protect himself, and find a way of holding himself together, protectively.

This was my concern about Clare's baby, Tom, who was five months old. I had worked with Clare since Tom's birth, trying to support her attunement to the infant, but their relationship was not thriving:

> Clare was not sensitive to Tom's cues and calls. She seemed to alternate between intense rather intrusive play with him, or a lack of response when she appeared to ignore him. If the baby was upset, I found I was the one who responded to him. Tom did not seek out his mother's eyes. He would turn away, smiling at me, rather than relate to her. I was very worried that such a young baby was so avoidant. I wondered if he was afraid of the disturbance or anger he saw in her eyes.

My immediate concern was how to build a rapport between mother and baby before the baby gave up trying. Some detachment is typical of many parents I see, but this degree of disengagement was unusual. I thought I was also out of touch with the mother's feelings, both about her infant and seeing me. It is often difficult in parent–infant work to make sense of the feelings communicated by the infant and the mother, and to differentiate them. Here I could recognise the baby's anxiety, but I did not understand the strain in my relationship with the mother. I felt if we could put this tension into words, it might help Clare feel freer to bond with the baby. Yet

I sensed her mistrust of me made all my interventions futile. Intuitively, I feared that her hostile feelings towards the baby were not out in the open and she might secretly harm the baby:

I talked to Clare about my concerns that things were not moving, and that she was still very stressed with Tom. I said I thought that she found my comments critical and that she felt unsafe with me. She said this was true, but she felt like this with everyone and she thought I was trying to help her. This seemed to ease things between us, but made no difference between her and the baby. I watched their interaction, the determined way the mother played with Tom whom she placed on the mat, her face very close to his. At first, he was interested and pleased, but then he quickly tried to turn away. He cried and his mother put him in the buggy. I realised that there was no time when Clare had Tom close by, on her knee, just sitting while we chatted, occasionally inter-acting with him as parents often do. I thought of Winnicott's 'capacity to be alone', the experience of being with someone without any demands on the self. I realised that Tom never had that experience with his mother. Clare was terrified of being alone with him, particularly if he was distressed. I knew that if I tried to help her think about her fears of dependency and intimacy at this stage, she would become furious and resistant. Instead, I wondered if I could support her to be with the baby in an undemanding way, it might help their relationship.

In the next session, I suggested that Clare sit Tom on her lap while she talked to me. I encouraged her to respond if Tom looked at her or showed a particular interest. The baby became relaxed and looked around, absorbed in exploring the room with his eyes, while his mother also became calmer and easier in her contact with him. Later she was able quietly to give Tom a feed without the restless movement I usually saw. Next session, I suggested she read him a baby book, another way for them to be 'together but separate'. Tom loved this, babbling to the photos of the baby in the book, in a way I have never seen him do to his mother.

What was important here was that the baby was having the experience of being supported by his mother 'to explore the world' without intrusion by her needs. I had to be there for Clare to do this, helping her contain her anxiety about being close to Tom while recognising the achievement and enjoying it with her. I find sometimes that practical suggestions like these are needed by parents to give them an experience that might be quite new but can be added to their repertoire. The challenge for me is to discover an intervention that will match the unmet need in the parent–infant relationship. The fact that my relationship with Clare became easier made it possible for us to explore together the difficulties in relating to her son. The therapeutic relationship became a space, like Winnicott's transitional space, where at times we had a freedom to play with ideas and see what might help.

Sometimes, a small infant's dawning individuation cannot be tolerated by the parent. This can happen when the mother's ego is fragile and she has felt totally absorbed in the new baby as part of herself. The idea of separation is then a threat and the mother rejects the baby when he develops into a little person, different from herself. He becomes a persecuting, rejecting figure who cannot be tolerated. This occurred with the young mother, Anne, whose relationship with Jack began to deteriorate when he began to sit up and have a personality of his own. She could not tolerate the growing sense of separation and she became quite paranoid. I will describe the sad sessions when I saw her begin to distance herself from the infant and treat him cruelly:

Anne's alliance with me was tenuous, and it began to become very strained in the fifth month when she found it increasingly difficult to care for Jack, who often would not sleep at night and could be fretful when he was teething. Although Anne could not settle Jack, she refused to give him a soft toy to cuddle, saying she had never needed one as a child. She became persecuted and withdrawn, rebelliously refusing to think or listen if I expressed concern. Moments of warm relating to the baby were interposed with cruel rejection. She would avoid eye contact with Jack, talk about him in a derogatory way and poke at his nose angrily with a tissue until he cried. When she was upset, she would turn the baby upside down in a mechanical way that the baby tolerated but which brought no pleasure. In these moments, it seemed as if the baby was no longer a separate person from her but had come to represent an infantile side of herself she found strange and distasteful. I wondered if she was repeating her own early experience as a baby with a mentally ill mother. My attempts to think with Anne about this deterioration were now angrily rejected and seemed to make her even more hostile to the baby, whereas previously she had responded to my attempts to support her with the care of her child.

This behaviour was awful to observe, and it was difficult to know how to intervene without making Anne feel more criticised, increasing the cycle of persecution and poor mothering. I thought about what had led to this downward spiral, her own mother's refusal to support her through this time, the baby's gradual separation, her heightening transference to me as her therapist bringing her hostile dependency to the fore. From early on, I found it difficult to puzzle out the baby's experience of his mother as he appeared contented. Had Jack been in touch with a more active responsive side in his mother that she hid from us or did he remain undemanding, so as not to rock his fragile relationship with his mother? If he did feel the hostility and paranoia we saw at times, how damaging was this for him and his future capacity to relate?

These questions reminded me of Winnicott's concept of mirroring (Winnicott 1967). He believed that what a baby sees in the mother's face is a picture of himself through her eyes. When things are going well, this is a creative process. However, if the mother's face is rigid or unresponsive, there is no enriching exchange and the infant may give up. Sometimes, the response will be so variable that the baby learns to study the mother's face to predict her mood and judge whether it is safe to be spontaneous or not. Winnicott goes on:

> Immediately beyond this in the direction of pathology is predictability which is precarious, and which strains the baby to the limits of his or her capacity to allow for events. This brings the threat of chaos and the baby will organise withdrawal, or will not look except to perceive as a defence.
>
> (Winnicott 1967: 113)

I think this happened with Jack. As the days progressed, he became compliant, and fearful of his mother. We decided that we needed to protect the infant from his mother's disturbed projections, and he was placed in foster care. Here he became more relaxed and responsive, although he was distressed by her leaving after contact visits.

After Jack left, Anne was grief-stricken. Only then could she think about the impact of her persecuted state on her baby. When they were together, she could not see his needs as separate from her own but, apart, she had to face their separateness. Anne's adolescence made the task harder as she was still immature and her volatile moods accentuated her ambivalent feelings. After several weeks, Anne was able to face things more realistically, and accept help again from those around her. Then it become possible to think of returning Jack to her to see if she could build a more empathic relationship with him with therapeutic help. When he returned, Anne did develop a more lively relationship with him, enjoying his progress as a toddler, and they finally returned to supported care in the community. But I remained anxious about her future capacity to respond to Jack's changing needs as he grew more challenging and independent.

It had been painful to observe this relationship deteriorating. One of the strains of parent–infant work is recognising that a mother is failing, and separation might be necessary to protect the infant. I find it harder when I have been working with a parent–infant couple for some time and I have become fond of both. When I realise that I am becoming a persecuting figure, and the mother cannot share anxieties or think about our concerns, it often means that the infant is no longer safe. In an in-patient setting like ours, I would hope that others in the treatment team have retained a working alliance with the mother, the mother's therapist or the family nurse, and that together we can rebuild some trust, but often this is not possible and a breakdown in one area of treatment is mirrored in the work of others.

This work with Anne also emphasised how important the support of a mother is to a new parent. If a mother is mourning the loss of her own mother when her baby is born, it is known that she will be vulnerable to depression. To have a parent alive, but unavailable, is equally stressful. The parents we see have often been abused or neglected as children, but there is often the hope that a new infant will win back the love of rejecting parents. The disappointment if this does not happen can undermine a mother's attachment to her new infant. It is equally difficult when a mother is still enmeshed with her own family and meeting their needs. They then become rivals with the new baby. As a therapist, I can easily find myself in a 'tug of love' situation trying to support the mother to engage with her baby while knowing sadly that the pull back to the family of origin is stronger. Attempts to work on this mother–daughter relationship directly can help, but if the enmeshment is too entrenched, this is likely to fail and the baby will be rejected in favour of the mother's need for her own family.

INDIVIDUATION

The toddler presents new challenges. He has an independent will, a need to be separate and relate to others, and a wish to explore. This can be a relief to some parents who have found the infant's dependence too demanding, but enjoy the liveliness and sturdiness of a toddler. For others, it raises issues about ambivalence, their love and hate for their child and the problem of setting boundaries without being too harsh. There are new issues for the therapist too: how to help parents differentiate undue hostility from ordinary ambivalence; how to set boundaries for parents who are harsh without undermining their authority and confidence. These issues arose with two mothers I saw, each struggling with an intensely ambivalent relationship with her toddler, but with very different outcomes. With both parents, a key task was to help them find a way to talk to their child to rebuild their relationship.

Lee had been separated from his mother in his first year, after a near psychotic episode when she had been fearful of killing him. At 2 years, he was now being reunited with her to see if they could live together again. In their early sessions, Lee would turn his back on his mother, as if fearful of her and angry at their separation. She was terribly upset by his avoidant behaviour, but relieved that he would often peek at her, as if wondering whether there was some hope in this reunification.

I encouraged Diane to find ways to get closer to Lee, inviting him to play and telling him she understood he was upset that she left him. Putting this experience into words helped her discover that she could talk about difficult feelings with Lee, and it helped her begin to see the past from his point of view. Lee became interested that his mother was now trying to understand him. He would seek her out to play, although he could also retreat, anxiously remembering the frightening times when she had been ill and angry. Diane was able to comfort Lee, but she was reluctant to face the past and the guilt it made her feel. The crisis came when Lee began to want more closeness to his mother and reassurance that she loved him. He also began to challenge her more, letting her know how angry he felt at their separation and testing her ability to set limits. Diane backed off, fearful she could not sustain this growing relationship.

Diane found being in touch with her son's feelings unbearable and she was frightened of her destructiveness if they became close again. Sadly, she decided that he should return to his foster carers, so that an adoptive home could be found for him. These situations are hard to bear for everyone involved, seeing the child's disappointment and confusion, as well as the parent's distress. Diane's decision was realistic, as she knew she could not give her son the mothering he needed. This made it possible for a permanent home to be found for Lee, knowing that everything had been tried to reunite them. But when rehabilitation fails, we inevitably go through a period of self-questioning and mourning, finding it hard to let go of the family and the hope, after all the work involved.

Another difficult aspect of this work with severely disturbed parents is the experience of observing their volatile feelings towards their infants, the moments of hatred so split off from their loving feelings. I am aware how angry I can become towards the parent, seeing the infant's distress, and wondering how to intervene appropriately. It is usually only after the sessions that I can stand back emotionally and see how such moments fit in the wider picture of the parent's relationship with the child. Surviving such feelings and making them understandable to myself and the parent is an important part of the therapeutic process. Winnicott discussed this in 'Hate in the counter-transference', saying the therapist has to know about the hatred engendered by the patient and contain these feelings until they can be usefully shared with the patient (Winnicott 1947).

My work with Sally tested my ability to contain my anger, until she could acknowledge the impact of her aggression on her child and try to understand it:

Sally's son Bob, aged 2, was returned to her care at the hospital from foster parents after a period of separation due to her early cruelty and neglect of the child. They were both unused to each other and avoided close contact. I often felt angry towards Sally, in the early days. She talked in honeyed tones about loving her son, but I would see her spitefully pulling his hair when she brushed it, while her son winced. She complained about her son's greediness and attention seeking, not acknowledging her own desperate need for attention. I often did not know whether she was talking about herself or her child, they were so entangled in her mind. I recall one time when she arrived, complaining that Bob had grabbed food from another child after returning from a weekend away with her grandparents. I remember thinking how awful it must be for Bob returning to this self-absorbed mother after a weekend of good care. It was only when I was able to help Sally talk about her feelings of loneliness and rejection, having to leave the hospital community at the weekend, that she could soften, and see that she was angry with her son for expressing the needy feelings she could not accept in herself. Then she felt sorry for Bob and gave him the comfort that he so badly needed.

Bob was a cautious, withdrawn child at first. As he became more secure with his mother, he became more spontaneous and lively. In his sessions, he could show Sally how hurt and neglected he had felt, pretending to be a doctor caring for a sick baby. He used the toy stethoscope to check if his mother was ill, letting us know that he was not sure yet of his mother's state of mind. I put this play into words, acting as an interpreter between mother and child. Bob now came to his sessions with enthusiasm, pleased to find he had a way to communicate with his mother. As Sally became more emotionally responsive to her son, she often picked up his cues before I did. Gradually Bob was able to share with his mother the frightening experience of her anger, and his distress at their separation. For a while, these feelings spilled into other settings. He was aggressive to other children, biting and pushing them as if replaying his own experience of being bullied. He could also be challenging, tipping things up to see if his mother would lose her temper. Sally learnt to respond firmly but with some humour to Bob's testing behaviour, finding she could set limits more calmly, as she gained confidence in her son's affection for her.

This mother worked hard in our weekly sessions. She learned to understand the fury motherhood had brought to the surface and how she had treated her child as an unwanted aspect of herself, re-enacting her own experience of feeling rejected and unloved. Bob became secure enough to work through the distrust and anger that had held him back from a close relationship with his mother. My task was to act as container and facilitator for them both to help them rebuild their relationship.

CONCLUSION

In 'The capacity to be alone' Winnicott focuses on a time in therapy when the patient can begin to think alone, supported by the presence of the therapist (Winnicott 1958). He linked this with a creative phase in development when the infant is able to play alone, in the presence of a supportive parent. My work with families has shown how hard it can be for parents who have been severely deprived or abused in early life to offer this experience to their child. I explore how parent–infant work with parents can be adapted to help parents reach the point where there is both a space for the child to play and explore imaginatively, but also for the parent to be able to think, a space to reflect. Much of the therapeutic work aims at achieving this quiet thinking space. A parent needs from the therapist a parallel experience of a thinking reliable presence to help her make sense of the 'unthinkable anxiety' she experiences as a mother to allow her to explore her relationship with her infant. Sometimes the interventions have to be more active than this implies to challenge worrying behaviour and protect the infant or provide different models of relating to the infant. However, if therapy is to succeed, it is working towards the time when the therapist is able to sit back and let mother and baby 'go it alone' and discover their own relationship, supported by her presence in the room.

References

Daws, D. (1999) 'Brief psychotherapy with infants and their parents'. In M. Lanyado and A. Horne (eds.), *The Handbook of Child and Adolescent Psychotherapy*. London: Routledge

Fraiberg, S., Adelson, E. and Shapiro, V. (1980) 'Ghosts in the nursery, a psycho-analytic approach'. In S. Fraiberg with L. Fraiberg (eds.), *Clinical Studies in Infant Mental Health: The First Year of Life*. London: and New York: Tavistock Publications

Hopkins, J. (1992) 'Infant–parent psychotherapy' *Journal of Child Psychotherapy* 18: 5–18

Miller, L. (1992) 'The relation of infant observation to clinical practice in an under fives counselling service' *Journal of Child Psychotherapy* 18(1): 19–32

Murray, L. (1996) 'The impact of postpartum depression on child development' *International Review of Psychiatry* 8: 55–63

Winnicott, D. W. (1947) 'Hate in the countertransference'. In Winnicott (1958) *Collected Papers: Through Paediatrics to Psycho-Analysis*. London: Tavistock

Winnicott, D. W. (1958) 'The capacity to be alone'. In Winnicott (1965), *The Maturational Processes and the Facilitating Environment*. London: Hogarth Press

Winnicott, D. W. (1960) 'The theory of the parent–infant relationship'. In Winnicott, *The Maturational Processes and the Facilitating Environment*

Winnicott, D. W. (1962) 'Ego integration in child development'. In Winnicott, *The Maturational Processes and the Facilitating Environment*

Winnicott, D. W. (1963) 'From dependence towards independence in the development of the individual'. In Winnicott, *The Maturational Processes and the Facilitating Environment*

Winnicott, D. W. (1967) 'The mirror-role of the mother and the family in child development'. In Winnicott (1971), *Playing and Reality*. London: Tavistock Routledge

5   The concept of mourning and its roots in infancy (1988)

Victoria Hamilton

In the essay 'On transience' (1916), Freud describes 'a summer walk through a smiling countryside in the company of a taciturn friend and of a young but already famous poet' (305). During the walk, the young poet admired the beauty of the scene surrounding them but felt no joy in it since he was 'disturbed by the thought that all this beauty was fated to extinction'. A conversation ensued in which Freud, though agreeing over the transient nature of all things, disputed the pessimistic poet's view 'that the transience of what is beautiful involves any loss in its worth'. To Freud, it was 'incomprehensible . . . that the thought of the transience of beauty should interfere with our joy in it'.

In this dispute, Freud propounds the common philosophical argument against the desirability of immortality – namely, that the limitation raises rather than diminishes the value of enjoyment. Freud failed to make any impression upon his two companions and concluded that 'some powerful emotional factor was at work. . . . What spoilt their enjoyment of beauty must have been a revolt in their minds against mourning' (1916: 306). Freud went on to comment that 'mourning over the loss of something that we have loved or admired seems so natural to the layman that he regards it as self-evident' and yet 'to psychologists mourning is a great riddle'. Why the detachment of 'libido' from lost objects is such a painful process is 'a mystery to us'.

Freud tackled this new mystery in the same manner as that with which he has earlier delved into the mysteries of hysteria and dreams. He traced back the manifest puzzle to significant wishes and impulses arising in childhood. Since 1917 (when 'Mourning and Melancholia' was published), those psychoanalysts who have taken up the theme of mourning usually refer to developments in infancy. Like so many psychoanalytic concepts, the concept of mourning has acquired a specialised usage whilst still maintaining many of its everyday connotations. When I was a child, I learned the word 'mourning' in relation to the black band men wore on the arm of their jackets and the black border around an envelope. This meant that someone had died – or, more likely since it was wartime, that somebody had been killed. It would never have occurred to me to associate this word with a baby. In contrast, the generalised and rather loose psychoanalytic concept of mourning covers many quite distinct mental processes which follow upon a whole range of losses. In the furthest reaches of the psychological literature, mourning is often used to denote a process accompanying almost any change in the life cycle. Much of the psychoanalytic literature portrays mourning as a daunting task whether it is confronted in infancy, adulthood or old age. Furthermore, this task can seem insurmountable to those individuals who have not negotiated an internal position in relation to endings early on in their lives. Most psychoanalysts would list it as one of the more formidable tasks which lie in wait for a young baby. Mourning, which seems so appropriate to the end of life, appears to have a central role in its beginning.

I shall not attempt to give a historical view of the development of the concept of mourning in this chapter. Instead, I focus upon some of the distinctions which are absorbed in the present-day use of the term. Like other much used psychoanalytic concepts, it can be described as a 'pliable, context-dependent' concept (Sandler 1983).

ENDINGS AS EVENT

In order to get some grip on the concept and its application to a whole range of losses which befall a human being from birth until death, I make a distinction between endings as events and the internal processes characteristically associated with these events. This distinction is important and it is often blurred in the literature on bereavement, separation and mourning. When mourning is used to refer to events, it approximates ordinary usage, whereas the psychoanalytic concept of mourning refers to complex internal developments which extend far beyond a layman's use of the term. Nonetheless, the events which precipitate these developments have some significance for our internal, or representational, world.

Endings can be grouped under four categories which I believe are loosely related and yet distinct. In order of increasing misfortune these are *separation, loss, bereavement* and *one's own death*. All four involve events in the sense that an ending has a place and time in the outside world. Death is not the same kind of ending as the other three types – separation, loss and bereavement – since it cannot be an event which is experienced during the life of a person. Thoughts about death are necessarily beliefs about a future event as this is experienced in a person still living, i.e. in an embodied human being (Wollheim 1984). The other types of endings are events which can be experienced while life goes on.

When we turn to the internal processes which accompany these endings, many of the above distinctions break down. For instance, I said that the event of one's own death cannot be experienced while one is still living. And yet endings readily evoke feelings and thoughts which are linked through complex associations to our beliefs about the certainty of death. Whether or not we postulate the existence of a 'death instinct', many of us believe that the new-born infant has an imminent sense of his own mortality and experiences moments of a terror of extinction. As the young child becomes more self-reliant and extends his circle of dependent relationships, he is able to mobilise a whole range of external and internal protective defences against such primitive fears. Paradoxically, when looked at from this point of view, the child gets further away from the possibility of death as he grows older. Death is something which happens to other people, to very old people perhaps. For a few years, a child in a stable and happy home is allowed a sense of immortality. A child who is preoccupied with death seems 'morbid'.

During childhood, we hope that a child will face neither bereavement nor death. We know, however, that parting, through innumerable experiences of separateness, separation and loss, is an essential part of his everyday life; a child deprived of such experiences seems ill-prepared for the years ahead. Attachment research has provided us with numerous empirical observations of the importance of separation in the moment-to-moment life of a young child. The child who 'weathers' a separation from his mother without protest is no longer automatically regarded as having a secure relationship.

Of the four types of events which are generally associated with the processes of mourning, separation is the least unfortunate. Separation *per se* need not be a tragedy. Death and bereavement refer to a loss that is final. In itself, a loss may be as we say 'no great loss' to a person. Losses can be mixed blessings. A separation, however, which is not final implies a sense of continuing relationship; it need not evoke a threat to one's personal exist-ence. Separations can be occasional or frequent, timely or untimely, foreseen or precipitate. Separation can refer to an event which is short in time or space – as for example, when a mother moves out of sight of an infant. On the other hand, a separation can be long in space and time. A separation can turn into a loss which is permanent as, for example, when a refugee is forced to leave his homeland never to return. And, of course, there are a whole range of mental states such as maternal depression which can lead to experiences of abandonment where physical separation is not an issue.

In other words, whereas bereavement refers to something which is final and irreversible and thus contains a greater potential for tragedy, separa-tion can develop along many diverse pathways. Even brief separations can be traumatic. As with bereavement, the way a person deals with a separa-tion has a great deal to do with the kind of relationship existing prior to the moment of parting. Specific and transient events elicit a train of internal processes which become, or already are, part of a person's disposition.

MOURNING AS A DISPOSITIONAL STATE

In his paper 'Failure to Mourn, and Melancholia', Pedder (1982) gives a clear exposition and review of the psychoanalytic view of mourning. He quotes from Winnicott as follows: 'If in an individual the depressive position has been achieved and fully established, then the reaction to loss is grief, or sadness. Where there is some degree of failure at the depressive position the result of loss is depression' (Winnicott 1954). Drawing on the work of Freud, Klein and Winnicott, Pedder puts forward the view that satisfactory mothering in childhood leads to the establishment of a 'good-enough internal object . . . which though threatened by later loss will enable healthy mourning to take place and a satisfactory internalisation of the lost object in time to be achieved'. When, however, 'there has been some degree of failure in childhood, later loss will bring difficulties in mourning and possibly depression' (Pedder 1982: 329). How, then, does the infant bear the pain of loss? This is the prototypical situation for the development of the capacity for mourning – for sadness, internalisation and renewal.

THE INFANT'S CAPACITY TO BEAR THE PAIN OF SEPARATION

I shall first raise some conceptual issues relating to separation within the infant–mother relationship and discuss some ways in which these concepts are treated both by psychoanalysts and by researchers in developmental psychology. Then I shall describe a piece of 'clinical' work with a mother and infant in which I was asked by a colleague to do an assessment of a 1-year-old boy who had developed a form of rocking which his parents found peculiar and disturbing.

The infant

If I think about the principal terms of the question – the infant, bearing pain, and separation – I have to ask myself what sort of person or being this infant is. There are as many infants in psychoanalysis and psychology as there are theories. We need only consider the work of two leading child analysts of this century, Anna Freud and Melanie Klein. The infants they describe inhabit different worlds. Similarly, the infant described by the developmental psychologist Jean Piaget several decades ago is different from the infant portrayed by contemporary developmental psychologists such as John Bowlby, Terry Brazelton, Daniel Stern and Colwyn Trevarthen. However, there is one phase used by Winnicott which, in principle, unites most contemporary psychoanalysts and developmental psychologists – namely, 'we cannot describe the baby without describing the environment' (Winnicott 1970: 248).

With Winnicott's statement in mind, I can rephrase the question as follows: 'How do the infant and his parents (usually mother) bear the pain of separation?' In this chapter, I use the words 'mother' or 'caregiver' instead of 'environment' as these expressions are more succinct and convenient for my purposes. Researchers find that it is the 'specifically experienced environment, as opposed to the general family environment' which is the greatest predictor of later behaviour and pathology in the individual. Two siblings can grow up with two very different models of relationship. The 'specifically-experienced environment' concerns the infant–caregiver relationship (Emde 1987). This rephrasing of the question in terms of the infant and the mother does not imply that the experiences of the mother and infant are the same – although they might be very similar. But, as Winnicott pointed out, the baby is being a baby for the first time whereas the mother is bringing many experiences to the situation, not least of which is the experience of herself as a baby. As demonstrated in my clinical vignette, such powerful previous experience can be the mother's greatest ally and greatest hindrance.

Thus, the consideration of the first term in the question – namely the infant – has led to a rephrasing in terms of a relationship. This relationship is one of inequality or asymmetry in the areas of experience, control, regulation, and cognitive capacities such as intentionality. For instance, an observer of early infant–mother 'attunement' (Stern 1985) might think that both partners intended to fit in with one another. However, the attribution of intentionality to others always has an inferential component; this is particularly important to bear in mind when we talk about an infant of a few days or weeks of age. We have much less reservation about attributing intentionality to the mother's behaviour. Most of us assume that a caring mother intends to attune herself to the infant's cues. But, as far as the infant is concerned, we can say that the newborn seems 'prepared' or 'preadapted' for participating in human interaction. For instance, at birth the infant demonstrates a propensity for participating in eye-to-eye contact and for showing prolonged alert attentiveness to the features of the human face and voice; he is also in a state of responsiveness to being activated and soothed by human holding, touching and rocking.

Bearing pain

My focus on the relationship between mother and infant has consequences for the question of bearing pain. Bearing pain is not something that the infant does completely alone. What pain means to him, how it feels, its intensity, duration, terminability or interminablity, depends upon the relationship which exists between himself and his caregiver or mother. In addition, the baby's experience of pain, his ability to tolerate negative feelings such as rage and anxiety, depend upon his age and developmental capacities. Obviously, separation at one month is very different from separation at 6 months, 18 months, 3 years and so on throughout the life cycle.

Thus the intensity or duration of the pain of loss depends upon its bearability. In bearing pain, a *mature* person draws upon internal resources, his previous experiences of loss and comfort and upon his capacity to draw on external resources in the present. And of course the availability of comfort turns upon an individual's ability to trust and turn to others in times of stress. Bereavement studies emphasise greatly the availability of comforters as a predictor of either disordered mourning or favourable outcome. A solitary child has a hard time finding a comforting shoulder in later life. In their series of films on childhood separation, James and Joyce Robertson emphasise the crucial role of comforters in temporary separations of young children from their mothers. When a constant, familiar comforter is available, the level of distress is of a wholly different magnitude. The point is that to suffer alone is unbearable; and it is this unbearability which can lead to the states of detachment, denial, or manic-depressive illness described in the literature on mourning. The comforter – father, child-minder, or older sibling – plays a central role in the infant's ability to tolerate separation from his mother.

The pain of separation

I now turn to the object of the question – namely separation. How is the pain of separation borne? Is the infant's pain of separation similar to the adult's? Is there any difference between the pain of separation and the pain incurred by another kind of loss? To me the crucial difference between separation and bereavement is in *beliefs* about the possibility of reunion. Generally speaking, unless for religious reasons we believe in immortality or reunion after death, we do not regard it as a healthy sign if a bereaved person cannot reconcile his beliefs that loss is both final and recoverable. In normal childhood, however, we expect a quite young infant to develop the sophisticated belief that when his mother leaves the room, she will eventually return.

By the time a child goes to nursery school at about 3 years of age, we expect him to be able to enjoy himself for two or three hours away from his mother, provided he is in the care of people he likes and trusts. When a child is anxiously attached and clings tearfully to his mother to avoid separation, or alternatively denies himself the perception and experience of separation, we tend to feel that he does not hold the same beliefs about separation and reunion as most other children. In normal development, therefore, the tolerance of separation and the belief in reunion seem to go hand in hand and, when things go wrong, we usually find some confusion between these two beliefs. In bereavement, it is the juxtaposition or tandem relationship of these two beliefs that we are asked to forgo. At the root of the pain of grief is the demand that we give up something so natural and apparently essential to human growth and development, namely the anticipation of reunion.

Thus far, I have suggested that the endings involved in separation, loss, bereavement and death call forth different responses in so far as different *beliefs* must be entertained. I imply that the pain of separation is more easily borne when beliefs about reunion can be entertained and physical and psychological comfort is at hand. However, if we think simply of the pain of separation, do we find parallel differences in the affective responses which endings bring in train? Perhaps not.

Here I return to the distinction I drew at the beginning of the chapter – the distinction often blurred in the literature on mourning between loss as an event and loss as an internal process. Of beliefs we can say that they are true or false; they point towards shared knowledge. Affective responses are guided by beliefs and in turn empower beliefs. But we do not ascribe truth and falsity to feelings in the same way that we ascribe them to beliefs. Feelings and beliefs can be appropriate or inappropriate both in relation to events and in relation to one another. For instance, to a person recently bereaved, feelings of expectation and accompanying beliefs about the recovery of the lost one seem appropriate even though the beliefs are false. The process of mourning illustrates this complex interrelationship between belief and feeling because of the central position played by the belief in reunion in the resolution of mourning. In looking to infancy as a sort of template determining later experience, psychoanalysts focus upon the pain of loss and the many ways in which individuals deal with this pain by unconsciously arranging their internal world and their beliefs to deny or exclude the painful reality. Satisfactory mourning requires that 'natural' beliefs about extinction or reunion be foregone. A baby must learn that when his mother turns her back, she is not gone for ever. He will survive her departure and anticipate her return. A bereaved person must learn that the 'mate' who has returned every day for thirty years or so is indeed gone for ever.

The pain of loss or separation from a loved one is universal and may in itself allow of little variation in the degree of suffering. When we feel this sort of pain, we do not usually say 'I feel a little pain today' or 'I felt more pain yesterday'. The pain of loss tends to come and go, to become frequent or intermittent; it lessens, as it becomes more tolerable. Here it seems legitimate to ask whether the suffering of a wife for the recent loss of her husband is qualitatively different from that of a very young infant who has been set down in his cot whilst his mother fixes his bottle in the kitchen? Both can be struck by a sense of finality. There is a threat to existence. The infant flails about; the adult feels numb and frozen. The adult has a more or less sophisticated repertoire of beliefs, a few trusted friends and so forth to help her cope. By comparison, the infant is in a sorry state.

Nevertheless, the infant has at his disposal a complex repertoire of behaviours designed to evoke powerful responses in his caregiver. Principal amongst these, particularly in the first few weeks of life, is crying. Crying is a response to complex states of arousal – for example discomfort, hunger, loneliness – but it is also the most powerful stimulus for caring responses. As we know, parents greet the first smiles with happiness and with relief. Now they can respond to a new range of stimuli other than crying. In cases of child abuse, the infant's constant crying is often the main factor in tipping the parent with meagre resources over the edge. Bowlby and other researchers have pointed out that the expression of crying and anger over bereavement in adulthood and separation in childhood is crucial to the resolution of mourning – that is the capacity to bear the pain of loss. Perhaps the infant has an advantage over the grown-up in that he can directly express his anger and protest through behaviour such as crying and hitting, whereas the adult has the advantage of an inner set of beliefs and experiences. The adult can think, 'I am a person leading a life', whereas the three-week-old infant cannot think this way and as yet has not led a life. He cannot be said to be a person leading his life in the sense that leading a life implies having a past, present and future.

Where, then, shall we focus our research for the template, as it were, of the mourning process? If we regard endings as essentially akin to 'normal' separations in infancy, we will look at the characteristic ways in which infants respond to separations and we will try to build up some picture of the internal model they create in order to represent their experiences to themselves. Should we, then, focus upon the mourning process of a six-month-old baby? Or should we suspend the backward looking passage of our thoughts and pause at a later age, say, when the child has developed the capacity for representational thought and can be said to hold within him an internal working model of the world around him?

THE DISTINCTION BETWEEN SEPARATENESS AND SEPARATION

Some of the lack of clarity in the literature on mourning stems from con-fusion between separation and separateness. As observers, we can fairly easily draw up a list of differences, not least of which is the physical presence or absence of the person from whom the baby has been separated. However, as with bereavement, this objective distinction becomes blurred when we consider the range of internal responses to separateness and separation.

A brief look at two models of mourning can highlight the distinction and overlap between separation and separateness. Melanie Klein and John Bowlby have looked to childhood and infancy for guidelines upon which to map adult responses to bereavement (Klein 1940; Bowlby 1980). The theories of mourning of both thinkers originate in observations of a child's responses to separation from his mother. For Klein, the crucial issue was less reponses to actual separation than to the infant's conception of his mother as a separate person. Klein conceptualised the resolution of the mourning process in terms of the infant's negotiation of a position or stance in relation to his mother as a whole and separate person outside his omni-potent control. The achievement of this position – the 'depressive position' – enabled the infant to begin to cope internally with some of the pain of separation. During the second half of the first year, the young infant grieves for the loss of control over his mother – the breast – and also for an earlier mental state of ruthless or self-centred illusion. Klein believed that, once gained, this position stood the child in good stead in life but that experiences of separation and separateness, at any age, were of an essentially painful and persecutory nature – hence their potential for pathology. To me, the term 'depressive position' describes a disposition rather than a developmental stage. In coping with the task of mourning, a person manifests underlying, persisting dispositions.

Klein's emphasis has immediate clinical appeal. Many disturbances in the mourning process relate to faulty negotiations of the unavoidable fact that other people are separate from ourselves and thus not under our control. Our ways of relating to other people can reveal a lack of belief in their existence as separate persons. Problems about separateness often surface and become urgent in the context of a separation. Prior to an actual separation, mental and physical boundaries between persons may be so blurred that separateness goes unacknowledged. Bowlby has written less about the negotiation of a position of separateness and difference within an attachment and has focused instead on prototypical responses to separation. Essentially, he draws a parallel between the typical course of mourning and a child's response to separation from his mother. In the event of separation or loss, characteristic affective responses are evoked; these are numbing, yearning, anger, despair, and disorganisation and, optimally, reorganisation and renewal.

Frances Tustin has described the crucial issue of separateness in therapy with autistic children and with neurotic patients who hide an encapsulated autistic part of the personality. Before or following the birth of these patients, their mothers have usually been acutely depressed. This has

> caused mother and baby to experience the strain and stress of bodily separateness in a particular poignant way, which made them cleave to each other. . . . Thus, the awareness of bodily separateness was a particularly devastating happening for such a baby which (s)he took steps never to experience again. In addition, the depressed nursing mother could not help her infant to bear the strain of panic, rage, grief which awareness of separateness occasioned.
>
> (Tustin 1988, personal communication)

This discussion of the overlap between the concepts of separation and separateness brings me back to my rephrasing of the original question – how do the infant and his mother bear the pain of separation? Obviously the answer will devolve on how both mother and baby negotiate their separateness and the inevitable separations of everyday life. A sense of separateness buffers the pain of separation; at the same time the capacity to bear separation seems central to the sense of oneself as a separate person.

We could say that the infant comes to bear the pain of separation as he gains a sense of his separateness. If we then think of the situations in which a baby develops the sense of separateness, we are immediately reminded of the many contexts other than separation in which separateness is worked out. There is the obvious issue of control, for instance over feeding. In her detailed observations of the 'rapprochement' phase in the development of separation–individuation, Margaret Mahler describes the many inevitable conflicts which surround the negotiation of both separateness and separation (Mahler 1975). But there is another class of situations in which an infant's separateness matures – this is the area describes by Winnicott as 'mutuality' and by the researchers as 'attunement' (Stern 1985), 'matching', 'social fittedness' and 'mutual referencing' (Emde 1987).

To us as clinicians, the pain of separation is a subject of primary concern. We rarely think about 'joy', 'surprise' or 'interest'. But the 'positive' emotions are extremely important in development from earliest infancy and, according to researchers, are organised relatively separately from negative emotions. Positive emotions can be swamped by negative emotions and states of prolonged distress. Nevertheless, researchers have found that pleasure and interest are major indicators of emotional attunement between mother and infant and that the most sensitive clinical indicator of emotional availability in infancy is the presence of positive affects. The sharing of positive affects and interests is typical of infant–parent interactions towards the end of the first year (Emde 1987).

This emphasis on mutuality, on the sharing of emotions and interests, has important repercussions for the concepts of separateness and separation. Mutuality does not mean sameness. Playing, turn taking, the development of an interesting theme depend upon some notion of separateness. In the first three months, mutuality can mean, for example, attunement, responsiveness, harmony, containment of the unbearable. These are essential aspects of the task of mothering. But the ingredients of mutuality change. For instance, researchers have observed an important shift in the baby's focus of attention when he reaches three months of age. Trevarthen (1983) notes that babies may even avoid the gentle, seductive, soft talk which characterises the synchronous type of exchange of the first months. They begin to take great interest in the world around the mother. This means that the baby twists away, looks beyond his mother's face, seems much less enraptured by close eye-to-eye contact with her. Researchers note that visual curiosity, watching others, is a sort of vicarious learning which precedes any capacity to reach and grasp and manipulate objects. Learning about the world is at first done vicariously. From the psychoanalytic viewpoint, Ferenczi described this primitive form of learning as 'introjective identification' (1909) and Klein described a similar and parallel process in terms of 'projective identification' (1946).

But turning-towards also means turning-away. What does this mean to the mother? What does she feel when the infant no longer gives her his undivided attention? Does she let him look around, does she compete, does she withdraw because she feels rejected? Does she turn around too? We tend to talk about the baby's adaptation and to underestimate the formidable task of adaptation required by the mother of a new baby. Things are moving at a remarkable speed. Each shift demands a type of mutuality different from the early kind of close-fittedness of the first three months. At six months we can talk about the interplay of two subjects. Trevarthen describes the play as having a much 'rougher', 'teasing' quality. Nevertheless, the 'privileged' and exclusive nature of this relationship is immediately apparent if a stranger or more or less anyone other than the mother attempts to play these games. From the infant's point of view, this will not do. By nine months, things have become even more sophisticated. Through gesture and vocalisation, the baby brings his interest in an object and his interest in his mother together. The mother and baby look at something, for example, a book, together. They can both point, look, then communicate about something. The outside world towards which the baby turned away from his mother becomes a shared world. Togetherness is restored – but, again, this is of a different order from the precise synchrony of the first three months.

I describe some of the changes which go on during the first year of life in order to suggest additional imagery with which to envisage a baby's developing sense of being a separate person. Though closely related, separateness is learned in contexts other than separation. Many of these contexts are not experienced as painful. Thus, when mourning is used to refer to an underlying disposition or mental 'position' (as described in Klein's concept of the depressive position) in relation to separateness, it is important to consider the range of activities and communications in which separateness is learned. Mourning refers to the painful aspects of change. Although an incapacity to mourn may interfere with a person's ability to change, the term mourning should not be applied indiscriminately to change *per se*. The following clinical example illustrates the very close connection between the pains of separation and separateness as these were experienced by a mother and her 1-year-old girl.

CLINICAL EXAMPLE: 'MRS LLOYD' AND 'BEATRICE'

I shall describe two interviews with Mrs Lloyd and her baby Beatrice who was just under 1 year old at the first interview. Mrs Lloyd has been in therapy with a colleague and intended to stop therapy that Easter. I did not discuss Mrs Lloyd's history with my colleague prior to meeting her; nor did I look at her file. I wanted to come to the situation fresh. I knew that the first six months had been relatively happy and harmonious for both Mrs Lloyd and Beatrice. However, in recent months, Beatrice had developed a curious form of rocking which would go on for two hours at a stretch. She did this mostly at night, or at times between sleeping and waking. She appeared quite content whilst in the rocking state, rarely objecting to being put down by her parents who had been awakened by the noise and had picked her up.

Mrs Lloyd was pleasant to meet. At first Beatrice looked at me a bit shyly from her pushchair but slowly began to smile and look more at me. She seemed a friendly child. She was rather sweet to look at, a neat face and body. Her mother took her out of her pushchair while explaining to me about her lamb – a soft white cloth lamb. She has about five of them, all identical. Mrs Lloyd keeps buying them because they get dirty. Beatrice began to suck on her lamb as her mother told me about her rocking. Beatrice turned away from us and started to rock with her lamb in her mouth, making a sort of humming–groaning noise. Mrs Lloyd said 'That's it' and went on to comment that it was unusual for her to do it in the day. Beatrice soon stopped and hoisted herself up on the arm of her mother's chair and buried herself in her knees. Mrs Lloyd comforted her while continuing to talk to me. Beatrice then looked at me, smiled again and started to look around the room. Mrs Lloyd got out a big soft ball for her and she set off to get it and quickly became engrossed in crawling back and forth with her back to us over the edge of the carpet and the lino in my room. This seemed to intrigue and please her. Quite quickly her mother distracted her with the ball and she came back to the centre of the room and looked in the toybox I had brought.

Mrs Lloyd described how Beatrice goes to sleep quite easily at 7.30 in the evening, often rocking, but wakes at about 1 in the morning. Mr and Mrs Lloyd hear Beatrice making the rocking noise through the baby alarm. She sleeps at the end of the corridor. After a while one of the parents gets up. Usually Beatrice is wet and needs changing; often she is asleep when they go in and seems to be in a trance. At about 4 o'clock they are again awakened by the rocking noise, although they sometimes turn off the baby alarm. I noticed that on three occasions when Mrs Lloyd described Beatrice's night-time rocking, she told me as an aside that they had turned off the baby alarm although they could still hear Beatrice. To get more of a picture of Beatrice's life, I asked Mrs Lloyd to describe the baby's daily routine. She wakes up at about 7.30, usually in a good mood. Mrs Lloyd gets her up to have breakfast. She then puts her in her playpen for about an hour between 10.00 and 11.00, while she does other things. She takes her out and plays with her for a while until she has her sleep between 12.00 and 2.00. Beatrice sometimes rocks herself to sleep but falls asleep quickly, as she does during the night. On the days Mrs Lloyd has therapy, Beatrice goes to a child-minder who also picks up a 9-year-old boy from school. The babysitter is 'wonderful' and has been available since Beatrice was very small. On the other days, Mrs Lloyd will take Beatrice out to the park.

Beatrice was continuing quite happily to go back and forth over the edge of the carpet and the lino and had also picked up a plastic giraffe out of the toybox. She took this off to the lino and enjoyed dropping it and listening to the sound. She would come back and hoist herself up on the chair periodically and 'talk' to her mother but did not need her to pick her up or attend to her more than that. I asked Mrs Lloyd about Beatrice's early life. She told me she had breastfed her for about six months, although she had introduced the bottle early on because she did not have enough milk. Beatrice had not particularly taken to a bottle and had started on solids around this time quite happily. I asked Mrs Lloyd if Beatrice sucked her bottle at all, like at night, or when going to sleep, and was told no. However, it later emerged that Beatrice does wake up thirsty and likes to have a drink in the night; but she uses the bottle purely for drinking and not sucking.

I asked Mrs Lloyd when the rocking first started and she told me that it was around the time when Beatrice was beginning to crawl – at about five to six months. Mrs Lloyd then connected this time with the end of the breastfeeding. When I asked if Beatrice had complained about this, Mrs Lloyd said no and went on to say that Beatrice hardly ever cried. She never had. She wondered if this was a bit odd. I asked her if Beatrice cried in the night and she said that she rarely does. Sometimes the rocking noise turns into a cry but generally Beatrice seems quite happy and not to need them; it is they who cannot bear it. I questioned her further about crying, both now and when Beatrice was little, for instance when Mrs Lloyd went out of the room. She replied that although Beatrice may whimper when she first leaves the room she quickly forgets about her and gets on with her own things. I wondered out loud whether the reasons Beatrice did not get upset was that she forgot about her mother or because she knew that somehow her mother would return. Mrs Lloyd said that she could see this and went on to remark that she hardly ever left Beatrice but she thought that anyway Beatrice just forgot and was too busy with her own things.

By now Beatrice had gone over to the door and was enjoying banging on it with her hand, making quite a noise. She came over readily after a bit when her mother called her and she re-interested herself with the plastic animals in the toybox, which she took out and put in her mouth and then banged on the table. When I asked Mrs Lloyd who Beatrice stayed with if she and her husband went out, she said they never went out. They had gone out once, leaving Beatrice with the child-minder who is keen to babysit, but they have to get back early – at 11.00 – which means they cannot go to a party or have a proper evening. Mrs Lloyd then told me how she hates to leave Beatrice and has never wanted to leave her. I asked how Beatrice got on with her husband; she told me that Beatrice adored him, adding, 'As you can see, she is a much loved child.'

Beatrice now moved into the centre of us and started to investigate the book-cupboard which has glass doors. She was interested in seeing herself in the glass and Mrs Lloyd remarked that she was very vain. Beatrice banged on the glass, making quite a noise with the doors banging against each other. After a while Mrs Lloyd stopped her and tried to distract her with her lamb. Beatrice looked a bit confused and displeased but then did seem quickly to 'forget' about what had so engrossed her and returned to sucking her lamb vigorously with a rather anxious expression on her face. She complained a bit as if she might cry but did not do so. She seemed a bit restless and distracted and at this point she returned to the carpet–lino edge. Her going back and forth resembled a rocking movement although she was actually moving over space. There was a short lull and Mrs Lloyd returned to her preoccupation with the rocking. I felt that I was meant to come up with a solution in relation to her worry and I voiced this feeling. Mrs Lloyd replied, 'I know that all children have things like this, bottles and so on, but suppose it goes on till she is fifteen or something.'

I was interested that Beatrice slept at the far end of the corridor and commented questioningly on this. Mrs Lloyd told me that she had moved Beatrice when she was three to four months old. She said that she could not bear to be separated from Beatrice and decided that she must just move her out of their bedroom or else she never would. She emphasised how much she loved to have Beatrice there. I asked whether Beatrice had remonstrated about this move and again Mrs Lloyd said, 'Not at all, Beatrice never cries.'

Beatrice now seemed rather unhappy and was sucking on the plastic giraffe; she then put the top of her head on her mother's knee and sucked rather desperately on the arm of the chair. This interaction seemed quite mixed, in that Beatrice went to her mother for comfort but did not ask to be picked up and held or cuddled. Mrs Lloyd told me that Beatrice does not particularly like to be cuddled now although she did when she was small. Beatrice started to suck vigorously on the tassels of her mother's shoes. As it was near the end of our time I suggested to Mrs Lloyd that Beatrice had found a way of calling out to her parents in the night which was in keeping with her character as described by Mrs Lloyd. Namely, Beatrice gets her parents to get up in the night and come to her but she does not cry directly for them. In fact, she appears not to need them but to be quite happy with the rocking, which she can do by herself. Mrs Lloyd accepted this. I then said that perhaps Beatrice felt that she did not need to cry if her mother was always close by and came immediately when she cried. She agreed with this and reiterated how she does not like to leave Beatrice.

I remarked that Beatrice seemed a lively child in many ways, although the rocking seemed expressive of various anxieties and I asked Mrs Lloyd if she felt she had difficulties in separating. I asked her about her own childhood, what it was like when she was Beatrice's age. Mrs Lloyd said, 'Oh well, I was fostered so I don't know, I grew up in children's homes.' This led to her telling me about how worried and over-concerned she is over her baby and how desperately she does not want Beatrice to be as unhappy as she was. I agreed with her when she commented that she was trying to be a better mother than any ordinary mother who does not have to make up for such a deprived past. Beatrice was by now making quite a noise and Mrs Lloyd stopped her very gently. I asked her what happened if she said 'No' to Beatrice when she goes to see her in the night. At first, Mrs Lloyd looked at me with surprise. So I said that I expected Beatrice would know what 'No' meant and went on to explain that I meant something like picking Beatrice up and saying, 'No Beatrice, go back to sleep' while settling her into sleep. Mrs Lloyd replied that she did not think that Beatrice would understand 'No'.

As Mrs Lloyd got ready to leave and we arranged a second appointment, she quickly told me one or two things she thought I should know about Beatrice. She does not like lumpy food. I said that perhaps Beatrice wanted everything to be smooth, to iron out the lumps and gaps as she does with her rocking. We talked more about the way Beatrice stays in this in-between state and how she is not like a child who wakes up and cries out. As Mrs Lloyd tried to dress Beatrice, she struggled and was quite annoyed, in what seemed a very natural way for a 1-year-old. Mrs Lloyd said twice, 'You see, she doesn't like it' and again remarked on how Beatrice does not like to be cuddled and held. I said that perhaps Beatrice's annoyance was understandable for a child as curious and interested as Beatrice and that she was fed up with her mother for interrupting her and distracting her from her business. Mrs Lloyd could see this and went on to tell me that when Beatrice gets cross or she herself is in a bad mood, she has to leave the room. She goes out and stays by herself, has a cigarette or something until she has quietened down. She cannot bear to shout. She thought this was because she had been beaten by two of her foster mothers. I suggested that she was trying to deal with her own past and this made her fearful that she might really get angry and beat up Beatrice but that perhaps she also felt that Beatrice should not get angry or show frustration by crying and getting cross with her.

It seemed to me that Mrs Lloyd was in a dilemma which led her to oscillate between feeling and acting as if she and Beatrice were inseparable and, on the other hand, leaving Beatrice to her own resources, expecting her to 'forget' about her mother as soon as she was out of sight. I wondered whether the template of their relationship was contained in the rocking and the baby alarm: in order to separate, Mrs Lloyd had to put Beatrice in another room at the end of the corridor but then had a baby alarm to awaken her. Beatrice, in turn, did not cry out as if she were alone, separated from her mother and needing her to come to her. Instead she rocked, made a noise which was nevertheless unbearable for her parents.

The second meeting was easier. Again, Beatrice was initially friendly, smiling at me cautiously, turning to her mother and looking back again. She seemed more alert. Mrs Lloyd gave Beatrice her white lamb and went on to describe her rocking. She now rocked more frequently, more during the day but for shorter periods of time. She also rocked more noisily, really banging with her head on the cot so that they could even hear it in the kitchen. As Mrs Lloyd talked to me and we focused less on Beatrice, Beatrice gave me a rather wan smile, as if trying to be friendly, but then started her rocking on the floor between us. She rocked very persistently, back and forth, while sucking and biting on her lamb. The rocking was certainly more driven than the last time, a quicker more desperate movement. It looked to me as if she was trying to reach her mother − her rocking being close to her mother's knees − almost butting into her yet pulling herself back. It was curious and looked like an arrested crawling movement, as if the natural movement would have been to crawl towards her mother's knees and demand attention. As she rocked, she moaned in a repetitive, complaining way, very close to a cry.

This went on for over five minutes. We continued talking but both of us looked at Beatrice, acknowledging the rocking. Mrs Lloyd pointed out that her eyes were closed – she could see Beatrice's face whereas I could not. Beatrice was much more obviously distressed than the last time when she had rocked away from us, on the edge of the carpet and the lino. In this session, she was right in the middle of us; her rocking was more disturbing and self-absorbed but the noise was much closer to a proper cry.

Mrs Lloyd described two rows she had with her husband. This was unusual. They rarely fought and never in front of Beatrice. Mrs Lloyd thought Beatrice had been affected. The cause of the row was Beatrice's rocking, which had been criticised by a friend with whom they had spent the previous weekend. Beatrice had been compared adversely with the friend's baby of the same age who seemed perfectly normal. Mrs Lloyd talked about her worries over leaving Beatrice to come to her own sessions. I then pointed out how when she and I talked, Beatrice turned to her rocking. I suggested that Beatrice might be protesting about us talking together and not paying attention to her. I pointed out that Beatrice seemed happy to begin with when we both paid attention to her, offering her toys, but perhaps we then became like two parents at night, talking together and ignoring her. I also said that Mrs Lloyd seemed very distressed and guilty about leaving Beatrice and about her rocking.

By now, Beatrice seemed to have recovered her equanimity and was fairly happily exploring the room, first the door and then the plants which we had to move out of her reach. She then began to explore the desk and the papers and books so these also had to be moved. Luckily we found some plastic spoons and I gave her one of these which she *dropped on the lino floor*. She very carefully lowered herself from the desk and picked up the spoon and proceeded with this dropping game until she was in danger of banging her head on the desk.

As Beatrice played with the spoons, Mrs Lloyd spoke to me about a recent visit to one of her foster mothers. Although this foster mother was the nicest of her foster mothers, she got fed up with Beatrice when Beatrice wanted to touch things on her table (this paralleled the plant and papers in my room). However, in contrast to her experience in my room, where Mrs Lloyd said she felt at ease, her foster mother had written to her after the visit with advice that now Beatrice was 1 year old, Mr and Mrs Lloyd should start to train her. This meant that they could give Beatrice a slap with the outcome that, on future visits, the foster mother would no longer have to move things out of Beatrice's reach. Mrs Lloyd became tearful as she recalled her foster mother's attitude towards her. This opened the discussion about how sensitive she is to any criticism and also how very difficult she finds it to separate from Beatrice and to say 'No' to her. She acknowledged that she was trying to do everything right for Beatrice. I had, of course, noticed the tense and immobilised way in which Mrs Lloyd had watched Beatrice's exploration of objects in my room and her considerable relief when I stopped Beatrice and re-directed her attention without appearing to be either punitive or unable to act.

Mrs Lloyd commented on how Beatrice seemed to like to play by herself and did not particularly want to play with her mother. Mrs Lloyd pointed to Beatrice's play – by herself with the spoons. However, as Mrs Lloyd spoke to me about this, she did in fact tap Beatrice's spoon with her spoon and Beatrice did not ignore it. I noticed Beatrice smile to herself, although she did not continue or elaborate on the game. I asked Mrs Lloyd whether Beatrice did not join in when she played with her; did Beatrice always ignore her? Mrs Lloyd said that Beatrice likes to play ball with her that requires two people. She then commented that Beatrice hated to be cuddled, she always had. Mrs Lloyd seemed tearful again and went on to talk about how hard she does find it to leave Beatrice even though she loves the babysitter and her family. Beatrice always had a wonderful time with her. They played with her. She came back exhausted. But Mrs Lloyd always felt guilty when the babysitter said how much Beatrice enjoyed going to the park or going to the swings. She took this as a criticism that she too should be doing this, that she did not take Beatrice out enough; she should do more with her; she should have afternoons off. I commented on her readiness to feel guilty and inadequate and that she seemed to feel that she had to be the perfect Mum who did everything for her child and could not feel that it was a good thing that Beatrice enjoyed being with her and yet also enjoyed doing different things with different people. She said that she had thought about this but found it hard to believe. She went on to describe how she had felt rejected by Beatrice for a considerable length of time. It emerged that Beatrice's turning away form her started at around three to four months. Mrs Lloyd had talked to her husband and the babysitter about this but they could not see it and did not think that Beatrice was actually rejecting her.

By now Beatrice was making more direct overtures to her mother to join in and this seemed to evoke sad thoughts about Beatrice's birthday the day before. Now, Beatrice was 1 year old. Mrs Lloyd became tearful when I said that she seemed to feel very sad about losing the first three months' close relationship with Beatrice and about her growing up. Mrs Lloyd absolutely agreed about this, saying that she loved Beatrice to be grown up. She enjoyed all the things she could do, she felt proud of her but she really felt terribly sad about losing those first three months when there was just she and Beatrice and nobody else. I said how difficult it was for her to accept that Beatrice still loved her when she turned away from her but at the same time towards other people and things that interested her. This turning away from her and towards other things felt like a rejection of her and a failure on her part. She cried quite a bit about this, saying that long before Beatrice was born she had often said to her husband, 'Oh I wish I could have a baby', to which he replied, 'Yes but it won't be a baby for long; they soon grow up.' Now a year had gone by, so quickly, it was all past now, that special time. This emotional exchange seemed to give Mrs Lloyd relief and she went on to discuss her concern about her own future. She had been thinking about whether to go back to work or study part-time and whether it would be all right to leave Beatrice and continue with the babysitting arrangement for the afternoons. She then told me that she had decided not to stop her own therapy that Easter.

I was able to draw some parallels between Mrs Lloyd and Beatrice, pointing out how closely she and Beatrice are in harmony in a way that they shared a similar conflict, both wanting each other and yet wanting to do things independently. I suggested that she found this difficult to deal with in herself and in relation to Beatrice because of her fears of rejection and being rejected. I remarked on how the early special and exclusive relationship was so precious to her. She acknowledged this, saying she felt that Beatrice was the only person in the world with whom she had this relationship – 'my own flesh and blood'. She had a real mother and two half-brothers or half-sisters somewhere but did not know them. Beatrice is her 'one blood relation'. She then told me about her one meeting with her real mother and about how very rejected she felt.

We talked a little more about the rocking in relation to her feelings of guilt about separation and separateness. I suggested that the rocking was Beatrice's way of trying to deal with separation from her and of giving up this exclusive relationship with her. I linked this with Beatrice's rocking in our two sessions – how she rocked at the beginning when we talked to each other. I also said that perhaps it was important that Beatrice now protested more loudly. I said that I knew that Mrs Lloyd found this daunting and I thought she might find what I was going to say daunting as well – namely, that Beatrice would probably continue to be preoccupied with these issues for the next two years, or at least until nursery-school age. I said that this was an area of development which Beatrice had to struggle with and how perhaps she felt that there must be something she could do to save Beatrice from these difficulties and inevitable conflicts. Mrs Lloyd accepted this and said that she had been thinking that it was really she who had to work further on this herself.

POSTSCRIPT

Since these two meetings, I have had no further contact with Mrs Lloyd and Beatrice. However, my colleague who has continued to see Mrs Lloyd in individual therapy has told me that she became less anxious about Beatrice's rocking, which subsided. Apparently, Beatrice had become more openly defiant, crying more and complaining more vehemently. From the point of view of her physical development, Beatrice began to walk fairly soon after I saw her and this in itself may have contributed to the cessation of the repetitive rocking movement. As I suggested, the rocking movement seemed to represent both an internal state of conflict and an urge to crawl forward towards her mother, which met with both motor and psychic frustration.

References

Bowlby, J. (1980) *Attachment and Loss*, vol. III, *Loss: Sadness and Depression*. London: Hogarth and Penguin; New York: Basic Books

Emde, R. (1987) 'Development terminable and interminable'. Paper read at 35th Congress of the International Psychoanalytical Association, Montreal, July 1987

Ferenczi, S. (1909) 'Introjection and transference'. In Ferenczi, *First Contributions to Psycho-Analysis*. London: Maresfield Reprints, 1980

Freud, S. (1916) 'On transience'. *Standard Edition*, 14. London: Hogarth Press

Freud, S. (1917) 'Mourning and melancholia'. *Standard Edition*, 14. London: Hogarth Press

Klein, M. (1940). 'Mourning and its relation to manic depressive states.' In Klein (1975) *Love, Guilt and Reparation and Other Works 1921–1945*. London: Hogarth

Klein, M. (1946) 'Notes on some schizoid mechanisms' *International Journal of Psycho-Analysis* 27: 99–110

Mahler, M., Pine, F. and Bergman, A. (1975) *The Psychological Birth of the Human Infant: Symbiosis and Individuation*. New York: Basic Books

Pedder, J. (1982) 'Failure to mourn, and melancholia'. *British Journal of Psychiatry* 119: 329–37

Sandler, J. (1983) 'Reflections on some relations between psycho-analytic concepts and psycho-analytic practice' *International Journal of Psycho-Analysis* 64: 35–45

Stern, D. (1985) *The Interpersonal World of the Infant.* New York: Basic Books

Trevarthen, C. (1983) Talk to Association of Child Psychotherapists delivered in March

Winnicott, D. W. (1954) 'The depressive position in normal emotional development'. In Winnicott, *Collected Papers: Through Paediatrics to Psychoanalysis.* London: Hogarth Press, 1975

Winnicott, D. W. (1970) 'The mother–infant experience of mutuality'. In E. J. Anthony and T. Benedek (eds.), *Parenthood: Its Psychology and Psychopathology.* Boston: Little Brown & Co

Wollheim, R. (1984) *The Thread of Life.* Cambridge: Cambridge University Press

6 Reflections on 'The concept of mourning and its roots in infancy (1988)'

Victoria Hamilton

This chapter is a commentary on an earlier work reprinted as the previous chapter in this volume, using clinical and personal experiences that have intervened since 1988. Into this narrative, I weave influences on training in the Independent tradition of psychoanalysis as practised in Britain at the end of the last century. I alert the reader to the different levels from which I approach this commentary. It is necessary for the reader to think hierarchically, and to distinguish statements about earlier thinking and clinical work from hypothetical interventions that I might make in clinical practice today. As Gregory Bateson liked to point out, 'the map is not the territory', we do not eat the menu, nor does the word 'cat' scratch us (Bateson 1970). Thus, when I describe personal experiences that inform this commentary *about* previous clinical work, I do not describe what I would actually say to a patient in therapy. I am not a proponent of mutual analysis and 'self-disclosure'.

In order to situate my comments, I preface this chapter by describing the contexts, past and present, in which I wrote the paper in 1988 and write my commentary today.

PREFACE

1988

In 1988, I had returned to London after working for several years as a child and family psychotherapist in Los Angeles. As my practice grew, I received an increasing number of adult referrals. Back in London, I eagerly undertook further training in the Adult Department at the Tavistock Clinic, where I had earlier completed my Child and Family Psychotherapy training in 1972. The most important influence on my adult work was the weekly supervision I was fortunate to have with Dr Harold Stewart who was then both a consultant in the Adult Department and a highly respected and distinguished analyst and author in the Independent group of the British Psychoanalytical Society. I also benefited greatly from the weekly clinical meetings that took place in the unit to which I was attached under the consultancy of Dr David Taylor. These meetings were attended by therapists of all denominations within the British psychoanalytic scene, by trainees from countries all over the world and from varying professional backgrounds – psychiatry, psychology, social work, nursing, pastoral counselling.

During this training period, I had frequent contact with two 'mentors' with whom I had developed both personal and professional relationships since the beginning of my child training in 1968 – John Bowlby and Frances Tustin. Bowlby and Tustin were large figures in my life and perhaps have exercised the most formative influence on my clinical understanding and thinking. Though very different in terms of their personalities and educational and professional backgrounds, both were truly independent thinkers and teachers, devoid of any desire to preach and convert their students to either their way of thinking or any 'school' with which they were affiliated. Their style is something that comes naturally to me, but one that I also wish to emulate.

Coincident with additional training in adult psychotherapy, I was fortunate enough to be one of the first intake of PhD students in the Psychoanalysis Unit at University College, London under the professorship of Joseph Sandler. As all my clinical and theoretical training had taken place at the Tavistock, I knew very little about the work of Anna Freud, of the Ego Psychologists, even my reading of Freud was patchy, and I was largely ignorant of international psychoanalysis particularly as it was practised at that time in the US. Joseph Sandler's scholarship and international experiences (he was then President of the British Psychoanalytical Society) were invaluable to me, I was fascinated by the new perspectives which his weekly seminars opened up to me. In addition, I was learning to think as a psychologist, with some knowledge of statistics, as well as a psychotherapist with a background in art and philosophy.

2004

Although I cannot articulate their effects, three large events in my personal and professional life weigh heavily on my thoughts on mourning and affect my writing of this commentary (*about* an earlier work).

On 1 January 1999, my husband received the diagnosis of metastatic lung cancer. He died seven months later, three weeks before his 50th birthday. We had lived and worked together for 27 years, writing each day side by side, editing each other's work, growing up together.

At the end of November 1999, on Thanksgiving weekend, I closed my practice in Los Angeles. I had worked as a therapist since 1965 when I got my first job as an art therapist at the Marlborough Day Hospital in St John's Wood, London. The decision to close my practice had been made independently of my husband's illness and was the outcome of several years of planning and thought. To leave a practice and teaching position is a huge and weighty decision because of the responsibility and respect for human lives to which we have dedicated ourselves.

I now live in New York City. I live in close proximity to other people in ways that are very different to residents of London and Los Angeles; close and continuous human contact has drawn me into a new kind of relating and befriending. There is no way out: no British reserve, no Los Angeles automobile, inside which one can immure oneself from the onslaught of the sound and touch of fellow human beings. A year and a half after I moved to New York, September 11th broke into our lives. Like most New Yorkers, I immediately thought of what I could do to help: anything to be involved and not stay frozen and helpless at home, watching the horrors unfold on the TV screen. I soon found a place at a Red Cross centre where I could interact with children and families who were survivors of the fallen Twin Towers.

In the short time I have lived in New York, I find myself immersed in the lives of immigrants – highly educated men and women who have lost their countries, their families, their livelihoods and homes.

COMMENTARY

The life events described above confirm much of my earlier thinking on mourning as it was centrally influenced by Bowlby's work on loss, separation and attachment. However, in reviewing the 1988 paper from a conceptual point of view, I think I would now place greater emphasis on the following elements:

1   Mourning, like trauma, follows upon a specific *event*. Yes, stages in the life cycle and in development inevitably call forth capacities for mourning, resignation and acceptance. But, for me, mourning should be reserved for something closer to ordinary thinking – i.e. it should describe a process which is preceded by an event in the outside world. Since these events are usually highly specific, occurring within a particular location and time, experiences of loss and ways of grieving can be very diverse. However, there is often communal or intersubjective consistency in the descriptions given by survivors of a particular event. This accounts, I believe, for the fact that survivors often prefer to congregate together and talk with one another rather than to the professionals who may be 'flown in' to advise.

2   Untimely and unexpected loss calls forth extreme responses that test both emotional and *cognitive* thinking. I underline the conscious act of will that is required in order to redirect attention away from familiar working models. I call this redirecting a 'steering' of the mind, very different to the commonly used psychoanalytic terms 'denial' and

'defence', but close to Bowlby's concepts of 'cognitive bias' and 'selective exclusion' (1973). I believe that these are survival strategies that are commonly used by survivors of trauma and bereavement; as far as I am aware, these tactics have not been described in positive terms within the psychoanalytic literature on mourning.

3   Loss of homeland and professional identity usually coincides with movement to a strange environment, and, as a consequence, the loss of familiar surroundings and the absence of comforters that naturally play such a crucial role in the mourning process. Today, I would focus more on the effects of being *uprooted* from one's country of origin, and, as illustrated in the case of Mrs Lloyd, from one's original mother.

When I wrote the 1988 paper, I tended (as I would today) to first organise my thoughts by a conceptual analysis as I had been trained to do when I was a philosophy student at University College London in the mid-1960s. Thus I broke down 'endings' into four categories 'in order of increasing misfortune' (Wollheim 1984): separation, loss, bereavement and one's own death.

To these I now add a new category: *uprooting*, a sub- or cross-category perhaps of the first three described in the 1988 paper, but nevertheless distinct from these in the capacities for reorganisation that are called forth in order to survive. Uprooting involves the removal from one's homeland and the precipitous relocation to an alien, strange environment. Flight, exile, terrors of leaving and escaping, and abrupt relocation in a foreign land entail a loss of self and of the activities that have defined one's identity up to the moment of uprooting. Language barriers are enormous; where possible, we try to find others we can talk to in our language of belonging.

A poignant example of this uprooting and relocating is the elevator man in my apartment building here in New York, who escaped with his immediate family from Sarajevo following the massacres there in 1993. He is Bosnian and Orthodox, a former sociology professor of 35 years and author of 5 books. His wife was a judge and a Muslim. He witnessed the killing of 12,000 fellow citizens, 5,000 of whom were children. Now he lugs garbage bags into the basement of this 225 apartment building. One day, I asked him if he was writing another book. He put his hand over his heart and said, 'No, I cannot, my heart is dead.'

The loneliness of uprooting feels different, I believe, to the aloneness that follows the death of a loved one. The country is still there, often family members are still at home, and yet they remain out of reach. Perhaps this loss has some similarity to the agonies of a person suffering the aftermath of an unwanted divorce. As I mention in the 1988 paper, bereavement studies emphasise the crucial *role of comforters* as a predictor of either disordered mourning or favourable outcome. In a foreign land, comforters are not at hand, and even when they are, language constraints can be crippling. The philosopher and historian of ideas, Isaiah Berlin, quotes the observation of a friend who came from the Balkans and had lived in England for 40 years: 'Solitude doesn't mean when you live far from other people. It means when people don't understand what you are saying' (Jahanbegloo 1992).

Bowlby always emphasised the overriding importance of the parameter 'familiar/strange' in the development of human beings from the cradle to the grave. From infancy on, we tend to orientate towards the familiar and away from the strange, a trait that has survival value for human beings and other species. This deeply rooted pattern links with Bowlby's concept of 'cognitive bias' and sets a formidable task for immigrants, exiles and refugees. Isaiah Berlin, quoting Herder, states: 'nostalgia, craving for home, is universal and "the noblest of all pains"'. To belong 'means that people understand what you say without your having to embark on explanations, that your gestures, words, all that enters into communication, is grasped, without mediation by the members of your society' (Jahanbegloo 1992). For this reason, Berlin was an early and fervent supporter of Zionism.

The Czech poet and writer, Milan Kundera, poignantly describes this state in his book *Ignorance*: 'the most moving Czech expression of love translates as "I yearn for you", "I'm nostalgic for you", "I cannot bear the pain of your absence"'. Etymologically, in the Czech language, 'nostalgia means something like the pain of ignorance, of not knowing. You are far away, and I don't know what has become of you. My country is far away, and I don't know what is happening there' (Kundera 2000).

The Scottish psychoanalyst Ian Suttie (a powerful influence in the early days of the Tavistock Clinic) and the Scottish philosopher John Macmurray (an equally powerful influence on the thinking of many of the first British psychoanalysts, particularly the fathers and mothers of the British Independent group) stressed that the urge to belong to a community, for companionship and tenderness, is a basic human need. *To be uprooted is to no longer belong.*

Returning now to 1988 and setting up the mourning paper, I followed the scholarly approach taught by Joseph Sandler: in order to understand the meaning of a concept, we first explore its historical development and usage within a particular tradition and culture. For instance, in my thesis on patterns of transference interpretation, I had made a chronological study of the concept of transference, starting from its early use by hypnotists in the nineteenth century from whom Freud developed many of his ideas on hysteria. This historical approach accounts for the introductory paragraph to the mourning paper in which I refer to Freud's papers 'On transience', 'Thoughts for the times on war and death' and 'Mourning and melancholia', all of which were written during the First World War, the tragedies of which ravaged European society for decades, certainly throughout Freud's lifetime.

Commenting on the section of the paper in which I describe *mourning as a dispositional state and the infant's capacity to bear the pain of separation*, I would now focus more on the *mother's* dispositional state and her habitual ways of dealing with the pains of separation. Referring to Winnicott, I state: 'the baby is being a baby for the first time whereas the mother is bringing many experiences to the situation, not least of which is the experience of herself as a baby' (1970). Using the idea of 'uprooting' outlined above, and my experiences, clinical and personal, with people who have been adopted and fostered, I would emphasise that Mrs Lloyd was being a mother for the first time in the special sense that she had received no mothering from her biological mother. She was forging new pathways of mothering out of early experiences of being uprooted – a person without roots in mother earth or mother nature.

Today, I would make more of her remark that Beatrice was the only person in the world with whom she had 'a flesh and blood' relationship. Beatrice was rooted in her mother in a way of which Mrs Lloyd had no personal experience. I am reminded here of the wise words of Frances Tustin who once said of my son when we moved first to London and then back to Los Angeles where he was born: 'he has been uprooted, he has lost his roots'. This observation stemmed from her work with autistic children and their families in which she described the trauma of feeling 'uprooted' from the ordinary flesh-and-blood world.

Reading through the two sessions with Mrs Lloyd and Beatrice, I think I would try to connect Mrs Lloyd's experiences of adoption and fostering, the recurrent theme of uprootedness, with her responses to both *separation and separateness*. Away from Beatrice, her one blood relative, she could easily have experienced herself as orphaned and alone in the world. Our discussions tended to return to issues of separateness and individuation. These are conveyed in Mrs Lloyd's anxieties about leaving Beatrice with her much-loved child-minder for occasional evenings and enjoyable outings to the park. Mrs Lloyd acknowledged that Beatrice's 'turning away' from her in order to 'go towards' other people and things that interested her (a natural development in infants over three months of age) had felt like a rejection and a response to her failure as a mother. Mrs Lloyd told me that Beatrice was so busy with her own things, she quickly 'forgot' about her mother. Mrs Lloyd's experiences as a child, moving from one foster home to another, meant that she was only too easily forgotten. She belonged nowhere and to no one. She had to learn for the first time that she could be a mother that Beatrice would not forget.

In part of the second interview in which Mrs Lloyd tells me about discussions with her husband and babysitter about feeling rejected by Beatrice, I would now focus attention on the role of the *father* in terms both of separation/individuation and in the encouragment of positive emotions and exploration of the wider outside world. I gleaned from the interview that Mr Lloyd adored Beatrice, and that he could see no signs of Beatrice's rejection of her mother. I would have liked to invite Mrs Lloyd to come in with her husband and Beatrice. Mrs Lloyd was seen individually by a male therapist, but I believe that Beatrice's father could have been more actively engaged and supported in his position within the nuclear family.

Returning to the 1988 mourning paper, I follow Bowlby in the emphasis placed on the complex interrelationship between *mourning and beliefs in reunion*. Today, this relationship still stands out as one of crucial and paramount importance. In infancy and childhood, painful experiences of loss and separation are enormously assuaged by developing beliefs in reunion. Following the permanent loss of a loved one, natural beliefs based on thousands of experiences of reunion are overturned and thrown to the winds. Reorganisation requires the complete reversal of the cognitive bias towards reunion.

However, recent experiences have alerted me to a large difference between those individuals who entertain religious beliefs and those, like myself, who believe neither in reunion after death nor in any sort of a spiritual connection on earth. Beliefs in reunion and presence can be specific in that they are ordered by a particular religious tradition, or they can be wider and looser in that they refer to a spiritual connection. Examples of the latter are: 'X would be so proud of you, so happy to see you now', 'X is looking over you, he/she is guiding you'. For me, these kinds of beliefs are indeed comforting but they refer to memories, often body memories and conversations. But, beyond vivid, palpable memories, I have no sense of an actual presence. In practice, when working with a bereaved person today, I would pay greater attention to whether he or she is overtly religious or more widely 'spiritual'. In adulthood, beliefs in reunion shift and ameliorate the pains of bereavement, just as in early childhood, they soothe and calm the pains of separation and separateness. But for non-believers like myself, the last breath and silence that follows can be an agonising reminder of the vast impenetrable line across which the departed will never return.

I now turn to the section of the 1988 paper on the baby's 'repertoire of behaviours designed to evoke powerful responses in his caregiver'. I note that principal amongst these and key to the role of comforters is *crying*. I refer to the work of Bowlby and other researchers who point out that expressions of crying and anger over bereavement in adulthood and separation in childhood are crucial to the resolution of mourning. In the clinical section of the mourning paper, I quote Mrs Lloyd's observation that 'Beatrice never cries'. Beatrice did not remonstrate when she was moved out of her parent's bedroom nor did she complain when breast-feeding stopped at six months of age when she was beginning to crawl. However, the rocking symptom started at this time and seemed to replace, or rather forestall, crying and complaining. The hypothetical connection I made between the rocking symptom and crying and crawling, which I discussed with Mrs Lloyd, was later supported in the individual therapy with my colleague. In a session, Mrs Lloyd reported to her therapist that Beatrice had become 'more openly defiant, crying more and complaining vehemently'. The stage of motor development captured in the rocking movement (crawling on all fours) was superseded by Beatrice's learning to walk, at which point the repetitive rocking ceased.

I believe that Mrs Lloyd, like many survivors of loss and trauma, found it impossible to witness those emotions that are so naturally expressed in crying. She wanted to avoid and redirect the pain of separation at all cost, to save both her child and herself from the agonies of uprooting and rejection. Since September 11th and my acquaintance with the lives of immigrants and exiles, I have been struck by what I might call the smile and laugh of the traumatised. Here, I parallel Sinason's work on the 'smile of the abused' (Sinason 1992), a smile that is both specific and reactive. Frequently, interactions are initiated by a cheerful smile, joke and laugh. I believe that this laugh/smile expresses a compromise between conflicting emotions and behavioural repertoires. It is a bit like the 'freezing' of an animal who wants both to escape and yet remain unseen, a successful camouflage. Prolonged, unstoppable crying in children and adults can evoke rejection, even cruelty, as is well documented in cross-generational studies of abused children. Even when comforters are available and willing, crying becomes wearing and disturbing. Witnesses can feel helpless, hopeless and ultimately frustrated. The saying 'Laugh and the world laughs with you, cry and you cry alone' has some truth. Survivors of exile and uprooting have learned to attune themselves to this observation of human nature.

As noted in the 1988 paper, the sharing of 'positive emotions and interests' plays a crucial role in experiences of togetherness and mutuality. In order to be welcomed into a new culture, positive feelings are very important. It is hard not to feel rejected if a person talks endlessly about previous losses – his or her longing and nostalgia for the person or country that has been lost or left behind. After a traumatic loss, as I observed in 1988, negative emotions and states of prolonged stress can swamp positive emotions such as joy, surprise and interest. I think these feelings play a key role in being welcomed into a new culture; they contribute to experiences of 'matching', 'social fittedness' and 'mutual referencing'. Expanding on Bowlby's observation, 'turning towards' the new involves a 'turning away' from the old and the familiar. The immigrant's laugh or smile can be an expression of both genuine curiosity and enjoyment and a camouflage of the opposite – the urge to cry and withdraw into memories of the familiar.

Last September 11th, I was talking with a Serbian immigrant who was helping me decorate my apartment. He is a singer and dancer, full of jokes and good humour. Our conversation drifted back to where we were and what we were doing on 11 September 2001. Within seconds, my companion's eyes filled with tears and the whole cheerful veneer collapsed. The story of his flight from Yugoslavia, the murder of so many friends and family, the terrors of being downtown waiting in line for his green card interview at 9 o'clock on the morning of September 11th, flooded over. Excessive drinking, smoking, working non-stop often seven days a week, churchgoing and community work, were ways of staying upbeat and of reaching a point of exhaustion that might sometimes bring a few hours of sleep and respite. The feelings of abrupt loss and severance from everything familiar were palpable and excruciating and shared by many on this anniversary. I was again alerted to the cheerful front well presented that day by the doormen and concierges of my apartment building.

Today, following the more recent work of Fonagy and Target (2002), I would try to assess a person's capacity for self-reflection and the development of his or her 'reflective functioning' as a guide to clinical intervention and as a predictor of favourable outcome of treatment. As an infant, Mrs Lloyd had had little, if any, experience of being the object of reflection, of being held in mind by a caring adult. To my question about what it might have been like for her when she was Beatrice's age, Mrs Lloyd responded, 'Oh well I was fostered so I don't know, I grew up in children's homes.' It seems to me that, despite so many deficits, Mrs Lloyd showed a great capacity for self-reflection. Her reflective functioning in relation to Beatrice expanded during therapy, building as it did on her great desire to be a new kind of mother, one who not only loved, but who understood and could correctly interpret her baby's experiences. To me, Mrs Lloyd also portrayed the creative and transforming capacities that are described by Christopher Bollas in his seminal paper on 'The transformational object' (1979).

CONCLUSION

In the 1988 paper, I discuss the concept of mourning and its roots in infancy in terms of finding a possible 'template' for later experiences of loss and bereavement. I think that the writing of this commentary has loosened any belief I may have entertained in a set of conditions that can be generalised or universalised. Yes, good experiences in early childhood, such as finding 'a comforting shoulder' to cry on, stand one in good stead and can act as buffers against the many disasters and pains of later life. But the pathways to recovery that follow so many types of loss under the rapidly changing conditions of modern society are nevertheless both highly individual and specific to social and ethnic groups. However firmly a 'secure base' (Bowlby) or 'depressive position' (Klein) is established in early childhood, all can be thrown asunder by traumatic, often violent, events that can throw unimaginable hurdles onto the course of mourning. Disbelief, despair, protest, unspeakable agony remain universals . . . perhaps. But how such unbearable feelings, images and memories are negotiated and transformed seems to me to be a highly individual and creative endeavour.

If I try to relate my theoretical and clinical thinking to the thinking of child and family therapists and analysts in the British Independent group, the influences of Bollas, Bowlby, Stewart, Tustin, Winnicott are obvious. I think the kind of interventions I made in 1988 were also organised by thoughts from the seminars given by Winnicott which I attended in 1971 during which he so beautifully illustrated his belief that, ultimately, 'mother knows best'. Our job is to elicit the mother's reflecting and transforming capacities by revealing the fullness of her own potential. Many Independent analysts – Michael Balint, Marion Milner, Charles Rycroft also come to mind – have focused on the creativity of the patient and the role of the analyst in bringing forth capacities that have been fettered and blunted. In his later work, Winnicott wrote about the role of waiting and of silence, of not rushing in with active and pointed interpretations before the patient is ready for them. This is something I have also learned from Pearl King, herself influenced by the practice of meditation and the Quaker background of her analyst, John Rickman. I thank my Independent training as well as my musical education for transmitting to me the value of listening in clinical practice and everyday life.

References

Bateson, G. (1970) 'Form, substance and difference'. In Bateson, *Steps to an Ecology of Mind*. New York: Ballantine Books, 1972

Bollas, C. (1979) 'The transformational object' *International Journal of Psycho-Analysis* 60: 97–107

Bowlby, J. (1973) *Attachment and Loss*, vol. II, *Separation*. New York: Basic Books

Fonagy, P. and Target, M. (2002) *Affect Regulation, Mentalisation, and the Development of the Self*. New York: Other Press

Kundera, M. (2000) *Ignorance*. New York: HarperCollins

Jahanbegloo, R. (1992) *Conversations with Isaiah Berlin*. London: Peter Halban

Sinason, V. (1992) *Mental Handicap and the Human Condition*. London: Free Association Books

Winnicott, D. W. (1970) 'The mother–infant experience of mutuality'. In E. J. Anthony and T. Benedek (eds.), *Parenthood*. Boston: Little Brown

Wollheim, R. (1984) *The Thread of Life*. Cambridge: Cambridge University Press

Part II
Latency and adolescence

7 A question of balance

Working with the looked-after child and his network

Iris Gibbs

This chapter draws on material from the therapy of children who come into the category of being 'looked after', placed in care settings through the intervention of the local authority. It addresses the challenge for the therapist in how to position herself *vis-à-vis* the child, the carers and the network of professionals who often hold the balance of power regarding the therapy. Part of the challenge for the therapist lies in determining what aspects of the therapy remain confidential and what need to be shared. This can create a tightrope situation. If she shares too much information too quickly, the therapist runs the risk of losing the cooperation of the child. On the other hand, she may also risk losing the child from therapy if she is seen by the network to be too withholding or too exclusive in terms of her relationship with the child.

The child may also be accustomed to an absence of confidentiality and express no concern about this. He may be used to exposure – perhaps from lack of privacy in the network, perhaps from a perverse early experience. The child in this situation needs attunement and care on the part of the therapist, especially when sharing information is undertaken, as this has to be with the child's informed knowledge and consent and not be part of a re-enactment of past disclosure.

Psychotherapeutic work with a child in the care system is thus often wider and more complex than the relationship between therapist and patient. From the start, therapy happens in a context where several people are involved in decision-making about the child's current and future life. These may include social services teams, court representatives, foster carers and the organisations employing them. Some children continue to have regular contact with their birth families even in situations where neglect and abuse may have led to their removal. In her work with these children, the therapist's dilemma is often about balancing the needs of the child in a context of the many competing external forces.

Whether in the care system or not, a child needs privacy, space and time to struggle with issues at his own pace. This work may be 'out of synch' with the timescale of the professionals involved. Often therapy is viewed as a quick fix for a child who may have had several broken placements, or be seen as a panacea for curing all the psychological problems of the child – and of the system that is meant to support his development.

Professionals referring children for therapy often have specific ideas about what the therapy should address: for example raising self-esteem, reducing aggression, moving on from attachments to neglectful and abusive early relationships and forming new attachments. All will clearly be part of the remit of child psychotherapy; however, the process of achieving these goals will be affected in a number of ways. Nevertheless, the therapist first has to form a working alliance with the child. This may be defined as a basic willingness in the child to come and be involved with the therapist (Sandler *et al.* 1980). It also involves a degree of basic trust and mutual interest between the therapist and the child. All the above are prerequisites for the forming of a therapeutic alliance and approaching the hoped-for goals of insight and understanding in the child regarding his problems.

How and whether these goals are achievable are important considerations, given that many of this population of 'looked-after children' have severe developmental delays and deficits due to the traumas they have experienced (Hurry 1998). The term 'developmental therapy' evolved at the Anna Freud Centre as a specific way of working with such children. In her developmental role, as 'developmental object', the therapist is more evidently 'herself' and is (or needs to be) more spontaneous than in her interpretive role. These children often require the therapist to be creative, both in her timing and the techniques she employs. She may have to take a role in their play, to carry those externalised aspects of the child's self that cannot yet be integrated, or to enact the role of feared or longed-for inner objects.

Writers such as Lanyado (2004) emphasise the non-interpretive aspects of the therapeutic relationship while others such as Stern speak of the 'something more' than interpretation that is needed (Stern *et al.* 1998). This 'something more' is seen as a 'shared implicit relationship' which develops in the intersubjective environment between therapist and child. These authors draw on insights from parent–infant interactions and the 'moments-of-meeting' in which each partner recognises that there has been a 'mutual fittedness'. Anna Freud was aware that developmental deficit called for help via relationships and that this help took precedence over revival of the past within the transference. She nevertheless drew attention to the fact that most children do not present a pure clinical picture and therefore require a range of therapeutic procedures. This view also allows for 'selection' by the child. By selection is meant that the child may also choose what to bring or to engage within the therapeutic arena.

The 'looked-after' child in the therapeutic setting may not therefore comply with the wishes of the external professionals and carers in 'telling' the therapist about his problems. This can create problems for the network when the child's behaviour either worsens or does not improve quickly enough. In situations like this, good inter-agency communication is essential.

Joan Hutton (1983) commented on the different ways that social workers and carers may conceive of therapy, i.e. as something to idealise or to be suspicious of, rivalrous rather than complementary. The author speaks coherently about the benefit of 'face-to-face' experience between the therapist and the network. It means that the therapist, contrary to historical practice, may do the necessary work herself, dealing constantly with the split transference, and selecting those areas where either child and carers appear to be responding to the dictates of the transference (i.e. they may both be acting out) or the child is arousing issues in the inner world of the carer or other members of the network.

When working with such deficit and deprivation, the therapist draws on her psychoanalytic understanding not only with the child, but in enabling the network to recognise their impact and presentation: an inability to trust, projection, over-activity, silence and other defensive behaviours will be discernible. Hoxter (1983), in an important chapter, writes of the complex nature of experiences relating to children who have suffered deprivation. She notes that a capacity to process external events into internal experiences becomes central when considering what it means to come to terms with severe loss. This capacity, she considers, depends crucially on the opportunity to identify *with carers who are themselves* able to 'feel and think'. The thinking, in Hoxter's opinion, involves the capacity to bear experiencing the child's feelings and one's own accompanying feelings, until these have undergone a process of internal modulation, enabling the adult to make a response in keeping with what the child has communicated, rather than a reaction driven by the adult's own emotions.

WORKING WITH THE CHILD IN THE NETWORK: FLEXIBILITY

Jenny, aged 11, was removed from home because of neglect and abuse. In the first term of her therapy, Jenny's way of communicating was largely through elaborate role plays in which she involved the therapist. Outside the sessions, the foster carers were being pushed to the limit by Jenny's aggressive and sexualised behaviour. They thought that the therapist was being fooled by Jenny who presented as polite in her sessions. In her work, the therapist had to be prepared to represent to the carers the interests of the child and her profound need for a protected space to struggle with her issues at her own pace and in her own way. However, she had to do this without isolating the carers or the network of professionals involved with the child. At a practical level it involved regular meetings with the foster carers. This offered the opportunity for the therapist to highlight aspects of the child's behaviour that were rooted in past relationships and which would need time to shift. Here the therapist is introducing the network to processes in the child which, though largely unconscious, continued to have an insidious influence on behaviour and the child's view of her object world.

Jenny's carers were pleased when she started calling them mum and dad quite early on in the placement. They saw this as evidence that Jenny was settling and beginning to form attachments. However, Jenny's history demonstrated a series of rapid yet shallow attachments that were easily dismissed when the placements ended. In her work with the carers, the therapist was careful to highlight the positive aspects in her attachment – that Jenny had not given up hope of a good relationship with caring parents. Here she was identifying an island of health in the behaviour. It was nevertheless important that the carers understood and helped Jenny to promote her own identity. First they needed to acknowledge the long list of separations and abrupt endings in Jenny's life. Secondly, were these unresolved issues to remain ignored, they would continue to interfere with Jenny's capacity to form meaningful and more profound attachments. The therapist's work with Jenny continued alongside the work with the carers. In addition, the therapist encouraged the initiation of life-story work to enable Jenny to begin the work of ordering and mourning her experiences.

Barrows (1996) writes that when the deprived children we treat can be enabled to develop a coherent sense of their own life stories, this should prove a way in to break the cycle of deprivation. Coherence, in Barrows' opinion, depends upon the interchange between internal and external reality, which in turn allows the child to assimilate new experiences and ultimately a sense of hope.

Jenny's early care had been highly tantalising and varied according to her mother's state of mind about the people in her life. These mainly consisted of a series of brief relationships with men who were violent and aggressive. Jenny therefore had no consistency of care at a time in her life when the building blocks of a secure attachment should have been in place. Instead her relationships with others reflected the disorganised patterns written about by Ainsworth and her colleagues (Ainsworth *et al.* 1971). Jenny had been left to live in this unpredictable environment for the first nine years or so of her life, with brief respites in the care system. This meant that by the time she was placed on a full care order at the age of 10, many of these ways of relating had become structured into her personality.

In her foster placement her behaviour veered from being perfect to exploding in spectacular temper outbursts, which were often accompanied by violence to others. She would then expect things to carry on as if the outburst had not happened. She showed little remorse, and seemed not to have any idea of the impact of her behaviour on the other. In working with Jenny, her therapist had first to join in with the role play and yet stay sufficiently outside these activities to retain her observing and reflective stance. This was not easy as Jenny could become totally immersed in the games and at times could be very dissociated from the real situation in the room. Nevertheless all these roles, though elaborated, meant something to the child. For example, the therapist had to endure being shut out of the room, threatened by security guards and imprisoned. Often she would have been set up by Jenny who, as the social worker in her play, seduced the therapist (mother) into thinking she would have her child returned. Jenny's play was symbolic in that it touched on many aspects of her history and longings. Nevertheless the therapist had to be mindful of the situation outside the therapy room and the potential it had to break the placement.

Meetings between the carers and the therapist helped to lessen their guilt that they were letting Jenny down: they thought, for example, that they were not 'good enough' parents and were relieved to find an arena to think of this in the context of Jenny's projections onto her objects. Such meetings also offered encouragement and support for their attempts to set manageable boundaries and expectations about behaviour at home. A further consultation with the school enabled the teachers to stick with Jenny and to find ways of keeping her in school (thus not re-enacting her early experience of being sent away) while protecting others from her violence. Here the reliability of the others involved as well as the sensitivity of the therapist to the external situation was crucial in protecting the child's treatment. In addition, understanding how the network can be driven to re-enact the internal world of the traumatised or acting-out child (Davies 1996) was vital in this work.

When these systems of communication work well, the therapist can be a key person in decisions about the child's current and future needs. For instance, she will be appropriately placed to inform the network about the child's state of mind and relationship to objects both internal and external. In situations where this involves a change of placement, the therapist would be in a unique position to advise about the child's level of preparedness and the level of support needed after a move.

This does not mean that Jenny's treatment was plain sailing, even with this flexible and supportive framework. Many adjustments had to be made to technique as Jenny continued to act out her wishes and distress. This put her safety in jeopardy: when following a very involved role play, Jenny ran down the street screaming and laughing hysterically about being put in prison. The carers, who had been waiting for her, were not amused as Jenny ran into the busy road, seemingly unaware of the danger to herself. The adjustment to technique was that the therapist then left plenty of time at the end of the session to enable Jenny to re-establish herself and regain touch with the reality of the situation. With Jenny's permission, the therapist also effected a handover to the parents, passing her into their physical care and giving verbally a brief sense of what Jenny might be struggling with as she left the session.

Jenny was able to continue and make progress in her therapy because of this flexibility in the therapeutic approach. At times she opted to involve her carers actively in the therapy by insisting that they come in for part or all of the session. They were bemused by this but gradually began to see that, as Jenny gained trust in the therapeutic situation, she began to show through her actions and behaviours in the room something of her real conflicts. It is not easy for a therapist to work in this way. Nevertheless the capacity to make some of her thinking transparent, and to be observed as she struggles and sometimes makes a fool of herself in the process, can ultimately work to the benefit of all concerned.

A SECOND CHANCE FOR EMMA: KEEPING DEVELOPMENTAL ISSUES IN MIND

Emma was referred for psychotherapy at age 6 'to be made "adoptable"'. She had been previously adopted at age 4 but after 6 months was returned to the care system with the label of being unlovable. Emma faced the difficulties in her development, described by Jill Hodges (1982) in relation to adopted children, of coming to terms with being born to and relinquished by her birth parents. Emma had to face this dilemma not just once but twice, when her adopted parents also gave her up. After 18 months in once-weekly therapy, Emma was adopted again, this time successfully.

Emma's play in the first six months of therapy reflected a high level of preoccupation with dirt and a frantic effort to scrub things clean. The sink was the main area of play for much of that time. Emma would demand more and more washing up liquid or cleaning material. However much she scrubbed the sink and the dishes, they were never clean in her eyes. Repeated scrubbing began to take its toll on Emma's skin. Externally, I was able to supply a large plastic apron to protect her clothes, but had to bide my time before Emma was able to listen to my interpretations about feeling hopeless and unworthy. Emma then attempted to scrub me and I became concerned about damage to *my* skin. I began to see this as an attempt to externalise onto me, her black therapist, her feelings of unworthiness. In one painful session, I was invited to close my eyes. When I opened them Emma had painted the white doll black. The doll was pushed roughly in my arms and tears were visible in Emma's eyes as I tenderly wrapped the naked doll in a paper towel blanket.

In this play there were obvious questions about who Emma could be in relation to me. Did she have to become like me to be accepted by me? It was therefore important that I did not reject the baby, who I believe represented Emma's fantasies about her early relationship, first with her birth mother and later her first adoptive family.

During the second six months of treatment, more of the real Emma came into the room. Her behaviour became challenging: for example she would jump on the chairs and invite me to stop her. Emma was demonstrating her need to be held, but her behaviour also invited reprimand. When I verbalised this, her mood changed and she became the small child who wanted a mummy to tuck her up in her cot. This baby also fooled the mother into thinking she had gone to sleep but when the mother had fallen asleep the baby would sneak out of the door. Could I be an attentive mother? Could she merit such a mother? I struggled to interpret this play and my counter-transference feelings were that I should be vigilant.

I spent a lot of time commenting on the part of Emma that longed for a mummy who kept her eyes on the baby so that she did not come to harm. It was equally important but more difficult to link this to the baby Emma who grew up expecting to be punished and who pushed until it happened. This led to Emma recalling angry confrontations with her adoptive mother and the painful memory of father not intervening to rescue her from mother's anger. Emma then began to speculate that the same thing must have happened when she was with her first parents. As the therapy entered its tenth month, Emma came to the conclusion that she had been given the wrong parents. Although this in some respects could be interpreted as a defence against the pain of rejection, it was also the beginning of a shift in Emma's thinking that she was not totally responsible for her abandonment by two sets of parents and it was vitally important not simply to focus on the defence at this point.

It was now possible for Emma to begin to fantasise about having the *right* kind of parents. The right kind of parents in Emma's mind consisted of a father who would spoil her and a mother who did lots of cooking. In drawing her ideal family, Emma was clear that they would have a skin colour similar to hers rather than the brown skin of her therapist. Emma nevertheless needed the therapist's permission and good wishes to have such a family. She had reached this point because she had been able to make an attachment to her therapist and to form some identifications. In the context of this relationship, she had begun the task of knowing who she was and what she wanted.

From the start of Emma's therapy, her therapist had to work with an extended network of carers and professionals as well as attend to Emma's struggles to make sense of her experience. For the network, the therapist had to represent Emma's wish to take her 'second chance'. This meant engaging actively with the network to shift their position of extreme caution. Emma's social worker had been anxious about moving too soon towards a second adoption. Here the ghost of the earlier failed attempt was rearing its head. In saying that Emma was ready, the therapist drew heavily on Emma's material, which now showed that she was prepared and able to take this risk. The following are excerpts from a therapy report written at the time:

> Emma is as prepared for a move to adoption as she is likely to be but needs the permission of the adults to get on with her life and the forming of new attachments. I expect Emma's move from her present carers to be painful for both her and them. However it is essential that she does not have to feel the responsibility for the carers' pain as well as

her own, or feel she has to hold back from taking the plunge into a new life. It is nevertheless vitally important that Emma keeps in touch with these important attachment figures in her current life.

The right kind of parents

The search for an adoptive family for Emma began in earnest after this. After the family was found, the therapist continued to occupy a vital role *vis-à-vis* the foster carers and the adopted parents during the transition from one home to another. As with Lanyado's patient, ultimately the transition was made easier by the therapist's continuing involvement at this time of change (Lanyado 2004: ch. 6). Further, Emma was greatly supported by her social worker who had been with her throughout her time in care. In this respect Emma was lucky in that there was a constant person who knew all about her and her history, offered continuity and was committed to seeing her settled and happy.

When Emma heard that an adoptive family had been found, she was immediately concerned that her therapy would end. The therapist confirmed that their work together would be continuing while Emma settled into her new life. Relieved, Emma announced that she would paint a picture. She started by mixing colour, grey, black and white. She considered the result for a moment and then added a splash of red. Emma stirred this and said, 'Now we are the same, the colour of strawberry milk shake'. The therapist picked up on Emma's wish that she could be her mummy instead. Emma agreed. She brightened, however, when the therapist said that they could talk about Emma's wishes about her newly identified mummy.

Emma hoped she would have brown hair and hazel eyes like her. She should not be too tall, otherwise Emma would not be able to reach to give her a hug. The therapist challenged the idea that the onus was on Emma to do the reaching. She said that it might be even better to have a mummy who reached down to hug Emma. Emma liked this idea. She then began a new drawing of a house. It had a garden and a long path, which was dotted with black spots. The spots represented the therapist walking up the path to see her. The caption was: 'This is the house I would live in.' It was signed to her therapist with love from Emma. She then returned to play seen earlier in the therapy when the baby would climb out of the cot when the mummy was not looking. Here Emma could agree with the therapist's comment that she was very anxious about what lay ahead for her.

Over the next few sessions, Emma began to bring dreams about her birth mother. In her dream her mother had dark hair and wore lots of rings. She did not recognise Emma when they met. Emma seemed very sad. This dream seemed to indicate that a process of mourning had begun for the lost mother of Emma's early childhood. Mixed into this was also an anxiety that her therapist might forget her. Emma needed to remember consciously and to mourn this painful period in her life. I believed this enabled her to take the risk of making an attachment to her therapist and ultimately to her new parents.

In the session after her first meeting with her new parents, her main concern was how to be with her foster carer and yet get to know her new mum at the same time. The conflict was about showing love to two sets of people. Are you going to make one set angry? This highlighted continuing feelings in Emma that the onus was still on her to make situations and relationships work. This concern was passed on to the social worker who had further work to do with the foster carer to ease Emma's transition to her new family. Emma clearly had enough of her own conflicts to struggle with as the following extract shows. It follows her first overnight stay with her new carers:

On the journey in the car Emma was anxious to stay completely awake. She wanted to fix her own seatbelt. She described waking very early the first morning and lying in bed cuddling her teddy. 'I was waiting for someone to tell me what to do.' At breakfast she said she felt so hungry, but it didn't matter what she ate, she could not get full.

The attempts to be self-sufficient showed both her difficulty with trust and her defences against possible disappointment. They also replayed Emma's desperate sense, under stress, that *she* had to make things work. Later she was afraid that she would get things wrong. Emma did not think she could knock on the parents' door to say she was awake. Her overeating was a further sign of anxiety (it had been evident earlier when the first adoptive placement broke down).

The first six months in an adoptive home is very difficult. Emma pushed her mother to the absolute limit. She began to have dreams that she was handed back to Social Services. Emma refused to let her new mother do personal things like comb her hair. She would come from school to her sessions with holes in her new tights and clothes. She kept falling off her bike and was covered in bruises. In the sessions Emma deliberately played up to me and was often cruel and denigrating to her new mother, yet she insisted that her mother came in for part of the session. Gradually the situation began to shift. I watched Emma's painful attempts to get close to her mother by playing with her hair, by touching, sniffing and licking her. This was difficult for her mother but she impressed me with her capacity to tolerate it. In this respect Emma was like a small baby discovering the smells and sounds and tastes of Mother for the first time. In another way, she was taking a chance in showing her own imperfect, damaged, unworthy bits.

Emma began to find her place with her new family, which meant that some rejection of me was inevitable. Her play at that time was mainly about her new family – a white mummy and daddy, sitting together, watching the children play. The parents in the play were anxious to ensure that the children were well strapped in on the swings. Emma was beginning to take a chance on owning her new family and relinquishing the stance whereby she had to be responsible for her care and safety.

Several factors helped to make this adoption successful. The parents told Emma that they would keep her no matter what. Gradually, Emma gave her parents permission to tell me some of the things she forgot to bring to her sessions, for example when she had been naughty at home. I had to tread a difficult line at times as Emma used me in a manipulative way to undermine her mother's attempts to set limits. I was nevertheless impressed by the tenacity of these new parents. They brought Emma reliably to sessions in all weathers, travelling many miles in the process. They joined an organisation for adopting families. They tried desperately hard to maintain links with the foster carers who, sadly, had been unable not to attempt to undermine the adoption efforts and who were now stepping back from the arranged contact.

Essentially one of the major differences in favour of this adoption working was that Emma continued to have her space in therapy to struggle and puzzle, regress and move forward. Externally she has been lucky with her parents who have used all the supports available to them to love this child who was once designated 'unlovable'.

THE IMPACT OF ADOLESCENCE ON CHILD, CARER AND THERAPIST

Jonathan at 13 was referred for a psychotherapy assessment. He was on a full care order and had been living with his carers for 18 months. At home he had become surly, withdrawn and uncommunicative. When challenged he became angry and complained that his carers did not understand him.

Jonathan came into care when teachers informed Social Services about his high rate of absence from school. On investigation it came to light that his single mother had been mentally unwell for some time. Her illness had built up gradually through Jonathan's early life and over time he had assumed the role of carer, both for himself and for his mother.

Jonathan's first year as a 'looked-after child' was fine in that he seemed to thrive on having a father and mother who looked after him and allowed him to be a child. This suggested that some of his early dependent, developmental needs had been met before mother became ill. The concerns about his behaviour seemed to coincide with the onset of adolescence. Jonathan still craved the attention of his carers, particularly his foster father, but his behaviour sent out contradictory messages (I need you, but do not get too close). The carers struggled unsuccessfully to negotiate a comfortable level of contact with Jonathan, resulting in severe strain on the placement.

Hoxter (1964) states that the specific feature which differentiates the adolescent from people of other ages is, of course, the experience of puberty. Much of the adolescent's behaviour in the community may be seen as an external expression of the unconscious anxieties and conflicts aroused by pubertal sexual development. Furthermore some of the community's reaction to the adolescent expresses the anxiety of the adults when faced with this. Other key tasks faced by the adolescent include becoming more responsible for the self, modifying the reliance on parental ego-support, turning more to relationships and identifications with the peer group. These are generally considered amongst the normative tasks of adolescence. However, for children like Jonathan, with unsatisfactory early relationships, negotiating these tasks presents additional challenges to both the child and the carers. The capacity to help and guide these troubled adolescents presupposes some working through of the carers' own adolescent conflicts. In conducting Jonathan's assessment, which also included interviews with the carers, the therapist found this not to be the case.

His carers had little difficulty with the little boy Jonathan who wanted to cling and was content for decisions such as what he ate and wore to be made for him. The young man who had become concerned about his image and who worried about his masculinity presented a different kind of challenge. It meant that the carers had to find new ways of discussing and sharing information with him, accessing advice and providing sympathetic support without alienating or patronising the young person whom he had become.

Tonnesmann views the environmental provision as one of the crucial factors in helping the adolescent to have his 'second chance' to master and integrate conflicting aspects of his development. If this is not 'good enough', the author cautions that this second chance is likely to fail (Tonnesmann 1980). Failure in this context could be adolescent arrest, or foreclosure – a rigid defence structure – with premature pseudo-adaptation to adulthood.

In assessing Jonathan, it was clear that he had the capacity to use psychotherapy and was motivated to accept help. This suggested that there were sufficient intra-psychic organisation and ego resources to engage with the therapeutic process. Jonathan's fear in coming to therapy was that the therapist would be stern and silent and would consider him to be mad. The transference could already be seen to be in operation – a common fear for adolescents experiencing the dramatic changes and challenges of puberty but, for Jonathan, perhaps also involving feared identification with his mother and projection on to the therapist. The capacity to form a trans-ference relationship was important as it allowed for the possibility of Jonathan revisiting and re-working his infantile ties to his mother, one of the necessary tasks of adolescence.

The issue of time to work through these issues, in addition, had to be weighed against the current distress in the placement. In recommending therapy for Jonathan, the therapist was also concerned that some work would be needed with the carers, prior to or alongside the work with Jonathan. In a clinic setting this would have been done by another therapist experienced in helping parents/carers to think about the impact of the child's development on them. There was no one immediately available and it fell to the child's therapist to fill the breach. Aware of the risks in such work – perhaps more normal with a younger child – the therapist also recognised that in working with the system in this way, she was ideally placed to assess the carers' capacity to shift their position, to appreciate the complexities of adolescent development and to adapt their care accordingly.

At the start, the therapist was interested in learning something of the carers' own individual attachment histories. In doing this, she was engaging them in thinking and reflecting on their pasts and what might have been left unresolved – and therefore be acted out – in their relationship with Jonathan.

Jonathan's carers had come to fostering with good ideas about offering troubled youngsters a better experience of parenting. However, they had been totally unprepared for the resurgence of their own adolescent conflicts. Because these had not been resolved, the carers had no strategies for helping Jonathan to manage his. There were six meetings, at the end of which the carers felt sufficiently encouraged to go on and seek their own individual therapy. Both had suffered traumatic early experiences and had thought they had put these firmly behind them until Jonathan came along and began to 'press their buttons'.

The role of the foster carer

The foster carers' task, once considered so natural as to require little in the way of training or special expertise, has had to be re-evaluated because of the complex needs of the children in their charge today. The book *Companion to Foster Care* gives extensive information on what is now required to care for this group of children:

> Foster carers require training in child development generally and attachment theory in particular. They should have an understanding of how the various unfortunate experiences that most of the children they care for will have undergone have affected their development and they should have some knowledge of how best to help them recover. They need to have techniques available to help them to assist the young person in building trust and self-esteem. In addition to training, foster carers need to be professionally supported in order to meet the needs of their charges.
>
> (Wheal 1999: 3)

Child psychotherapists working with looked-after children can and do offer professional support to carers. This extends beyond their physical management of the child to thinking and understanding the processes of re-enactment that occur in systems around distressed and disturbed children. The psychotherapist thus holds a key position in helping the network to think about its impact on the child and vice versa. However, there are many pitfalls in this way of working. Splits and polarisations can occur, not just between child and carers but between the carers and the different organisations they work for. The therapist therefore treads a careful line. She has to maintain her therapeutic alliance with the child, promote the good things in the placement and at the same time highlight the areas that need to change and the timescale in which this should be done in the interest of the child's development.

CONCLUSION

In these three examples of therapeutic work with looked-after children one can see the adaptations of technique that are often necessary to reach such troubled and often traumatised children. This kind of adaptation is also discussed by Lanyado in Chapter 8 of this volume in relation to a late adopted patient. In all the cases mentioned the therapist also had to work actively with the network of professionals and carers without losing her central focus of her child patient.

With Jenny, her concreteness and alarming acting-out meant that the therapist had to be both sparse and careful with any interpretation she attempted. Containment and an openness to Jenny's pain and confusion about her early life was necessary for most of the first six months of therapy. The work inside the therapy had also to be partly transported into the outside environment as the therapist needed to verbalise Jenny's differing and confusing states of mind to her concerned carers. In this way the therapist often acted as a bridge between child and carers and in the process acted as a container for both.

In Emma's case, it was the child's creative way in engaging the therapist in work with her new adopted mother and Emma together that enabled a parenting partnership to develop – and the therapist's capacity to respond with flexibility to the child's creativity. Horne (2000), commenting on this approach, sees this as an important addition to a child psychotherapist's way of working in that it does not impose artificial boundaries of what is therapy and what is parent work, but allows the therapist to retain the capacity to be responsive.

In Jonathan's situation, the therapist had to acknowledge that therapy by itself would not move his development forward. The technique of working actively with both the adolescent and his carers was risky. The challenge for the therapist lay in her ability to maintain the adolescent's confidentiality, yet work with his ambivalence towards his carers and towards her in the transference. At the same time she had to be alert to the failures in the system and their ability to inhibit rather than promote the adolescent's development.

Many of the children in the care system do not have the privilege of being able to grapple with their difficulties in a supportive environment. Many are subject to frequent changes, both of placement and social workers. Often care plans for them are shelved or interrupted as each new worker tries to come to grips with their histories. Many of these children are left to drift. I agree with Hunter that therapeutic work with the child cannot take the place of a good care plan for the child. Rather it has to be an integral part of a package of care for the child (Hunter 2001). This package pays some attention to the external, but even in addressing the external environment it is predominantly geared towards the internal wishes and conflicts of the child and informed by a psychoanalytic understanding of these.

References

Ainsworth, M. D. S., Bell, S. M. V. and Stayton, D. J. (1971) 'Individual differences in strange situation behaviour of one-year-olds'. In H. R. Schaffer (ed.), *The Origins of Human Social Relationships*. London: Academic Press

Barrows, P. (1996) 'Individual psychotherapy for children in foster care: possibilities and limitations' *Clinical Child Psychology and Psychiatry* 1(3): 385–97

Davies, R. (1996) The inter-disciplinary network and the internal world of the offender. In C. Cordess and M. Cox (eds.), *Forensic Psychotherapy: Crime, Psychodynamics and the Offender Patient*, vol II, *Mainly Practice*. London: Jessica Kingsley

Freud, A. cited in A. Hurry (ed.) (1998) *Psychoanalysis and Developmental Therapy*. London: Karnac

Hodges, J. (1982) 'Adopted children in psychoanalytic treatment'. Contribution to the Conference of the Association for Child Psychology and Psychiatry 'Children in Turmoil', Dublin

Horne, A. (2000) 'Keeping the child in mind'. In J. Tsiantis *et al.* (eds.), *Work with Parents: Psychoanalytic Psychotherapy with Children and Adolescents*, EFPP Monograph. London: Karnac

Hoxter, S. (1964) 'The experience of puberty' *Journal of Child Psychotherapy* 1(2): 13–25. Reprinted in P. Barrows (ed.) (2004) *Key Papers from the Journal of Child Psychotherapy*. Hove, UK: Brunner-Routledge

Hoxter, S. (1983) 'Some feelings aroused in working with severely deprived children'. In M. Boston and R. Szur (eds.), *Psychotherapy with Severely Deprived Children*. London: Routledge & Kegan Paul

Hunter, M. (2001) *Psychotherapy with Young People in Care: Lost and Found*. Hove, UK: Brunner-Routledge

Hurry, A. (ed.) (1998) *Psychoanalysis and Developmental Therapy*. London: Karnac

Hutton, J. (1983) 'Thinking together about children in care'. In M. Boston and R. Szur (eds.), *Psychotherapy with Severely Deprived Children*. London: Routledge & Kegan Paul

Lanyado, M. (2004) *The Presence of the Therapist*. Hove, UK: Brunner-Routledge

Sandler, J., Kennedy, H. and Tyson, P. (1980) *The Technique of Child Psycho-analysis: Discussions with Anna Freud.* London: Hogarth Press

Stern, D. N., Sander, L. W., Nahum, J. P., Harrison, A. M., Lyons-Ruth, K., Morgan, A. C., Bruschweiler, N. and Tronick, E. Z. (1998) 'Non-interpretive mechanisms in psychoanalytic therapy: the "something more" than interpretation' *International Journal of Psycho-Analysis* 79: 903–21

Tonnesmann, M. (1980) 'Adolescent re-enactment, trauma and reconstruction' *Journal of Child Psychotherapy* 6: 23–44

Wheal, A. (ed.) (1999) *The RHP Companion to Foster Care.* London: Russell House Publishing

8   The playful presence of the therapist

'Antidoting' defences in the therapy of a late adopted adolescent patient

Monica Lanyado

Consider the following clinical situation. A severely deprived 8-year-old girl, whose plight had been repeatedly unseen and unheard by the authorities, was eventually fostered, but with poor case management leaving her vulnerable to further abuse. Several foster homes later she was placed with a foster family who were able to make a commitment to her and who fought for her to have therapy. In one of her sessions she spent a great deal of time and effort repeatedly trying to build a tent using a blanket and parts of the furniture in the room, in ways that would obviously fail. She couldn't accomplish this task on her own for straightforward mechanical reasons and yet she kept trying to achieve the impossible. She kept on and on trying to build a space that she could physically get inside, in a heartbreakingly futile way, and several times asked the therapist to help, but in a controlling and rather bullying manner which the therapist felt he could not agree to. Finally in desperation the child shouted at the therapist who had quietly observed these efforts, 'Why won't you help me?'

The therapist as well as the patient found the session distressing but the therapist felt that the girl's expression of helplessness and despair was important and needed to be contained and heard, but not actively responded to, and so decided not to help the child to make the tent. Nevertheless the therapist also felt uncertain about where the therapy was going and what he was trying to achieve and was concerned that he might at times be getting caught in a re-enactment of the past (by not helping when help was so clearly needed) that was not therapeutic for the child.

From an Independent perspective, it can be argued that this was a situation where, despite the patient's controlling behaviour, the therapist could have responded to her cry for help, and thoughtfully joined the girl in her play. In this way it might have been possible to acknowledge the child's desperate need to maintain the controlling defence, whilst also recognising the intensity of the pain that necessitated such a severe and unrelenting defensive structure. However, at the time, the therapist was more highly aware of the child's sadistic efforts to control everyone around her and the problems that this defence was creating in all her relationships. His view was that there was a pressing need to experience and contain the underlying anxieties in the transference relationship and resist what could be seen as a collusion with the defensive structure the patient had erected.

This is a common dilemma and indeed at the root of a significant technical and theoretical divergence about how to analyse anxieties and the defences around them. Traditionally, Kleinian therapists would directly try to analyse the underlying anxiety, whereas Anna Freudians would be analysing the need for such controlling defences. The therapy of severely deprived patients, whom I find it helpful to think of as suffering from 'multiple traumatic loss', seems constantly to present these kinds of technical choices and challenges (Lanyado 2002, 2003, 2004).

Another argument for the therapist agreeing to help the child could have been the opportunity to help the child in her highly significant wish to build rather than to destroy, which was her more usual way of being. Having witnessed the child's struggle, the therapist might even have offered help before being asked, and waited to see whether the child could accept that this kind of building, practically as well as symbolically, was the kind which could not be done alone. It needed two people. The recognition of the need for adult help is another painful experience for children like this, who will behave omnipotently and controllingly in situations in which they actually feel terrifyingly helpless. Indeed, this is a classic defence used by children who are described in attachment terms as being 'detached' or 'disorganised' (see Solomon and George 1999). Thinking in terms of the girl's attachment disorder, it was a significant achievement that she dared to ask for help. It could therefore also be argued that it was possibly a technical mistake *not* to respond to this with a therapeutic gesture that recognised her need for someone who would try to protect her, and help her to build rather than destroy.

Underlying these differences of perspective about what are the child's primary therapeutic needs is the important further question of 'therapeutic priorities' and how to respond to them. In this instance, it can be argued that by appearing not to see, hear or respond to the child's desperate cries for help, the therapist could indeed have been perceived by the child as repeating what had happened in the past when the adults were around her, and the authorities had not responded to her cries for help. The child believed that the authorities had turned a blind eye to her suffering by not taking her out of care situations which they had placed her in, in which she was being neglected and abused by adults. For children such as these, for a long time in therapy, the therapist's actions can speak louder than words and are needed as an evident accompaniment to the constant therapeutic efforts to contain, internally and externally, the child's pain, trauma and anger.

Additionally, there are times when a reluctance to follow the flow of counter-transference intuition, as a means of exploring what is happening in the transference relationship, can result in the therapist being unnecessarily withholding or even unwittingly sadistic or cruel towards the patient – often in the name of a perceived technical 'correctness'. By contrast, responding more intuitively to difficult clinical and technical situations, can be likened to taking a 'participant-observer' stance within the transference relationship, from which further information is directly experienced and then thought about through the medium of, at times, highly unusual experiences in the consulting room.

This example helps me to approach one of the central technical questions of this chapter: to play or not to play? Much of my thinking is based on Winnicott's seminal work, *Playing and Reality*, which is an extremely valuable source of thought about the importance of 'playing' in the psychotherapeutic process (Winnicott 1971). In this book he develops his ideas about how playing is at the root of all everyday creative and cultural activity and places this process at the heart of the psychotherapeutic process. His key statement about playing, which is explained and explored in great detail throughout the book, comes in a chapter titled 'Playing: A theoretical statement' and is a typically dense Winnicottian statement which has many layers of significance. He says

> Psychotherapy takes place in the overlap of two areas of playing, that of the patient and that of the therapist. Psychotherapy has to do with two people playing together. The corollary of this is that where playing is not possible, then the work done by the therapist is directed towards bringing the patient from a state of not being able to play to a state of being able to play.
>
> (Winnicott 1971: 44)

It is important to note that, in this statement about psychotherapy, Winnicott is referring to therapy with adults for whom playing with ideas is very central to the therapeutic process, as well as children. He has a very particular view of playing as taking place in an intermediate area of experience, which he also calls a transitional space, between the internal and external world. Winnicott argues for the value of the *paradox* of play being simultaneously both an internal activity in which fantasy is not constrained by reality, and an external activity as it is being enacted through the use of toys, activity and creativity in the broadest sense, in the outside world. The idea of tolerating this paradox is central to his thinking about the creativity of play.

Winnicott sees the ability to play as being facilitated at the start of life, by the presence of an adult who can hold the child's anxieties sufficiently for the child to be able to play in a *creative and free way*. I stress this quality of creativity and freedom in healthy play, because playing can often be very lacking in these qualities. Here I am thinking of the repetitive and ritualistic quality of the play of children who use autistic defences, or the self-destructive acting-out type of play of severely deprived children, some of which is described later in this chapter. Again it is important for the therapist always to remain discerning about the function of playing at any point in the therapy, and to be alert to the need to distinguish defensive play from creative play – when the actual content may be identical at times.

Of course, people are playful throughout life as seen in the many games and sports played by adults, the ordinary spontaneous play between adults and children, as well as in adults' ability to play with ideas and be creative in the arts and sciences.

THE VALUE OF HAVING A SENSE OF HUMOUR

As well as having this Winnicottian view in mind, there are other considerations that arise when thinking about playing. Playing, as thought about in a more everyday sense, is often accompanied by a sense of fun. The spontaneous use of humour in therapy, and whether or not it is 'right' to laugh at something that is clearly funny during a session, can cause some consternation, particularly to trainees or more newly qualified therapists. There can be a fear that laughter during a session may play into more manic defences in the patient and this may be true sometimes. However, Carlberg's research into turning points in child psychotherapy has suggested that spontaneous laughter in a session can 'open the door' to important therapeutic change (Carlberg 1997). Counter-transference sensitivity to the patient can usually help the therapist to distinguish between the discomfort that is felt when a manic defence against anxiety is operating, and a genuinely funny moment.

Nevertheless, some may lift their hands in horror at the possibility of anything as light-hearted as playfulness or humour in the context of the very serious problems that patients bring to their therapy. Others argue that being able to keep in touch with the relief and insight that humour and playfulness offer, by there being at times a lightness of touch in the therapist's way of responding to what the patient brings, is what may enable the therapeutic couple to keep on working together (Bollas 1995; Coltart 1992; Horne 2001, and see also Chapters 9 and 13 in this volume). This does not mean that the therapist is not taking the patiently seriously or spends his or her time cracking jokes with the patient.

Additionally, I have often observed that a sense of humour, even at times a rather 'black' sense of humour, can help people working with very disturbed, perverse or violent patients to maintain a humane perspective towards those in their care. Organisationally, this might be thought of as an adaptive social defence against the anxiety and pain that the organisational structure is trying to contain (Menzies Lyth 1988). Certainly a sense of staff in such organisations and units being 'good-humoured' is likely to help staff to continue to work with the most disturbing of patients, as well as be experienced in a positive way by the patients themselves.

Bollas thoughtfully discusses these issues in detail in *Cracking Up* (Bollas 1995). In his final chapter he draws attention to the ways in which 'a sense of humour grasps the absurdities in life'. He links this to the absurdities of unconscious life, particularly as seen in dreams – but of course also as played out by children when playing alone or with others. This is evident in the clinical example later in this chapter. Freud, of course, drew attention to the importance of jokes and humour and their links to the unconscious (Freud 1905). Bollas reminds us of the ways in which in ordinary everyday parent–baby relationships we can see the mother (and of course the father too) exaggeratedly 'clowning' with their baby to stimulate smiles and laughter. Whilst recognising that this comic approach can become 'too close for comfort' and rather manic in some relationships, in others he sees it as 'eliciting our true self's spontaneity' (Bollas 1995: 237). He goes on to say:

> Perhaps a sense of humour is essential to human survival. Amusement in the self and in the other may be a vital constituent part of a comprehensive perspective on life. The mother who develops her baby's sense of humour is assisting him to detach from dire mere existence, from simply being in the rather shitty world of infancy, for example. Such a child can, as an adult, ultimately find humour in the most awful of circumstances, benefiting from the origins of the comic sense.
>
> (Bollas 1995: 243–4)

In offering these persuasive arguments for the place of humour and playfulness within the therapeutic relationship, Bollas is in good company. Coltart, in her memorable essay *Slouching towards Bethlehem . . . And Further Psychoanalytic Explanations*, speaks of her impression that laughter 'can be felt to be dangerous in psychoanalysis' (Coltart 1992: 10) She quotes Bion in one of his São Paulo lectures as saying:

> I wonder if it is in the rules of psychoanalysis to be able to laugh at ourselves? Is it according to the rules of psychoanalysis that we should be amused and find things funny? Is it permissible to enjoy a psycho-analytic meeting? I suggest that, having broken through in this revolu-tionary matter of being amused in the sacred process of psychoanalysis, we might as well continue to see where that more joyous state of mind might take us.
>
> (Bion 1980: 94–5)

Coltart draws the conclusion 'to put it very simply, that laughter and enjoyment can be therapeutic factors in psychoanalysis. Certainly, I believe that one not only can but should enjoy psychoanalytic sessions' (Coltart 1992: 11). She goes on to describe the therapy of a man who could make people laugh and who although quite ill was really amusing in his sessions. She describes how she spent a lot of energy trying not to laugh and analysed the aggression in his jokes and so on. Many years on, she says that she would still analyse the material in this way, but thinks that she would now laugh first if she felt like it. She says that

> I am now of the opinion that I deprived both him and me unnecessarily by being so prim. I think I might have got nearer to some true shape or pattern in him *faster*, by responding with a natural reaction and *then* talking about it. If we are too protective of our self-representation and of what we consider grimly to be the sacred rules of True Psycho-analysis, then we may suffocate something in the patient, in ourselves, and in the process.
>
> (Coltart 1992: 12)

In thinking about the potential value of playfulness and humour, particularly in the therapist's way-of-being with the patient, what I think of as his or her 'presence', there are implications for the ways in which the therapist feels free to use his or her 'Self' during the sessions. The authentic interplay between therapist and patient in the present relationship, as well as the transference and counter-transference relationship, needs to be understood in every treatment. It is this unique constellation of each therapeutic couple, with its extraordinary complexity and essential humanity, that requires that when we talk about psychoanalytic technique, we are inevitably thinking about the therapist's use of a general technical framework as applied in a particular instance (Lanyado 2004; Tronick 2003). We are not talking about a manual.

FINDING AND EXPERIENCING THE UNIQUENESS OF EACH THERAPEUTIC ENCOUNTER

A patient whom I have written about elsewhere, whose letters I literally carried with me during a period of time when she was dangerously suicidal, I believe needed an unusual response like this from me (Lanyado 2001, 2004). She was in such a concrete state of mind at the time that she was unable to believe that she was in my mind between sessions, at this time of crisis. So I had to meet this concreteness, by actually carrying something of hers with me. It was not a problem for me to do this, and by this small therapeutic gesture I felt that I was, in her understanding, authentically meeting her primary and urgent need to feel emotionally held. She needed something 'special' – by which I mean something unique, specific, and not general – and she needed it for a particular purpose. I had not done this for any patient before her and so far I have not done this for any patient since. Checking the *Concise Oxford Dictionary* on the precise meaning of 'special' highlights that there are several different meanings of 'special'. I would argue that another therapist might have done something else 'special' in the above sense, for a patient in similar need which might have held the same *emotional significance* between them, but it would probably have taken a different form altogether, a point also made by Horne in Chapter 13 of this volume.

The question of a patient in some instances *needing* to feel 'special' to the therapist is a tricky one. Possibly this is because, in contrast to the type of specialness just described, there is another form of 'specialness' that *wishes and longs* for an exclusivity and a possessiveness of the therapist, which attempts to deny or get rid of the painful presence of other patients and people in the therapist's life. This kind of specialness implies a comparison with other people in which the would-be 'special' person is exceptional and more important than anyone else. There are controlling and tyrannical aspects in this kind of demand for specialness, which relate to its oedipal, three-person-type character (Bartram 2003). However, it should be remembered that these indications of growing particles of oedipal development are, for patients like these, a therapeutic achievement. But at the same time, these oedipal wishes cannot be met and therapy needs to address the pain of recognising this reality.

Where there has been neglect and poor emotional attunement to the baby from the start of life, there is likely to be a need, indeed a necessity in terms of emotional well-being, to feel special to someone. Developmentally, this need can only be met within a two-person relationship. If it is not, there is a deficit in the individual's emotional life at a basic fault level, to use Balint's terminology (Balint 1968). If this need emerges in therapy the patient may be unconsciously trying to experience feeling special to someone, possibly for the first time ever in a consistent way, within the therapeutic relationship as discussed by Hopkins in Chapter 10 of this volume. This is the form of regression that Balint would think of as therapeutic and could be described as a basic developmental need. It is an example of the therapist at these times being a developmental object for the patient, as described by Hurry and her colleagues (Hurry 1998). This kind of specialness relates to the earliest parent–infant experiences in which the parent recognises the unique individuality of their baby and all of his or her potential. To bring out this potential, some patients have a particularly intense need for their therapists to recognise this uniqueness.

Alvarez also draws attentions to this important distinction between needs and wishes and describes how the therapist uses language to express 'the grammar of wishes and the grammar of needs' in all his or her verbal communication (Alvarez 2000). I think of this as an aspect of the present relationship experience between the patient and therapist, which I have written about elsewhere (Lanyado 2004). Alvarez emphasises that it is not the words themselves but the underlying emotional understanding within the patient–therapist couple, of the difference between the patient's wishes and needs, that is crucial. Whilst it is better for the patient if the therapist expresses the awareness of the difference between needs and wishes within the language that he or she uses, Alvarez argues that the patient 'knows' in a mostly unconscious way what is in the therapist's heart, and is able to 'forgive us the grammar' if we get it wrong with the words themselves (Alvarez 2000: 18). Regarding this sense of specialness that could be thought of as a primary need, if I understand rightly what Alvarez is saying, she argues that trying to find a way to meet this rightful need can be a moral imperative, which is fundamentally life-enhancing. In effect I think she is saying, as indeed I would agree, that it may be a therapeutic mistake not to acknowledge or meet this need in some small, but emotionally significant way.

In this context of differentiating wish from need, I have been interested to note the ways in which other child and adolescent therapists describe their actions and words with some of the very damaged patients that make up the bulk of caseloads today. There is a growing literature on therapy with these children and young people (for example, Bartram 2003; Canham 2003, 2004; Edwards 2000; Hopkins 2000; Horne 2003; Kenrick 2000). Iris Gibbs in this volume (Chapter 7) discusses and describes the adaptations of technique that she has found helpful with looked-after children. Each of these accounts contains descriptions of unusual technical challenges and responses with which all who treat these children are likely to empathise. For example, Edwards' 6-year-old adopted patient developed an increasing tendency to 'throw himself headfirst onto the floor' and leapt dangerously around the furniture in the room (Edwards 2000: 361). This followed a period of time when the therapist was sellotaped to her chair and forced to witness the disturbing torture of one of the play therapy toys. Edwards says 'There was no question of my remaining in my chair holding Gary with interpretation alone: it was imperative that I follow him physically and link my interpretations to active physical contact at times of danger. In this context I thought of the earliest interactions between mother and baby' (Edwards 2000: 362). Her patient elicited a physical response, within the present relationship in which he additionally and significantly had the *opportunity* to experience this response being thought about in a therapeutic way. This is what Coltart is referring to in terms of the therapist first reacting naturally to the patient and then thinking and talking about it.

Bartram describes playing with her patient. 'She and I had to (pretend to) dress up in sparkling dresses and twirl around in front of Prince Charming' (Bartram 2003: 28). This game seems to have been important for the therapy and gives us a picture of the therapist playing with the patient in a natural and hopeful way as Zara was admired and increasingly chosen by the prince over Bartram. Bartram did not feel inhibited about engaging in this play and was able to see its therapeutic potential. Hindle describes the therapy of a very challenging patient who spent much of his session up a tree outside the therapy room, or rushing around the clinic (Hindle 2000).

Severely deprived and abused patients often put us in embarrassing, ridiculous and undignified situations, indeed as Bollas says, absurd situations, and seem to crow at us 'now what are you going to do about that?' This is a wonderfully effective way for the patient to explore the more intuitive and spontaneous side of the therapist, which they may need to know about much more than the cerebral aspect during the early stages of therapy. For children who have been severely abused by adults in positions of trust, this need to know who the therapist really 'is' is part of the child's life-preserving defences which sadly have had to be utilised in the past as a way of trying to avoid and/or survive abuse. They have had to use these antennae to try to judge, as one little adopted boy put it, 'who is for me and who is against me'. I have written about this in more detail elsewhere (Lanyado 2004).

The therapist may well try to digest what on earth has been going on in challenging sessions such as these after the session has ended, and if he or she is lucky, manage to make a bit of sense of it. Psychoanalytic understanding and if possible regular supervision are extremely helpful in sustaining the therapist through these demanding therapeutic experiences with the patient. However, often despite these therapeutic tools, the therapist is left with an increasingly incomprehensible therapeutic experience which can lead to the therapist – let alone the child – dreading the session.

These complex communications in action are rarely easily decoded. Embedded deeply within the extraordinary situations that these patients create in their therapy, there is an experience which the patient–therapist couple have to tolerate and survive before reaching any more thoughtful understanding or resolution. In the process, these patients inevitably get to know much more about the essence of the way in which the therapist's internal world works than patients who bring neurotic problems.

The clinical example which follows emphasises this idea of the opportunity that is contained within a crisis of this type in the course of therapy. It is through the creative challenges of situations such as these that windows of therapeutic opportunity can open and moments-of-meeting take place which are deeply healing (Stern *et al.* 1998; Lanyado 2001, 2004; Ward 2003).

THE PLAYFUL PRESENCE OF THE THERAPIST AND 'PLAYFUL' INTERPRETATION

Gail, the patient who made me think a great deal about the question of playfulness in the therapeutic relationship, needed us to develop a special, unconventional form of communication in therapy for a number of reasons which it took me a long while to understand. I probably played with her much more than any other patient before her. Of course, she did not know this consciously, but I think she did know unconsciously that what she received from me in therapy was something that grew inside me for her and her alone. It was specially for her therapeutic needs.

Much of what I wish to say about our work together only gradually made sense to me over time – a sort of crystallising out process from within the therapeutic process as a whole. I would not wish to give the impression that this was readily understood in this way as therapy progressed. However, as Gail made good developmental progress and became much happier and more able to discover who she was as she became a teenager, I was encouraged that what had happened between us had been helpful. I say this as a precursor to describing some unusual clinical events, because I think that whenever something technically unusual takes place in therapy, it is vital to look carefully at the consequences of these actions to see if they have been helpful or not. Whatever the outcome, the therapist will have to work with these consequences. If it has been unwise, there will be the need to repair the possible 'damage' done. If it has helped, it is important to try to understand why it has helped – and to share this with colleagues, as I hope to do in this chapter.

In Gail's therapy because of her quixotic unpredictability, there were many times when I awaited her sessions with considerable tension and trepidation. What would she do today that would take me by surprise, make me feel silly or touch me deeply? I am grateful to her parents for giving me permission to discuss the issues her therapy raised.

Gail was adopted when she was 8 years old. She had been severely neglected and traumatised by her biological parents and had an unusual 'syndrome' that may have impacted on her intellectual ability. Her biological mother had learning difficulties of her own. Both of her biological parents had been emotionally deprived in their childhood and father was considered to be personality disordered. In addition to these disadvantages in life, both birth parents were congenitally deaf. Gail was able to hear normally and her birth parents had 'signed' to her, but the severe communication difficulties that existed between them were mainly the result of the emotional neglect that took place during the first four years of her life. As a consequence Gail had no ordinary spoken language when she started nursery at the age of three but was able to 'sign' and 'speak' in a very rudimentary way. There were many complicated and very subtle repercussions from this situation as it is likely that Gail and her birth parents developed their own personalised and idiosyncratic communication system – a combination of signing and very simple speech. Facial expressions and gestures were probably an important part of this system.

Gail's adoptive parents had always made it clear to social services that they would want post-adoption funds to be made available for her to have therapy and this had been agreed. Because of this Gail came to see me privately in my home and the treatment was funded by social services. Gail started twice-weekly therapy when she was twelve and going into her first year at secondary school.

Although Gail was chronologically and physically well into adolescence, for the first two years of therapy play was our primary means of communication. I was concentrated in my wish to facilitate the process of play itself, as a means of communication between us. By this I mean that I realised that I needed to be as playfully present as possible to aid the development of communication between us. My demeanour, state of mind, attempts at openness and willingness to play out her scripts, however silly this felt at times, have helped us in this process. There were times, when she had been in therapy for over two years, when there were moments of humour in this that we both saw the funny side of, but that didn't stop us in our playful interaction. By then Gail could say, 'we're only playing' and just carry on, in a very unembarrassed way for a 14-year-old girl who was starting to appreciate ordinary 14-year-old girls' interests.

Early on in Gail's therapy, I was allowed to comment and interpret within and outside the transference relationship but I often felt that what I had said had not really got to the heart of the matter. Indeed, I suspect that, as I got better at understanding Gail, my words became much more threatening and indeed frightening at times. Just as I often wondered before and during the session what she would spring on me next, I am sure that she also felt this about my words. She told me to shut up, talked over what I said, or if that didn't work, simply left the room.

I learnt to keep quiet, but at times this was very hard, particularly when something in her play suddenly conveyed a powerful emotional message and I felt that I might 'miss the moment' if I didn't say something fairly soon. On these occasions I started to literally ask her permission to speak. So I would say, 'Gail, there's something I really want to say about what's happening at the moment. Can I say it?' When I first started to do this, I actually added that it was something 'very small' as I felt that the number of words I would be able to utter before being told to shut up was extremely limited. When Gail asked in a very slightly playful way 'how small?', I spontaneously literally put my hands apart in front of me indicating a small length of words. I can't say that she actually smiled at this, but there was a softening and a faint twinkle in her eyes when she said, 'Oh, alright then, but no more than that'. This dawning playfulness *between* us seemed to make whatever I had to say more palatable. This approach started after she had been in therapy for about four months. As time went on I came to see the expression of liveliness and creativity that this type of interaction between us allowed as a powerful *antidote* to her defensiveness. It seemed that by offering something that she could enjoy – playfulness – alongside something she found really hard to swallow, she was able to work with me to find a way of 'melting' or 'dissolving' the defences against emotional pain that she had needed so much in the past. I will come back to this idea of play as an antidote to defensiveness later, as well as thoughts about how defences can 'melt' or be 'dissolved'.

I want to give some more detailed material from a session that came a few months after we first started to communicate in this way. It illustrates therapeutic mistakes and what I learnt from them (Casement 2002), as well as windows of opportunity and a 'moment-of-meeting' (Stern *et al.* 1998). It was a session in which I think that Gail had a real experience of me as a person but in a way that I think helped her to feel that I could respond to her primary need to be special and seen and heard for who she really was.

When Gail had been in treatment for over a year and after a long holiday break she became increasingly desperate to go into all the rooms in my home that she was not allowed into. She felt that my home, and I, were full of doors that were closed to her. I had tried to talk to her about how excluded and rejected she felt by me and how under-privileged and unimportant she felt in comparison with other people in my life. These oedipal longings and rejections were really painful for her so I was particularly aware at this time of trying to keep the boundaries between my home and my practice well protected. Unfortunately, at the start of the session I want to describe, a number of unusual circum-stances led to her catching sight of other people in the house. I felt awful about this. She rushed into the therapy room, and, as on a number of other occasions, shut me out of the room, ostensibly to rearrange the furniture in the way she wanted it on that day – something that she did at the start of many sessions. This felt like a particularly poignant attempt, in the circumstances, to try to feel she could create a space which was uniquely hers and mine. It was also of course an attempt to make me feel as shut out as she did. Rather than trying to push the door open, I started to wait as I had done during other sessions, until she allowed me into the room.

However, in the confusion that had preceeded her session, I had inadvertently left a walk-in cupboard door in the consulting room unlocked. In my experience it is almost only children who have been fostered or adopted who have a need to keep on trying to get into cupboards and rooms which are 'not allowed'. I have come to see this as another way of expressing their constant sense of being excluded from the world of families – be they birth or foster-families in which they have such a paradoxical sense of being both a part of, and yet not belonging to the family. This was also her feeling towards therapy and me – she knew that she had her own, unique place within me, but was nevertheless painfully excluded from my family life.

I realised that Gail was in the walk-in cupboard by the noises that I heard from outside the room and went into the room to find her inside the cupboard but not as yet doing anything more than look at what was there. In the cupboard were boxes of therapy toys belonging to other children, a large filing cabinet and some clothes. I was angry with her and felt intruded upon – but also frustrated in my attempts to protect her from such obvious and painful evidence of the other relationships and aspects of my life. I said that she knew I didn't want her to go into this cupboard and she must have seen in my face and heard in my voice my anger at this moment. She came out of the cupboard, walked straight past me, ignoring me in the process and went to the bathroom, locking herself in. I think that this was the first time that she had succeeded in making me angry in such an obvious way – although she had tried hard to do so in the past.

I was now in the consulting room with the furniture all over the place and the cupboard door wide open. Gail was locked in the bathroom and was, I felt, hiding from my anger. These are the kinds of situations where the question of technique becomes increasingly difficult to frame. What to do now? In my view I had made several mistakes that were hurtful to her. She had glimpsed other people in the house, I had inflamed the already difficult dynamic over 'closed doors and open doors' and she had experienced me feeling angry with her. After a few minutes, I was again talking to her through a closed door – this time the bathroom door – asking her if she was upset that I had been angry. She said 'No', but I had a sense of her listening, so I said that I had been angry, but that I wasn't now and hoped that she would come back into the room so that we could talk about what had happened. To my amazement, a few minutes later, she came back into the consulting room. I was able to talk briefly about her distress, having first got her permission to do this in the way that I have already described. I think that she was probably also aware that I was upset at what had happened so far in the session and that this may have helped her to be curious about what I would do next.

After a few minutes of aimless rearranging of the furniture in the room, she suddenly said, 'I've got an idea for a game'. It was essentially about two girls sharing a room in a boarding school. She was a 'horrible' girl who kept tormenting the girl that I played, by waking her up at night, hitting her over the head, pushing her out of bed. Gail's character also raided the headmistress' office and vandalised it. No one liked Gail's character and the headmistress who had previously been sympathetic to her wasn't any more because of what the schoolgirl had done to her office. Gail wanted me to 'be' the headmistress and told me to tell the other girls at the boarding school that if Gail's character made any more trouble they were allowed to hit her over the head with a log. This play felt so wafer thin in its disguise of Gail's feeling that she was so awful, and that I was so angry with her that I would viciously attack her, that I really felt that I couldn't say this. (This is an example of one of the occasions when I decided I couldn't play purely on her terms.) I said to her that I couldn't say this as it felt wrong. She modified what the girls were allowed to hit her with and eventually changed it to the other girls refusing to be her friend, which I was prepared to say. However, Gail's character then raided the headmistress' office again and was caught red-handed.

I was told that as the headmistress I was to say that she was bad and that she had a 'bad heart'. This play was so powerful that before I knew it, I had blurted out 'But I couldn't say that. You've got a *good* heart!' – which is something I truly believe about her. I was really surprised by the spontaneous intensity of what I felt at this moment and the way that the words came out. Without being too fanciful, it really felt as if 'my heart went out to her', tears inadvertently sprang to my eyes, and I was touched by how deeply she was convinced that I would reject and discard her because I was so angry with her. I tried to explain that, although we were playing, we were also saying something very serious to each other and I didn't agree that she was 'bad', I knew that she had a good heart. Amazingly, the session, which had started in such a messy way, ended positively and I felt I knew her better – and I'm sure she felt that she had come to know me better. Most importantly, I think she also knew herself better.

Over time, we were able to build on this 'knowing' of each other through the medium of play. For example, I was very struck by the way in which I gradually realised that, figuratively speaking, I 'tip-toed up towards her' when I wanted to make an interpretation or comment about what was happening in the play. I continued to ask permission, but I could often build on the first permission and say, 'Can I just say a little bit more?' if I could see that she was open to this. This reminded me of a convoluted version of the children's game 'What's the time Mr Wolf'. In this game one child is the wolf and turns his or her face to the wall and the other children try to creep up on the wolf without being seen to move by the wolf, who can turn round at any moment. If they are seen moving, they are 'out'. The children ask the wolf the time as they creep up on him and he replies – 'one o'clock' then 'two o'clock' and so on until it is twelve o'clock. The aim for the children is to tap the wolf on the shoulder before twelve o'clock because at that time the wolf can turn round and chase them and eat them. If someone catches the wolf, he or she in turn becomes Mr Wolf. The fun is in the creeping up (for the children) or being the chasing devouring wolf (for Mr Wolf).

I wasn't sure whether this game meant anything to Gail, but felt it was a useful metaphor for our communication which it was worth trying out. She immediately recognised the ways in which the game paralleled the way we communicated and at her request we subsequently spent a lot of time playing this game as she gradually acknowledged how scary my words were to her. I was like a wolf who could suddenly rush at her and eat her up. I was similarly aware of how unpredictable I felt she was and how she could suddenly turn a session into a situation in which I felt attacked and intimidated. This is an example, like that of Edwards cited above, in which my natural response was followed by words in a manner that I think as a result was more communicative than the words alone, because it was couched in the medium of play that had become our special way of communicating.

We reached other extraordinary moments of understanding in this fashion. For a long time it was very hard for me to get a deep sense of what it might have been like for Gail to try to communicate, as a hearing infant or small child, with a profoundly deaf mother and father. My imagination, as well as the experience within therapy itself, didn't seem able to reach to this. It took me a long while to realise how deeply embedded this experience was in the unusual ways that we played together. I think I finally got the message through some play in the bathroom, where we would quite often play, in which I was asked to play in some particularly silly (but also funny) ways. By this time Gail often said, 'We're only playing' when she felt the play was a bit silly, but nevertheless important to her. She could also see the funny side, but the play had a serious purpose and she really needed me to go along with it.

Gail was the queen who wanted to make me her prisoner. She tied my hands with string (loosely, at my insistence) and told me to stand in the shower cubicle which was 'the prison', which I did. I felt very silly and unprofessional, and greatly reminded of the kind of silly play that goes on between parents and children at times and can be great fun just because of its silliness. She closed the transparent shower cubicle door and then started silently to gesticulate to me from the other side. Suddenly, I had a vivid image of two people trying to communicate through a sound barrier, but where it was still possible for them to see each other. I was stunned by this. All the months of talking to her at times through closed doors – to the therapy room or the bathroom –

suddenly made sense in a new way that connected emotional and intellectual understanding, and this had happened through being prepared to go along with a pretty unusual piece of playing. When I realised this, I was 'allowed' briefly to say how I thought that this could be what it felt like when she tried to talk with her birth mother and father, when they couldn't hear her and she couldn't get her message across. She agreed to this rather disdainfully as if it had taken me a very long time to finally understand this – and she was right.

My difficulty in understanding Gail continued and I felt sure connected with her learning difficulties. It was often painfully evident that Gail's understanding of the way the world works was limited. But she got much better at communicating verbally with me, and when some time later I tried to talk to her about how hard it could be for her to understand what was going on around her at times, she retorted, in a very deliberate and loaded way, 'No Monica, it is *you* who don't understand.' With this statement and the way in which she said it, I suddenly felt myself to be like a deaf mother who truly doesn't understand her child. It was an extraordinary experience and I shared it with her by saying, 'You're right. I really don't understand this properly yet. But what you just said has made me realise what it felt like for you not to feel understood by your birth Mum – made much more difficult by her deafness'.

This was a watershed session which led to a surprisingly 'ordinary' conversation in which for the first time she was able to talk with me about her early life with her birth parents, followed by going into Care and then being adopted. We had become able to talk about her traumatic early life from a more resilient position of emotional strength. This capacity to talk more about her painful past, and her growing ability to bear to think about and bear memories from the past, continued as her therapy progressed. I believe that the unusual playfulness of our earlier relationship, together with the spontaneity that this at times led to in the therapeutic relationship, paved the way for this development to take place.

PLAYFULNESS AS AN ANTIDOTE TO DEFENSIVENESS

My willingness to play with Gail enabled us to engage with a powerful creative process which emerged from the unique interactions and ways of communicating that became typical of our particular relationship. This creative process can be thought of as helping to melt, dissolve, neutralise and effectively *antidote* the painfulness of the raw and undigested memories and feelings that she carried in her internal world.

Drawing on this clinical example, I would like to hypothesise that the playful presence of the therapist can hold a key position in what can be thought of as a psychic detoxification process. We know that the extremely damaging past experiences and relationships that children like Gail are trying to recover from metaphorically poison the child's internal world. We now also have evidence from neuroscientific advances that the brain is actually changed and incapacitated because of early neglect and trauma (Schore 2003). We cannot remove the poison, but we can antidote it as best we can. Over time, a gradual change in the internal balance between creative development and psychic crumbling away as a result of this poisoning can then take place. When this starts to happen, it is as if these new experiences grow around the gradually decaying memories, and the damaged internal world from the painful past.

The session in which I spontaneously told Gail that I thought she had a good heart illustrates Stern *et al.*'s description of the therapeutic impact of a moment-of-meeting on the shared implicit relationship between patient and therapist (Stern *et al.* 1998). Their description of the impact of these special moments in therapy supports my view that it is possible to redefine the therapeutic process itself as one in which the losses and deprivations of the past are not (indeed cannot be) undone but, instead, something new in the present starts to tip the internal balance of the patient towards greater emotional health and well-being. This reframing of the therapeutic task is very helpful in providing a realistic therapeutic aim when working with children like Gail who have been so severely deprived, neglected and traumatised. Stern *et al.* describe this process as follows:

> In this model there is a reciprocal process in which change takes place in the implicit relationship at 'moments-of-meeting' through alterations in 'ways of being with'. It does not correct past empathic failures through the analytic empathic activity. It does not replace a past deficit. *Rather something new is created in the relationship which alters the intersubjective environment.* Past experience is recontextualised in the present such that a person operates from within a different mental landscape, resulting in new behaviours in the present and future.
>
> (Stern *et al.* 1998: 918; my italics)

I want to finish with some thoughts about why playfulness can be such an important feature of the present therapeutic relationship. From one perspective, I have in effect tried to demonstrate that by 'not playing' the therapist can be closing down therapeutic opportunities, possibly particularly for moments-of-meeting to happen. From another perspective I have linked the creative potential of playing as emphasised by Winnicott with the whole process of psychoanalytic work. Winnicott sees the therapist's ability to be playful as central to the process of therapy and Stern *et al.* emphasise the importance of the 'personal signature' of the therapist during the moment-of-change, which has to meet spontaneously the uniqueness of that moment. The moment of change notably is a two-way process. Without the openness of heart that playfulness requires on both sides, I think it is much less likely to happen.

References

Alvarez, A. (2000) 'Moral imperatives in work with borderline children: the grammar of wishes and the grammar of needs'. In J. Symington (ed.), *Imprisoned Pain and its Transformation: A Festschrift for H. Sidney Klein*. London: Karnac, pp.5–20

Balint, M. (1968) *The Basic Fault*. London: Tavistock

Bartram, P. (2003) 'Some oedipal problems in work with adopted children and their parents' *Journal of Child Psychotherapy* 29(1): 21–36

Bion, W. R. (1980) *Bion in New York and Sao Paulo*. Strath Tay, UK: Clunie Press

Bollas, C. (1995) *Cracking Up*. London: Routledge

Canham, H. (2003) 'The relevance of the Oedipus myth to fostered and adopted children' *Journal of Child Psychotherapy* 29(1): 5–19

Canham, H. (2004) 'Spitting, kicking and stripping: technical difficulties encountered in the treatment of deprived children' *Journal of Child Psychotherapy* 30(1): 143–54

Carlberg, G. (1997) 'Laughter opens the door: turning points in child psychotherapy' *Journal of Child Psychotherapy* 23(3): 331–49

Casement, P. (2002) *Learning from our Mistakes: Beyond Dogma in Psychoanalysis and Psychotherapy*. Hove, UK: Brunner-Routledge

Coltart, N. (1992) *Slouching towards Bethlehem . . . And Further Psychoanalytic Explanations*. London and New York: Free Association Press and Guilford Press

Edwards, J. (2000) 'On being dropped and picked up: adopted children and their internal objects' *Journal of Child Psychotherapy* 26(3): 349–67

Freud, S. (1905) *Jokes and their Relationship to the Unconscious. Standard Edition*, 8. London: Hogarth Press and Institute of Psycho-Analysis

Hindle, D. (2000) 'The merman: recovering from early abuse and loss' *Journal of Child Psychotherapy* 26(3): 369–91

Hopkins, J. (2000) 'Overcoming a child's resistance to late adoption: how one new attachment can facilitate another' *Journal of Child Psychotherapy* 26(3): 335–47

Horne, A. (2001) 'Brief communications from the edge: psychotherapy with challenging adolescents' *Journal of Child Psychotherapy* 27(1): 3–18

Horne, A. (2003) 'Oedipal aspirations and phallic fears: on fetishism in childhood and young adulthood' *Journal of Child Psychotherapy* 29(1): 37–52

Hurry, A. (ed.) (1998) *Psychoanalysis and Developmental Therapy*. London: Karnac

Kenrick, J. (2000) '"Be a kid": the traumatic impact of repeated separations on children who are fostered and adopted' *Journal of Child Psychotherapy* 26(3): 393–412

Lanyado, M. (2001) 'The symbolism of the story of Lot and his wife: the function of the "present relationship" and non-interpretative aspects of the therapeutic relationship in facilitating change' *Journal of Child Psychotherapy* 27(1): 19–33

Lanyado, M. (2002) 'Creating transitions in the lives of children suffering from "multiple traumatic loss"'. In L. Caldwell (ed.), *The Elusive Child*. London: Karnac, pp. 65–81

Lanyado, M. (2003) 'The emotional tasks of moving from fostering to adoption: transitions, attachment, separation and loss' *Clinical Psychology and Psychiatry* 8(3): 337–49. Special edition on fostering and adoption

Lanyado, M. (2004) *The Presence of the Therapist: Treating Childhood Trauma*. Hove, UK and New York: Brunner-Routledge

Menzies Lyth, I. (1988) *Containing Anxiety in Institutions: Selected Essays*, Vol.I. London: Free Association Books

Schore, A. (2003) *Affect Disregulation and Disorders of the Self*. New York: Norton

Solomon, J. and George, C. (eds.) (1999) *Attachment Disorganisation*. London and New York: Guilford Press

Stern, D., Sander, L., Nahum, J. P., Harrison, A. M., Lyons-Ruth, K., Morgan, A. C., Bruschweiler-Stern, N. and Tronick, E. Z. (1998) 'Non-interpretative mechanisms in psychotherapy: the "something more" than interpretation' *International Journal of Psycho-Analysis* 79: 903–21

Tronick, E. Z. (2003) 'Of course all relationships are unique: how co-creative processes generate unique mother–infant and parent–therapist relationships and change other relationships' *Psychoanalytic Inquiry* 23(3): 473–91

Ward, A., (2003) 'Using everyday life: opportunity-led work'. In A. Ward, K. Kasinski, J. Pooley and A. Worthington (eds.), *Therapeutic Communities for Children and Young People*. London and New York: Jessica Kingsley, pp.119–32

Winnicott, D. W. (1971) *Playing and Reality*. Harmondsworth, UK: Pelican/Penguin Books

9   Brief communications from the edge

Psychotherapy with challenging adolescents

Ann Horne

Where early trauma, overwhelming to the immature ego and not able to be processed, has featured, the young person subjected to it has often been left with early body-centred defences as a way of blocking out the primitive anxieties of annihilation, abandonment, disintegration, falling endlessly and merging. In the therapy room, consequently, we encounter in the patient the capacity to act in and out, and experience a counter-transference pressure to collude with the defence, to act ourselves or to become a harsh and critical superego-ish object. As Winnicott notes:

> the analyst must expect to find acting-out in the transference, and must understand the significance of this acting-out, and be able to give it positive value.
>
> (Winnicott 1963a: 210)

In such a transference we find ourselves in touch with fundamental primitive fears, cruel and punishing superegos, immature atoll-like egos, and defences designed to deny intimacy, attachment, affect and pain. We need to cope with not-knowing – often for long spells – and to be able to think both developmentally and psychoanalytically (Alvarez 1996; Fonagy and Target 1996; Hurry 1998), recognising when the opportunity of becoming a 'new object' glimmers, yet in touch with the dangers inherent in this for the patient (Loewald 1960).

INTRODUCING MATTHEW

Matthew was 14 years old when he abused the 7-year-old sister of a friend. The court requested an assessment as to the suitability of psychotherapy for Matthew in relation to his offence. I saw him three times around his 15th birthday, a colleague meeting his paternal grandmother and stepmother and then his father and stepmother. Once-weekly therapy began two months later.

Matthew's parents married when his mother was 17 and his father 18, his mother being six months pregnant with Matthew. Matthew's mother had been brought up in an abusive home and was sexually and physically abused by her stepfather as well as suffering severe emotional neglect. Her mother died when she was 13. Mr P (Matthew's father) had suffered serious depression from his early teens, attempting suicide twice and having a spell of adolescent in-patient psychiatric treatment. He had, according to his own mother, suffered most in the family when his parents separated when he was 4 years old. When Matthew was 3 years old his father's depression worsened and Matthew's mother ended their relationship. Mr P moved in with his mother, Matthew's grandmother, who came to the clinic. His wife moved a boyfriend, Sean, into the home with Matthew and her. There were violent episodes between the parents, occurring over Mr P's requests for access to Matthew, and an injunction was granted by the court banning Mr P from approaching the home. He spent a few weeks in prison, having destroyed their kitchen, and did not see his son for over a year.

Sean disliked Matthew. It was only following the referral that Sean's gross physical abuse of Matthew emerged as the family began to be able to talk of it. Matthew knows that this relationship was abusive but has blocked out his memory of it. He does, however, recall his parents arguing and fighting – the earlier and primary trauma for him.

When Matthew was 5, his mother was killed in a road traffic accident – she was knocked down by a car on a zebra crossing. Matthew was left in the 'care' of his abuser as his mother had stated that this was her wish in her will. There ensued a long custody battle, Matthew being made a Ward of Court, and at one point when he had been sent to stay with his abusive maternal step-grandfather he was kidnapped by his father and grand-mother, so anxious were they about his care. Matthew's father finally won custody. When Matthew was 6½, he and his father moved in with Mr P's girlfriend, Sammie, and her daughter, Emma, who is a year younger than Matthew. They now have a son, Alex, who is 11 years younger than Matthew.

MATTHEW'S PAST AND PRESENT FUNCTIONING

Mr P and Sammie approached their local Child and Family Consultation Service when Matthew was 7 years old, for help with his aggression, but it was felt that time to adjust to the new family was all that was needed. By the age of 9, Matthew had been expelled from six schools, sometimes for violence, sometimes for not being there. He described escaping out of school windows and commented, 'I thought that was mad – being expelled for not even being there!' There was no sense of a comprehending or a pursuing adult. Finally he ended up in a day school for children with emotional and behavioural difficulties, a school that creditably managed to hold on to him.

In school he was said to be 'bright' – brighter than most of his peers, 'capable of clear thinking but stubborn'. He could attack other children with words, and be rude, unpleasant and undermining to others. This verbal aggression remained worrying to the school and it tipped over into physical fights at perceived slights.

Peer relations were said by school and family to be poor, although it emerged in therapy that Matthew belonged to a group of delinquent lads with whom he spent much of his spare time. His descriptions of their meetings contained much excitement and activity, and were empty of thought or reflection. Matthew had an ambivalent relationship with his father whom he tried to like but who shouted at him, hit him and only rarely listened. He could have been allied to his stepmother, Sammie, as both are intelligent, but he felt excluded by the birth of his half brother, Alex. His paternal grandmother remained a 'good object' for him.

His offence occurred when he was at a friend's watching England being beaten by Argentina in the World Cup. This friend often had sexual intercourse with his girlfriend in the presence of a group of friends, which Matthew found exciting and disturbing. When he went to the toilet, his friend's 7-year-old little sister pounced on him from her bedroom to play, punching him and jumping on his back, and he threw her onto her bed. There he began to tickle her and what began as a game moved to his touching her genitals. When he found that he was trying to remove her pants, he stopped himself, wondered what he was doing, and went home. The others in the family, however, had a sense of something more sinister and asked the little girl what had happened later in the evening. Matthew was arrested at 2a.m. and taken to the police station. He told me his father followed but, in fact, it was Sammie who came to see him. Initially insistently denying everything, when faced finally with the video interview with the child he agreed that her version was right. He received a three-year Supervision Order, with a strong injunction from the judge that, should he appear in court on any count in future, he would be given a custodial sentence. When I saw him he was embarrassed to talk of it and ashamed of what he had done – hopeful signs. Like many violated young people, however, he was furious that the police had kept his clothes for analysis – as if he were trying to focus on the external to avoid thinking of the body, its actions and the internal.

THINKING ABOUT TECHNIQUE IN WORK WITH ADOLESCENTS

The key tasks of adolescence involve separation, individuation and becoming responsible for the self. In classical theory where psychosexual development is the main thrust, this means taking ownership of the body and sexuality at a time of great change. Where there has been early trauma and the immature ego has been overwhelmed, we have to think with care about technique. The defences available to the child are often pre-verbal, pre-representational, centring on the body-self, its traumatisation and its survival. What the young person does *with* the body, therefore, is significant:

1   in the offence of sexually abusing others (the victim's report is extremely helpful in letting us know just what is so intolerable that it has to be decanted outside the self);
2   in delinquency and putting the body at risk;
3   in violence or aggression where we often encounter either violent provocation designed to repeat an earlier experience of being violated, or self-preservative violence in Glasser's (1998) terms, designed to protect the fragile ego from perceived threat;
4   in the unconscious use of the body in ensuring one's exploitation. The prime example of this is the rent boy whose repetition-compulsion in relation to his own abuse is masked by a veneer of being in control of those whom he chooses to think he seduces and who are made to 'pay'.

Thus issues around the body, bodily conflicts and its use need to be addressed. Yet the adolescent task is to take over this body at a time when infantile fantasy and curiosity is revived. One solution for the therapist is to separate mind and body – 'Isn't it interesting what your body gets up to – being chased, being hit, being where it shouldn't be?' Addressing the func-tioning part to explore together the infantile part can help 'save face' and avoid humiliation. Sometimes, though, this is not enough. Edgcumbe (1988) approached such issues when thinking about the technical problems of interpreting (or not) in the transference with adolescents, and 'whether to take up defence, content or affect, and at what depth or level to deal with content of conflicts' in the light of 'the adolescent's heightened fear and shame about regression' (Edgcumbe 1988: 1). Following case illustrations, she concludes:

> I have stressed the importance of taking up material from the angle of the higher level conflicts which have engendered regression, rather than the infantile instinctual wishes and modes of relating which are expressed in the regression. . . . Shame and anxiety are likely to be best relieved by making sense of the situation which led to the regression. In this way the analyst can remain aligned with the part of the patient's self which is striving for growth, without denying the regression.
>
> (1988: 12)

It is just this kind of carefully thought-out, conscious choice of what to take up that often seems to have been totally misunderstood in the past in disputes between theoretical traditions. It led Winnicott in 1962 to an interim, transitional position that he called 'working as a psychoanalyst' when the 'anti-social tendency' (amongst other clinical issues) was present. Today, one hopes, we are clearer that this *is* psychotherapy and that it is, moreover, a question of conscious, sophisticated analytic choice.

In parallel with issues about the body comes the danger of relationships and especially of intimacy. Of particular importance in work with young people in search of a perverse solution (a survival technique) is Glasser's (1979, 1996) concept of the core complex. Here, one sees the search for intimacy as the start of what becomes a vicious circle. Gaining intimacy, the adolescent is overwhelmed by anxieties of a primitive nature – anxiety about merging with the object, of suffocation and loss of individuation. This arouses a violent response – violence in the service of protecting the immature ego – in order to escape anxiety; and a consequent sense of abandonment (again, a primitive anxiety) ensues with the necessity once more to pursue intimacy. And 'la ronde' continues. Glasser finds this to underlie all perverse psychopathology.

Psychotherapy requires a relationship of considerable intimacy, yet the adolescent process, too, is contrary to this. Apart from the danger in hoping that this relationship might be different from earlier ones, the adolescent can experience being understood both as a relief and as an enormous threat, bringing back just such primitive fears of merging with the object, of not being separate. One has to *pace* this experience of being understood and be aware of what is too intimate, and know that the young person may be driven to disparage it when it is desired, arousing as it does memories of vulnerability. Even pauses and silence need judgement: silence may become a threatening absence of the object, especially if this mirrors the young person's early life. At times, one has to be an 'enlivening object' (Alvarez 1992); otherwise one is perceived as abandoning and annihilating. It is 'either – or': there is little middle ground here – indeed, the process of therapy seeks to develop this. The 'all or nothing' quality Winnicott encapsulates in 'There is not yet a capacity to identify with parent figures without loss of personal identity' (Winnicott 1963b: 244) is exacerbated in the adolescent who has still to achieve a capacity for symbolisation, for whom emotional states *are* bodily experiences (Parsons and Dermen 1999: 341). The risk involved in 'hope', too, may be one reason why, with adolescents, one often gets 'brief communications' followed by escape.

We are all used to adolescents as escapologists. In a sense, this is a healthy adolescent process, distancing oneself. It contains elements of the toddler who has learned how to make the adults pursue him – except that with adolescents we are made to feel great uncertainty as to how much we should pursue. This capacity to put the grown-up into a 'double bind' seems to arrive with the hormones at puberty. Again, this requires delicacy: the conflict belongs in the adolescent, not in the therapist or network, and should be gently returned there. A very simple example would be the adolescent who invariably arrives 15 minutes late for his session. One can say how important taking control is, and how essential; it is a pity, however, that in taking this necessary step he costs himself 15 minutes of *his* time. That's an interesting dilemma he has there – and the conflict is quietly returned to its owner but not in the tone of his own dismissive and shaming superego. The other side of escapology is the defence of activity – a return to the body-self of toddler years. Activity often occurs as a way of blocking out thought, which itself involves unbearable recollection and memory. It is, in this context, unfortunate that the UK Government has instructed the Probation Service in England and Wales to breach offenders (i.e. to bring them back before the court) if they miss two appointments. One could point to a recourse to action and an absence of thought in government for this anti-adolescent decision. Thinking, too, in adolescence is a further aspect of intimacy – intimacy of mind – and

> The fear of thinking may derive both from conflicts over curiosity and from reluctance to let the analyst/mother intrude on painful private matters. Here, again, transference interpretation may have to be used sparingly, to free the patient's thinking.
>
> (Edgcumbe 1988: 13)

Creating a space for thought is not easy when the drive is to activity and not thinking. Making space for curiosity about the self helps, and one can often capture adolescents by picking up the paradoxes in their lives or offering the unexpected in comment, especially when the unexpected is in contrast to their dismissive, abandoning or punitive superego:

> Matthew described being on the back of a friend's motorbike (legiti-mately) in the park and the police cruising past. By their actions, the group made the police pursue them, but eluded them. I said that was interesting. Matthew had expected something more negative. 'How?' I said that he had really made the police pay attention. Perhaps he had wished people had done so when he was little. Matthew went on to say how his father often thought he was 'up to something' when he was not, then told of his favourite teacher, a female art teacher, who had taken his side in a dispute that he had actually caused, leading to another youth being punished. He grinned. I said that perhaps I needed to hear the warning – all is not necessarily as it seems? He grinned more widely. I said that this was another area for me to be curious about – he can change reality.

It is worth thinking here about the concept of 'therapist as developmental object', so well described by Hurry (1998) and a part of the work of the Hampstead Clinic for many years. The young person engages with a curious ego and supportive superego in the 'developmental object therapist' who *deliberately* takes up a position of *not* being used as a projection of the child's superego but is available as both ego support and interpretative therapist as needed. When one thinks of early trauma and the 'breaching of the shame shield' described by Campbell (1994) in the young abusers whom he has treated over 30 years, one sees a further reason for creating possibilities for alternative identifications and routes to a different ego ideal. Wilson (1999), writing about delinquents, put it rather well:

> The key therapeutic task is to resist the young person's implicit invitation to repeat the past . . . The . . . ability to find ways of responding that are different from what young people expect and which do not meet the dictates of the transference is essential. Ultimately, it is through the child psychotherapists' behaviour that they convey their understanding of the meaning of the young person's delinquency and provide the safety and boundary that the delinquent needs. Such behaviour, sustained by the child psychotherapists' own insights, constitutes interpretation and serves as a stimulus and basis for further verbal forms of communication and understanding.
>
> (Wilson 1999: 318)

It is also important, with the drive to acting out in adolescence and the risk of self-harm, that there is a functioning network that enables the therapy to continue, a subject addressed later.

Issues of sexuality appear throughout the treatment, often beginning in the form of remarkably crude jokes that show very early childish fantasies of destruction, inadequacy and incorporation in intercourse. The fantasies of adolescence, after all, overlay for such young people a very often traumatically abusive childhood reality. Work in this area tends, I find, to be consolidated nearer the end of treatment although it appears throughout – it is only after much work that the young person can, with confidence, face exploring the kind of adult sexual being that they would wish to be, and the fears and fantasies around that. Issues of a procreative body are acute for abusing and violated boys and girls. The necessary fusion of aggression, agency and sexuality for adult functioning is terrifying in its potential for destruction and much work on the positive role of aggression is necessary first.

Young people, defending against the memory of helplessness in the absence of a protective object, find aggression paradoxically difficult. It emerges in an uncontrollable fashion in their lives, overwhelming others and themselves. They need practice in appropriately assertive aggression and righteous anger, and a capacity to recognise and name emotions and affects, in order nor to be swamped by them. Identifying with the adolescent's victim role can mean the therapist missing aggression: it is important to have it in mind as a constant undercurrent, and to connote aggression and agency as necessary and, where it is problematic, to perceive the roots in an early defence against intolerable feelings. 'Anger management' strategies work well where there is a more integrated, functioning 'self'; where this is not so, the construction of an emotional vocabulary and 'anger practice' – the capacity to recognise agency and aggression, to note when they are appropriate and to begin to exercise them – are essential. Attention to such ego developments as affect recognition and affect tolerance is vital in psychoanalytic work with young people where the ego is immature and patchwork.

There are implications within all of this for assessment – the information one needs, the environment necessary for an assessment to be relevant and if therapy is to be considered, and the assessment encounter itself. These are beyond the remit of this chapter but must be flagged up: 'The essential thing is I do base my work on diagnosis,' said Winnicott to the British Psycho-analytic Society (Winnicott 1962: 169).

THINKING ABOUT MATTHEW

Matthew presents as not typical of young abusers but rather demonstrating the mixed symptomatology of mid-adolescents who arouse concern. Most abusing adolescents appear either to be rather isolated individuals with one clear *known* abusive incident, or to be multiple abusers with a real polymorphous feel. Matthew's history shows difficulties in equal peer relations (his mates are all less bright than he is), long-standing outbursts of aggression and seeking violent situations, delinquency and sexual abusing. His capacity for putting himself at risk is also becoming clearer.

With Matthew we can see the clear pattern of early violence where there is no protective figure, outlined in the Great Ormond Street Hospital research on young abusers: the two main factors correlating with abusing others are:

a   an experience of unpredictable and unprocessable violence and trauma, when the ego is too immature to make sense of it (Lanyado *et al.* 1995). Matthew witnessed early marital warfare, was beaten from the age of 3 and traumatically abandoned to his abuser at age 5.
b   having a mother who has herself been abused and unconsciously projects onto her male child the expectation that he, too, will abuse.

The memory of such victimisation (especially the humiliation and vulnerability) can be dealt with by developing a fantasy of abusing someone weaker and smaller, becoming powerful in the process and making someone else into the victim – identification with the aggressor. Part of the treatment thus involves exploring the patient's own 'victim' experience before one can reach the victimising.

There is also 'the ambivalence of the object' – a mother who consciously and deliberately leaves him with an abuser – and who turns a blind eye to his abuse when she is there. We should not be surprised that he 'tricks' the grown-ups in return and should expect this in the therapy. Thinking intergenerationally, Matthew's mother was abused and abandoned to her abuser on her mother's death and the scenario was repeated with Matthew. Matthew's father lost his father at age 4; his mother lost her natural father at a very young age; Matthew lost his for a considerable spell at age 3. Welldon (1988) has alerted us to the necessity of thinking across at least three generations where abuse is concerned.

We can also note the use of activity as a defence, beginning with his early escaping from school – but no one pursues, instead he unconsciously makes the process of his being abandoned happen repeatedly – and continuing in his delinquency. Indeed, one might find his delinquent activities to be a seduction of me, as therapist, away from the abusing that formed his offence, as well as a practised way of using excitement to mask depression. There is also the compulsion to repeat sensations of fear, as we will see in the clinical material: in some of his delinquent activities, Matthew scares himself. More profoundly, one might think about identification with the dead mother: it is unusual for a 22-year-old to have made a will and colleagues have suggested that her accident may have been suicide. Being alert as to Matthew's unconscious 'suicidal' behaviour therefore becomes a factor, and the meaning of an abandoning, not protective, even malevolent maternal object important.

Finally, it is worth commenting on aggression, an issue of long-standing for Matthew, noted first at the age of 7. This use of self-preservative violence has begun to turn into an enjoyment of others getting into trouble – the early beginnings of a sadistic quality – and it is essential for his development that work is done with Matthew on this.

AN ENCOUNTER WITH MATTHEW

This session occurred in early December, almost nine months into therapy. Matthew at this point is living with his grandmother.

> Matthew arrived early for his session, wearing a new, warm, padded jacket. (He had come the previous week in only a sweatshirt and with an awful cold.) Although his cold was still bad, he said that he was OK, that he had taken lots of soup. This comment came with a smile – in our last session he had told me that his grandmother was very good at making soup. (Paternal grandmother has transference implications.) He hadn't been allowed to take a day off school, however. I wondered if he could have been able to bear that – not being active and just sitting with

his thoughts. He agreed he could not, he would rather be in school. I reflected on this unusually intimate start and wondered when reaction would set in. When Matthew attends, he always takes time to re-discover his object: he seems, indeed, to expect a corrupt object.

There was a sustained pause. He looked very sad. I wondered if he were thoughtful now or just fed up? Fed up. His father had said that the moped was too much for his Christmas and he probably wouldn't get it. He expanded on how it would have cost £200. His father was giving his brother Alex a computer worth £200; Matthew would get a new mobile phone worth £100 and his sister, Emma, a present worth £75. There was a pause, half sad, half angry. I wondered rather weakly if that seemed unfair? *Yes* – Alex gets everything. (Alex, indulged at age 5, contrasts with Matthew who, at the same age, was abused and abandoned.)

After a further pause Matthew wondered if his father would give him the money and he could put it towards a bike himself. Then he deflated, recalling that his father preferred to pay things up week by week. I said that it seemed impossible for the adults to get things right for him. We reflected in silence.

'Do you know a Pa.. Po.. something like that – it's a bike.' It emerged as a Piaggio. 'They're *very* nice! I really like them. I was out last night on one!' I felt anxiety begin to rise and wondered inside about this need to make the adult anxious, and why. There followed a story of Matthew and five or six friends. Dave had brought the bike and all had tried it out in the local park. Steve did a 'wheelie' and drove into a tree. Matthew also tried it – 'It was really good!' He described sharp turns, sudden acceleration, mud flying, excitement. As he was in full flow, his mobile phone rang. He looked apologetic, muttered, 'Sorry', said the answering service would pick it up, and could not resist checking the screen. It was Dave leaving a message: 'He already phoned twice when I was on the train coming here! It's about meeting tonight.' The phone was switched off and put away. He continued with the bike tale – taking it out on the road out of town, a vivid description of Dave nearly coming off the back of the bike as Matthew accelerated, 'It can do 45 miles an hour!' and finally return to town.

I thought about the sense of life and energy in the midst of this extremely dangerous behaviour. 'You know, you really like being "on the edge", don't you?' Matthew looked questioning. I said that on the bike he liked being in control himself (he didn't like being on the back) but it could tip over – Steve had managed to hit a tree. I suggested he was also 'on the edge' with the police, were he found, and with the court as the judge had told him that his return to court on any count would mean a custodial sentence. And he had told me before (in an earlier session) that being on a bike could be scary and he didn't like that. 'Yes, that's why I won't let Steve drive.'

There was a pause. I interpreted then that it was interesting that this 'on the edge' excitement had actually followed a very painful description of him and Emma feeling 'on the edge' in the family. He gave me a very direct look. I offered that one way he had learned to be in control of these very difficult, sad feelings was through the excited 'on the edge' feelings, but they were risky. I wondered, too, about the excitement keeping *me* 'on the edge', not sure of his safety, and wondered if he was good at making the adults and me feel this. He smiled gently.

There was quite a long pause. Matthew launched into a story of his friend, Joseph, a very small 14-year-old. Joseph's passion was cars – with a particular emphasis on taking and driving them away. I noted to myself the connection between my interpretation of the pain in the family and his further recourse to excitement and danger, moving from bikes to cars, but did not interrupt. Matthew gave great detail of how Joseph would break into the black boxes behind the steering wheel panel, where to locate these in a Rover Metro, and diverted into a variety of ways to break into a car. Joseph had been doing this since he was 7 years old. The police knew him well – had been to see him the other day as he is the first port of call when cars go missing. 'He has been cautioned and the police know him. Pathetic!' 'Pathetic – who?' I asked. 'Joe. He knows they'll come to see him first. When he takes a car he drives with the headlights on full beam so that he can't be seen himself. He just gets very excited by cars. Once when I was with him he saw a Jaguar. I said, "NO!" but Joe kept talking about what it would be like to drive it when we were walking away.' I wondered if Joe had the same sense of excitement in relation to cars that Matthew had talked of with bikes. He looked surprised: 'No, he's pathetic.' I commented that sometimes things are both pathetic and exciting, reminding him of the 36 inch television set he said his father had bought that in one way seemed pathetic to him but in another seemed full of excitement and potential. This had been in an earlier session. He grinned – 'That's true!' I continued, 'So you know some things that are both pathetic-daft-dangerous and pathetic-exciting-"on the edge"?' He nodded thoughtfully.

The story of Joe continued. He had 'torched' a car. This felt suddenly very unsafe, as if the juxtaposition of 'pathetic' and 'excitement' had to be avoided. He had tried to break into a car in Tesco's carpark (the known area where local youth find and dump cars and bikes) but couldn't get at the black box. Realising that he had left his fingerprints all over the vehicle, he had found a cloth and jerrycan of petrol in the boot and poured it over the front seats, leaving the can in the car before striking a match. He had singed his hair. 'He's totally pathetic! He could have burned himself badly. He had the rag from the boot – he could have wiped off his fingerprints. He ran off and it went "Whump!" exploding. The fire brigade was called. He could have hurt people!' Matthew sounded very upset. I said gently that I thought he had witnessed this, been there with Joe. He nodded. I added that it was frightening that the excitement and 'on the edge' bits could tip right over into danger and wondered if he scared himself. He nodded, saying, 'He could have been harmed!' Yes. After a pause I added that it was interesting that such a memory of danger had followed my saying to him that he wanted me to feel 'on the edge' sometimes – that he was letting me know how dreadfully dangerous things sometimes felt for him and that it was right that we were both concerned.

He recalled a teacher at school, in car mechanics class, whom Matthew had asked something that implied how to hot-wire cars. The teacher had given him the information and not asked why he wanted to know. I said I thought he was letting me know about two things. First, grown-ups may not be straight but collude with exciting illegal things, like the teacher giving him the information. (I was thinking of corrupt objects again.) How, then, could he possibly know to trust me and my concern? Secondly, perhaps he was warning me that he could be tricky – tricking the teacher and perhaps other grown-ups, like me. He gave me a very direct, straight look. Collusion, of course, is one of the major pressures felt in the counter-transference with psychopathic patients (Symington 1980).

There was a further pause. Matthew said, 'The bike engine's still running.' The bike, of course, had been stolen and hot-wired. His friends were 'second time thieves', having come across it stolen and abandoned. They had bypassed the ignition and could not turn off the engine. They would have to cover the exhaust pipe, cutting off the air supply. (All endings, I thought, are traumatic – even for the bike.) 'Someone stole it last night.' I must have looked astonished. 'Yeah, when we'd gone home Dave had left it at his back gate and phoned to say it had been taken. We found Steve had taken it and had it at his place. It would have been pathetic if a nicked bike had been nicked – I mean we couldn't report it to the police, could we?' I said that I thought that was really interesting: that, when something has gone wrong in the past, the grown-ups will simply not take a young person seriously. Perhaps in some ways this was a little like Matthew – it is impossible for him to hope that the adults will be concerned *now* for his safety when they made such a bad job of it in the past. 'You mean Sean,' said Matthew, referring to his mother's abusive boyfriend. 'Yes, and every-thing that happened then. Now, as a result of that, you are making me into another of these grown-ups who hears very dangerous things but can't stop you. Sometimes it feels better to do that than for you to hope that it might be different.'

The following pause felt more thoughtful. 'I'll only go tonight if Steve has a crash helmet for me. I know he's got one. It *is* scary – but exciting scary.' ['Crash helmet' has become equated with me, interesting when one thinks about heads and minds.] I added that that was why he insists on driving, being in control: 'It's like not taking the risk that the adults won't protect you again, but it's also the same "on the edge" excitement of waiting for something to happen that was awful and too much for you when you were little.' Matthew nodded slowly.

It was almost time to stop. Matthew checked the clock and put on his jacket. He told me that he *was* careful as sometimes it could get too scary. Moreover tonight they wouldn't be on the road but in a farmer's field. I said that he was taking on some of the adult bits about protecting himself but still being 'on the edge'. He was leaving me with something to worry about – perhaps he needed to do that. He gave a quiet smile and 'See you next week!' I thought it was a promise to stay alive.

A NOTE ON NETWORKS

There must be a functioning, communicating network that is able to create a safe, holding structure if therapy for the young person who is a risk to himself and/or others is to be considered a treatment of choice. We all recall Winnicott's exhortation that delinquents need *placement first*, before psy-choanalysis, after he had the clinic basement flooded, his car jump-started and his buttocks bitten three times by his first child analytic patient (Winnicott 1956; 1963a). If there is not such a network, the issue is certainly placement. One could view this as offering practical 'containers' until the stage is reached where words can contain and anxiety be symbolised rather than enacted. This cannot be stressed enough. Our omnipotence – or pressure from the network – may take us into a therapeutic relationship that then fails because external containment and understanding are lacking, and we repeat and re-visit trauma upon a young person who unconsciously seeks it. In Matthew's case the problems of finding a good residential community did not arise. There was a functioning, thinking network: he was at a good EBD school, had a three-year Supervision Order from the court, which gave time to work, and had a good, involved social worker. His family moved a distance away but, with joint planning, Matthew stayed with his grand-mother through the week, sustaining attendance at the same school, and went to his father at weekends. Issues arose about leaving school: this is often experienced by adolescents as the school's abandonment of them, although they cannot articulate this, and the temptation is to get oneself thrown out or to leave it before it leaves you. This Matthew tried – and the network contained. He completed his exams successfully.

It is also important that the network be experienced as safe and 'holding' as, in therapy, the young person will inevitably get in touch with the early feelings of victimisation and humiliation that led to the offending beha-viour. Such a time may present a risk of suicide – as does the later stage when the adolescent begins to look at what he has done to others and guilt and shame arise – and a good support structure is essential. Equally, the defences, based on activity, may reassert themselves, as they did originally, to blot out such pain and the risk of further offending ensues. This has to be understood and *not* reacted to in a superego-ish way.

Networks suffer transference and counter-transference processes. All too often, this remains unconscious and damaging. It is *vital*, when working with young perpetrators, that a 'case manager' be appointed to work with the network and help the unconscious become conscious. This needs an experienced person.

When warfare breaks out in the network, or communication stops and unilateral decision-making appears, there seem to be three main processes at work (Horne 1999):

1   individuals in the network identify with and take up the positions of different family members (Kolvin and Trowell 1996). Such identifica-tions polarise – the young person is either viewed as a poor traumatised victim or seen as a dangerous perpetrator; the parents are said to be overwhelmed by their ungrateful evil child or perceived as dreadfully neglectful and abusive. Holding all views together and recognising the transference manifestations is vital.

2   the family system also gets re-enacted in the network – the myths, collusions and strategies for family homeostasis become replayed by all of us.

3   the internal world of the offender patient is realised in the network where we repeat the functions and attitudes of internal objects and freely reinforce unhelpful defences (Davies 1996), principally the drive to activity. This compulsion to act, to *do something*, is commonplace

and, as therapists, we will enrage other services at times by refusing to do this but requesting space to think together. The process of bypassing thought and reflection, after all, is the delinquent and abusing adolescent's prime defence, and he unconsciously tries to make it ours.

There is a paradigm from Transactional Analysis that is very helpful when thinking of networks. It comprises a triangle:

We move around it, not at will but propelled by others, taking up all positions. It is a salutary blow to one's omnipotence to be brought in as a 'rescuer' but quickly to be defined by the network as an 'abuser' (of the child by keeping him in therapy; of colleagues by not being able to say that he is no longer a risk) – and one becomes a victim oneself.

CONCLUSION

Keeping grounded and keeping sane are the two main tasks for the worker with acting-out adolescents. Regular clinical discussion is essential, both for support and survival but also to ensure that we are not seeing only one part of the young person or complying with 'the dictates of the transference' (Wilson 1999). A colleague can provide an oedipal third for reflection, an antidote to primitive pre-oedipal defences and anxieties. Pace and intimacy are important technical issues, and the level at which to take up conflicts (Edgcumbe 1988) is an important aspect of judging these. The impact of developmental deficit, body-based defences and pre-verbal trauma should inform our assessment and work, and a developmental and psychoanalytic framework is essential. Most importantly, 'thought not action' is the key for patient and psychotherapist – creating space for thinking and reflection.

Epilogue

A year on, Matthew's 'delinquent group' had become a social group. All were in work and the group included girls – opening up issues of sexuality in therapy. A sense of responsibility was a strong feature of his functioning. He dared to ask if there might be any flexibility when he is in work – could I still see him but at a later time? – a big risk, to ask for something, and on my letting him know that this was possible he promptly missed the next session (a telephone call –'I've lost my train fare!'). Intimacy continued to take careful negotiation.

References

Alvarez, A. (1992) *Live Company: Psychoanalytic Psychotherapy with Autistic, Borderline, Deprived and Abused Children*. London and New York: Tavistock/Routledge

Alvarez, A. (1996) 'Addressing the element of deficit in children with autism: psychotherapy which is both psychoanalytically and developmentally informed' *Clinical Child Psychology and Psychiatry* 1(4): 525–37

Campbell, D. (1994) 'Breaching the shame shield: thoughts on the assessment of adolescent child sexual abusers' *Journal of Child Psychotherapy* 20 (3): 309–26

Davies, R. (1996) 'The inter-disciplinary network and the internal world of the offender'. In C. Cordess and M. Cox (eds.), *Forensic Psychotherapy: Crime, Psychodynamics and the Offender Patient*, vol. II, *Mainly Practice*. London: Jessica Kingsley

Edgcumbe, R. (1988) 'Formulation of interpretations in clinical work with adolescents'. Unpublished paper given at the Institute of Psycho-analysis, London, October

Fonagy, P. and Target, M. (1996) 'A contemporary psychoanalytical perspective: psychodynamic developmental therapy'. In E. Hibbs and P. Jensen (eds.), *Psychosocial Treatments for Child and Adolescent Disorders*. Washington, DC: American Psychological Association

Glasser, M. (1979) 'Some aspects of the role of aggression in the perversions'. In I. Rosen (ed.), *Sexual Deviation*, 2nd edn. Oxford: Oxford University Press

Glasser, M. (1996) 'Aggression and sadism in the perversions'. In I. Rosen (ed.), *Sexual Deviation*, 3rd edn. Oxford: Oxford University Press

Glasser, M. (1998) 'On violence: a preliminary communication' *International Journal of Psychoanalysis* 79 (5): 887–902

Horne, A. (1999) 'Sexual abuse and sexual abusing in childhood and adolescence'. In M. Lanyado and A. Horne (eds.), *The Handbook of Child and Adolescent Psychotherapy: Psychoanalytic Perspectives*. London: Routledge

Hurry, A. (1998) 'Psychoanalysis and developmental therapy' In Hurry (ed.), *Psychoanalysis and Developmental Therapy*. London: Karnac

Kolvin, I. and Trowell, J. (1996) 'Child sexual abuse'. In I. Rosen (ed.), *Sexual Deviation*, 3rd edn. Oxford: Oxford University Press

Lanyado, M., Hodges, J., Bentovim, A. *et al.* (1995) 'Understanding boys who sexually abuse other children: a clinical illustration' *Psychoanalytic Psychotherapy* 9 (3): 231–42

Loewald, H. W. (1960) 'On the therapeutic action of psychoanalysis' *International Journal of Psycho-Analysis* 41: 16–33

Parsons, M. and Dermen, S. (1999) 'The violent child and adolescent'. In Lanyado, M. and Horne, A. (eds.), *The Handbook of Child and Adolescent Psychotherapy: Psychoanalytic Perspectives*. London: Routledge

Symington, N. (1980) 'The response aroused by the psychopath' *International Review of Psycho-Analysis* 7(3): 291–8

Welldon, E. (1988) *Mother, Madonna, Whore: the Idealisation and Denigration of Motherhood.* London: Free Association Books

Wilson, P. (1999) 'Delinquency'. In M. Lanyado and A. Horne (eds.), *The Handbook of Child and Adolescent Psychotherapy: Psychoanalytic Perspectives.* London: Routledge

Winnicott, D. W. (1956) 'The anti-social tendency'. In Winnicott, *Collected Papers: Through Paediatrics to Psychoanalysis.* London: Hogarth Press, 1975

Winnicott, D. W. (1962) 'The aims of psycho-analytic treatment'. In Winnicott (1965), *The Maturational Processes and the Facilitating Environment.* London: Hogarth Press

Winnicott, D. W. (1963a) 'Psychotherapy of character disorders'. In Winnicott, *The Maturational Processes and the Facilitating Environment.* London: Hogarth Press

Winnicott, D. W. (1963b) 'Hospital care supplementing intensive psychotherapy in adolescence'. In Winnicott, *The Maturational Processes and the Facilitating Environment.* London: Hogarth Press

10   Narcissistic illusions in late adolescence

Defensive Kleinian retreats or Winnicottian opportunities?

Juliet Hopkins

This chapter describes the development and gradual dissolution of narcissistic illusions, characterised by idealisation, grandiosity and merger, in the psychotherapy of Roberta, an 18-year-old girl.

Two different traditions regarding the understanding and treatment of narcissism originated in London. Klein and her followers (e.g. Steiner 1993) have understood illusions of self-importance to be defensive retreats from acute ambivalence that require immediate, active interpretation. Winnicott (1952, 1954) too accepted the defensive aspect of such illusions, but also believed that the regression to a transitional relationship to the therapist which they represented provided a developmental opportunity to 'unfreeze' previous developmental failures. This view, supported by Milner (1955) and Bollas (1987), leads to a more facilitating, less challenging, technical approach. Roberta's therapy was conducted according to the Winnicottian tradition and aims to illustrate its effectiveness.

REFERRAL AND BACKGROUND

Roberta was the second of three daughters born to parents who were national celebrities in the world of television. She sought help for depression and for a distressing feeling that she could never be satisfied. I found her to be a beautiful, vivacious adolescent of 18, fashionably and seductively dressed. Her account of herself was articulate and sensational and I was surprised to learn that she was training to be nothing more glamorous than a nurse.

Most of the details of Roberta's history emerged during the first year of her therapy. She wanted to achieve a coherent picture of a childhood fraught with conflicting experiences of adoration and rejection and of sexuality and violence.

Roberta had been her mother's favourite, a status which she had enjoyed because it protected her from the worst excesses of mother's violent rages, and which she had regretted because she had had to bear the brunt of mother's cloying need for admiration and caresses. Mother's impatience with her children and her need to pursue her glittering career meant that the children were cared for by a series of live-in nannies and were sent to boarding school from the age of 5 years. Father could be more nurturing than mother but he was very seldom available.

The parents' marriage was always stormy and sometimes violent. Roberta was allowed to sleep between them until she was 6. She harboured the fantasy that they would divorce and each marry her. She grew up wanting sexual relationships with both her parents and was surprised to discover that not everybody did. However, she was sure that her main reason to sleep with them had been in order not to be forgotten, since, for both her parents, to be out of sight was to be out of mind.

When Roberta was 15 her parents each revealed their possession of a lover and decided to get divorced. Roberta had come to believe that she was indispensable to her mother and she was outraged by her betrayal. She moved away to live with her father and his mistress in an extreme of vengeful hatred and vowed never to see her mother again, a vow which she had kept throughout the three years which had since elapsed.

THE DEVELOPMENT OF NARCISSISTIC ILLUSIONS

Roberta entered therapy three times a week with excitement. She allowed herself immediately to regress and to experience herself as a small child alone with a perfectly empathic parent. She seemed destined to be an ideal patient. Her material was always presented clearly and helpfully. She accepted deep interpretations and thought between sessions about what I had said. It seemed natural to her to suppose that while I fed her on therapy she was providing me with a delectable meal. From what she told me, as a child, she had worked assiduously to be a devoted 'carer-giver' to both her parents and her decision to become a nurse was an extension of this role. Within the therapeutic setting she clearly aimed to be my perfect daughter, to make me feel well loved as mother and brilliant as a therapist. She did this so successfully that I found myself reciprocating her idealisation. I could not help but find her 'special' and for a while our relationship resembled that between a doting parent and adoring child.

Roberta told me that she had always experienced her mother's kisses and touches as sexual. My words were soon experienced sexually by her too and she declared herself to be 'in love'. Her initial experience of therapy as mutual feeding became extended to experience it as 'marriage' and any threats to its continuation as 'divorce'. Although she was afraid of being overwhelmed by her homosexual feelings for me and always kept them carefully controlled, she somehow used them to emphasise her love for me rather than to make me feel in danger of being seduced. I supported this intention. For example, when she reported a dream of caressing my breasts, I emphasised her need for maternal care, rather than her wish to excite me.

Roberta expressed relief that, unlike her mother, I did not need to be excited. She claimed that when she was with me she felt safer than ever before.

It gradually emerged that Roberta's experience of safety with me was in part related to a grandiose illusion of unwarranted importance in my life. She was convinced that she was my only adult patient and that I could not possibly be married, otherwise I would not be able to give her such devoted attention. She basked in the certainty of our mutual love and assumed that I always felt exactly as she did. She also assumed that I always dressed with her in mind: clothes which she liked were selected to please her while other clothes were selected to stimulate her competitiveness. I later discovered that her grandiosity had reached the point of illusory merger with me when I stumbled across her unquestioned assumption that through therapy she was becoming a therapist; this preconscious conviction conflicted with her actual knowledge of the demands of training.

The start of Roberta's psychotherapy coincided with the start of a relationship with a new boyfriend, Tony, whom she later married. The most striking aspect of Tony's entry into Roberta's life was that I heard astonishingly little about him. Roberta did not believe that she could be special to both of us at once, just as it had seemed impossible to be special to both her parents together. She was convinced that, if she told me about Tony, I would be so overcome with envy and jealousy that I would destroy their relationship. Since I appeared not to mind, she thought I was either hiding my fury, or that I judged the relationship with Tony to be beneath contempt. She was unable to speak of her love for Tony for almost a year. Then I learned that she felt safe with him because he worshipped her and would always put her first in his life. It seemed that she felt that security was only possible through idealisation.

TECHNIQUE

In the early stages of therapy I did not try to modify Roberta's idealisation of our relationship, as I relied upon time and the disappointments of the analytic relationship to begin this for me. However, I did not always accept her illusions entirely either, but adopted a slightly quizzical approach, intended to help Roberta realise that I did not necessarily take her assumptions for granted.

It seemed that Roberta had been waiting for exactly this opportunity. Winnicott (1954) described this situation when he wrote, 'it is as if there is an expectation that favourable conditions may arise justifying regression and offering a new chance for forward development, that which was rendered impossible or difficult initially by environmental failure'. In the same paper he observed that in 'the return to early dependence . . . the patient and the setting merge into the original success situation of primary narcissism' (1954: 281). By this Winnicott meant that the patient returned to the period of development when the infant does not yet reliably distinguish between himself and the environment, that is between himself and the mother. It became a striking feature of Roberta's therapy that in certain aspects of our relationship, particularly with regard to emotions, she failed to distinguish between us; she developed an illusion of sameness, even of merger, within the transference. Winnicott used the term 'transitional' to describe the intermediate state between subjectivity and objectivity in which neither predominates. The illusion of merger could thus be understood as representing a self-created or transitional relationship to me as a subjective object (Winnicott 1969); surprisingly this co-existed with a more objective capacity to perceive me and my work, for at the same time she could show herself aware of some of my actual qualities and be able to make good use of interpretation. For example, she brought the subjective and objective strikingly together when I told her of the first holiday break. 'How can we possibly change from lovers to patient and therapist!' she tearfully exclaimed. At that moment she clearly expressed an awareness of both the illusion and the reality.

The benefits of allowing the development of illusion have been described by Milner (1955) in her account of the analysis of an 11-year-old boy. She describes the benefits of allowing him to use her as a transitional object. She felt that it was necessary for this boy both to experience and to become conscious of the need for fusion with her before he could relinquish this satisfaction and experience the relief of disillusion; this was a necessary therapeutic development because in his infancy he had experienced 'a too sudden breaking in on the illusion of oneness', so that he had had to adapt to the demands of external reality too soon. Her paper implies that it is technically important to allow the patient the unchallenged freedom to create the illusion of oneness, and not to press for acknowledgement of twoness until the patient shows signs of initiating this development himself. The reliable relief provided by the unchallenged illusion of oneness helps to make possible the subsequent toleration of twoness. As Winnicott wrote, 'disillusionment implies the successful provision of opportunities for illusion' (1952: 221).

Roberta's spontaneous recovery from one aspect of her illusion of oneness occurred early in the second year of therapy, when the repeated painful experiences of my holidays took effect. She realised that I might not be single but probably had a family of my own. In the context of this development I felt able to become more active in challenging her illusions and exploring more of their role in her relationships, as the following sections illustrate.

UNDERSTANDING THE NARCISSISTIC ILLUSIONS

Roberta's illusions can be understood paradoxically as having both defensive and developmental functions.

a Narcissistic illusions as defensive attempts to evade anxiety and to achieve security

Exploration of the function of Roberta's narcissistic illusions revealed that they were both a way of protecting her from the anxieties inherent in two- and three-person relationships and her chief means of ensuring the security of her parents' love. By imagining herself to be in sole possession of my love, Roberta avoided all competition with rivals. By imagining that we were the same, she avoided all rivalry with me. Roberta was very aware of the intense sexual rivalry which she had experienced with her mother and her older sister, and she dreaded repeating it with me. The illusory trans-ference successfully protected her from all the conflicts inherent in the three-person oedipal situation. It was the anxieties belonging to two-person relationships that became the first focus of our work.

Roberta was easily made aware of how her illusory transference pro-tected her from the anxieties which threatened to ruin her two-person relationships: 'either too little or too much'. By this Roberta meant the dread, on the one hand, of separation and rejection, and on the other, of exploitation and suffocation.

Roberta's terror of 'too little' was extreme. She could not tolerate being alone. In daily life she contrived to prevent this eventuality arising, but when it did she played the radio loudly to fill the void. In her memory, her parents alternately indulged and banished her, treating her at one moment like a princess, and at the next, relegating her to the nursery. The experience of being sent to boarding school at the age of 5 had been a final confirma-tion of Roberta's equation of separation with rejection. My holidays repeatedly re-aroused in her the desperate sense of being unwanted that she had suffered at boarding school.

It seemed that Roberta had been unable to achieve a normal degree of separation from her parents in childhood because the intense ambivalence which they aroused had prevented her from internalising representations of them as helpful people. She continued to depend for her sense of well-being on the physical availability of a caring adult. However, unlike her parents, I was in touch with her feelings, held her in mind, and gradually achieved with her a coherent picture of her history. As she felt understood and internalised by me, she began to internalise me herself. This meant that she was gradually able to relinquish the need to idealise and merge with me and was able to trust me with her hate. At first she risked hating me only for my absences, then for the inequality of our relationship, and only when she had discovered that I survived her hatred without retaliation did she allow herself the extremes of hatred with which therapy was to end.

Roberta's growing ability to internalise me helped to mitigate her fears of 'too little'. However, there was always a fine balance in the transference between the risks of 'too little' and 'too much'. If I said anything to indicate that her therapy might continue beyond the two years which she had decided to undertake, she was liable to be overcome with a fit of choking. She felt suffocated by my imagined need for her. She compared the ordeal with me to the daily hour she used to spend watching her mother bath before dinner. At these times she felt trapped, exploited and compelled to meet her mother's needs for flattery, caresses and massage. She dared not leave for fear of her mother's fragility and for fear of her violence. It must always have felt dangerous to frustrate the narcissistic needs of a mother whose murderous hatred could break through into violence unless she were charmed into the illusion of mutual adoration on which she fed. Roberta had developed social skills of charm, tact and empathy which enabled her to play her parents' game, to pander to their narcissistic needs and to be rewarded by moments of exclusive intimacy. In therapy her illusory infatuation allowed her to enjoy this security with me when she needed it, while at other times she was available to do interpretative work on the dangers of feeling sufficiently separate from me to risk 'too little or too much'. Within 18 months she became able to tolerate being alone at home and lost her symptom of choking in therapy.

The illusion of acquiring my skills as a therapist through merger was found to be a repetition of similar illusions which Roberta had developed with regard to both her parents. She had always thought of her mother as a sister and an equal and it came as a great shock to her to realise that she and I were of different generations. Likewise, she had previously believed that she had acquired her parents' most admired qualities simply through identification with them. It came as another shock to her to realise in therapy that she did not share their fame and status. It was Roberta's illusion that parental qualities could be acquired through merger which seemed to explain her life-long learning difficulties. She had supposed that she could acquire knowledge and success simply by being her parents' child. Consequently, in spite of high intelligence, she had failed to learn to read until the age of 11 years, and she had always done poorly at school. In therapy, Roberta realised with fury that she would have to work to obtain a degree before she could train as a therapist. She said she felt 'damned' and 'blown to bits'. Clearly, her identification with me, as with her parents, had protected her from intense feelings of envy and deprivation.

Not only had Roberta harboured unconscious illusions about sharing her parents' achievements and fame, she had also developed a conscious illusion about possessing her father's penis. Since latency Roberta had been aware of feeling bisexual and had imagined that she could change her sex by changing her clothes. When dressed in slacks she felt male and visualised her father's penis as part of her own body. Then she felt free, confident, outspoken and sexually powerful in ways which matched her childhood picture of her father's vaunted sexuality.

It seemed that father had contributed to this illusion by regarding Roberta in some ways as his only son, named after himself. The illusion may also have developed as a defence against her father's extremely sensuous relationship with her. Even when she was a teenager they still regularly bathed together, 'as chaps' father said.

When Roberta described her experience of intercourse her language conveyed that she experienced her lover's genitals as her own. Confrontation with this illusion led Roberta to abandon it. She lost the capacity to feel that she possessed her father's penis and she felt extremely angry with me for depriving her of it. This meant that she could no longer believe that Tony's penis was her own and she was sure that she would never enjoy sex so much again. But in spite of discovering intense penis envy, she gradually found that there were also rewards in making love as a woman.

At the end of her first year of therapy Roberta became aware of further aspects of the illusion of merger when for the first time she experienced Tony's kisses as coming from him and expressing his love. She then realised that she had previously experienced his kisses as if Tony were giving her own love back to her, just as during sex she had always felt she gave herself her own orgasm. This development followed work in the transference which had revealed that she experienced my love exclusively as a response to her own. She clearly had had no belief in the existence of her mother's spontaneous affection for her, but had always felt that she herself had had to initiate it. She once described her mother as a bottomless jug which she had had to fill up continuously in order to be sure that there would be just enough left inside for herself. By endlessly providing her mother with love in order to gain some for herself, she maintained the illusion of omnipotent control and evaded dependency while also eliciting her mother's love.

Throughout this period of work the needs of Roberta's parents for her collusion with their illusions was supported by numerous anecdotes. Both parents emerged as fragile people who depended upon their celebrity status for their self-esteem. Their ostentatious lifestyle featured in the media and they regarded themselves and their daughters as extremely special people. Roberta seems to have discovered that the only way of holding their benevolent attention was to share their illusions; there was security in unity, even if illusory.

In the course of therapy Roberta was surprised to discover that I did not need to be idealised and that I could reliably maintain contact with her through a range of moods. Envy, jealousy and hatred were particularly hard for her to share since she could not expect a parent-figure to tolerate the expression of such feelings towards themselves. Without the protection of mutual idealisation Roberta lamented that she felt 'abandoned' and 'orphaned' in the transference and fearful that I would end her therapy. Such anxieties are usual when patients are threatened with the loss of familiar, though pathological, means of feeling safely in contact with parents. Attachment theory explains why it can feel so dangerous to relinquish such 'secondary security' (Main 1995) which developed in childhood because actual security with emotionally available parents was unavailable. For a small child loss of emotional contact with parents is felt to threaten survival. Roberta's dreams at this time were full of life-threatening disasters.

b Narcissistic illusions with gratifying and developmental functions.

When Winnicott (1954) wrote of the regressed patient's capacity to return to the original success situation of primary narcissism, he emphasised the gratification which derived from the patient's capacity to recapture the early satisfaction of feeling at one with the environment. Roberta's great pleasure in her use of me certainly led me to believe that she must have found much satisfaction in her earliest relationship to her mother. She had apparently felt herself to be adored and had also had much physical satisfaction from cuddling and caresses.

Winnicott described how regression is used, not only to return to pregenital success situations, but also to return to developmental *impasse* which occurred because of environmental failure. Such failures can result in a 'freezing of the failure situation' until a new environment gives hope that the original experience may be repeated 'in an environment which is making adequate adaptation'. I believe that Roberta used her regression with me in an attempt to deconstruct or 'unfreeze' her paranoid, vengeful relationship to her mother. In the transference she re-entered the transitional relationship in order to enjoy for the first time, without the intrusion of her mother's demands for excitement and admiration, the close support which she had experienced only episodically in childhood. While she loyally repeated the mutual idealisation which had been the only means she knew to maintain contact with both her parents, she was simultaneously excited by her awareness of my difference from her parents – by my reliability, my respect for honesty and my capacity to hold her in mind. She was able to use interpretation to feel deeply cared about and understood in a way that, for a while at least, she experienced as genuinely ideal (Alvarez 1992).

When a patient uses a therapist as a transitional object (Winnicott 1951) it is interesting to know what sort of transitional object, if any, the patient had employed in infancy. Roberta had no knowledge of having used any special object in babyhood, but from very early in childhood she remembered 'being addicted to' her mother's empty scent bottle. She comforted herself by holding it to her nose. She had taken this uncuddly object with her to boarding school 'to keep the glamour alive'. Through its faint trace of smell, the scent bottle must have allowed Roberta to feel merged with her mother, which protected her from any awareness of the hatred associated with her mother's glamorous life through which she repeatedly abandoned and neglected her children. Instead of being able to pass through the transitional phase to establish a life which was increasingly independent of her mother, she had remained fixated on an idealised, glamorous, empty relationship. The therapeutic relationship provided her with a renewed opportunity to use dependence in order to move into independence.

Balint (1968) has made a valuable distinction between benign and malignant uses of regression in psychoanalysis. He considered a patient's use of regression to be benign when it was used for purposes of recognition, that is for enabling the analyst to recognise and verbalise significant aspects of the patient's internal problems. This enabled the patient to make a 'new beginning' and to recover. However, a patient's use of regression was considered to be malignant when its prime aim was to seek gratification. Such use was, in general, associated with demands for gratification by external action, with the development of addiction-like states and with signs of severe hysteria.

There is no doubt that, in Balint's terms, Roberta's use of regression was predominantly benign. She used it not only for the recognition of internal conflicts but also for the recognition of certain 'self-states' (Bollas 1987) which her parents had apparently ignored or denied. In particular, she had no experience of sharing calm and peaceful states of mind, whether of satisfaction or of boredom. 'Togetherness' in her family had always been associated with intimacy, excitement, drama and violence. In particular, as therapy progressed, she liked to share with me an unintegrated state which she called 'feeling scattered'. This involved lying silent for long periods while she enjoyed feeling held and letting her mind wander. Typically the silence ended in the emergence of a memory, often of some childhood contact with her mother's body. Apart from discovering the benefits of allowing herself the freedom to feel scattered, Roberta also discovered that it was possible to feel fully alive in my presence without feeling excited. In her family, she claimed, being alive and being excited had always been synonymous. She found it a great relief to discover that this need not be so. In this way she supported Bollas' (1987) finding that 'regression to dependence allows a person to form important insights from within the self via fundamentally intra-subjective means'.

While Roberta used me as an ideal mother she experienced her relationship to her own estranged mother as increasingly persecuting; she felt herself to be continuously contaminated and tortured by her preoccupation with her. As Searles (1956) described, intense vengefulness can actually be a means of keeping a relationship alive. Slowly, Roberta began to mourn both for the loved aspects of her mother whom she had lost, and for what her mother had never been able to give her; she relinquished much of her vengeance. She became aware of wanting to see her mother again and a reconciliation took place. Roberta was pleased to discover that she could use her attachment to Tony to create and maintain a necessary distance from her mother, while remaining on friendly terms. In this and other ways to be described, Roberta successfully justified the optimism which her idealisation had conveyed.

FURTHER ASPECTS OF DISILLUSIONMENT: TOWARDS
BECOMING A SEPARATE PERSON

As therapy progressed into its second year, Roberta's need to feel merged
with me lessened. She began to imagine me with a family and to notice
more about me. These changes made me feel able to confront her more
directly. For example, I questioned her assumption that I always felt the
same as she did. Roberta agreed that I might not do so, but was panic-
stricken to realise that she actually did not know what I felt. A few sessions
later she had reverted to the comfort of her earlier assumption.

None of her illusions was surrendered easily. Each one was reinstated
and had to be confronted again and again. Each confrontation led Roberta
to express hatred towards me for humiliating her and to renewed attempts
to create idealisation by other means. When she failed to produce the
tranquillising security of mutual idealisation, then Roberta resorted to the
drama and excitement associated with disaster or violence. She was aware
that such excitement provided a 'fix' and was better than the boredom and
frustration associated with disillusionment. She began to assault Tony and
to bring me sensational accounts of her cruelty to him. I understood this as
an attempt both to excite me into violence towards her, and to expose me to
her own childhood experience of being the passive witness of terrifying
scenes of violence. Roberta was horrified to discover her sadism but
experienced her destructiveness as her most authentic emotion.

Disillusionment was not only furthered by confrontation through interpretation. There were many other ways in which Roberta's illusions were
shattered.

My holidays have already been mentioned. In anticipation of each
holiday Roberta was tearful and worried about how she would cope, feeling
as though once again she was being forced to live a separate existence at
boarding school. During my absence she suffered from fears and night-
mares, particularly of my death. On my return she experienced acute ambivalence, which often left her trembling. She was simultaneously delighted to
be back, reassured by physical contact with the couch, bitterly tearful,
longing to punch me and furious that it was necessary to tell me what had
happened in my absence because I did not know. Her responses to reunion
provide a classic example of the 'anxious ambivalent' type of attachment,
observed by Ainsworth (1983) in infants as young as 12 months of age. Such
infants had had highly inconsistent mothering. Subsequently Main and
Hesse (1990) have shown that when an infant's experience of mothering has
been not only very inconsistent but also frightening, the infant at 12 months
shows features of extreme disorganisation under stress. As development
proceeds, the child is liable to react by becoming controlling of the parent,
either in a care-giving or in a coercive, punitive way. Roberta had mastered
both these techniques. The tender care-giving of her early response to me
was supplemented by coercive threats to punish and abandon me during the

last year of her therapy. Main's findings suggest that it was an underlying terror of disorganisation or disintegration which maintained Roberta's pursuit of intimacy.

Apart from my holidays which temporarily forced Roberta to become fully aware of my separate existence, Roberta was also very disillusioned by having flu and discovering that I did not come to nurse her. On another occasion she was shocked to realise that I must have colleagues who might be more important to me than she. But the deepest blow to Roberta's narcissism was experienced in the second year of therapy when I refused to come to her wedding.

The prospect of marriage had been used by her in therapy as an alternative exclusive relationship and an ever-ready means of escape, since Tony opposed her treatment. Roberta was adamant that I should come to the wedding ceremony to give her emotional support. She found it utterly unbelievable that I should refuse to attend this high society event which she had intended to 'enrich and enliven my life'. When at last it was clear that I would not move from my professional role, she lamented tearfully that she would never be able to feel loved by me again.

Roberta planned all the details of her wedding herself. While listening to her elaborate plans I told her that I felt like an onlooker of a game of 'Let's pretend'. This made her shocked to realise that the wedding was actually going to happen. She recognised that her plans felt exactly like the dolls-house games about an ideal family which she had played with her sisters in childhood. It seemed likely that Roberta had kept alive her capacity to enjoy transitional experiences in her play with her sisters, to whom she had felt very close in her parents' many absences. When arranging the wedding Roberta tried once again to make her imaginary world triumph over the vagaries of her family, and she was repeatedly disillusioned when they would not play the parts which she allotted to them. The disadvantages of illusion became painfully clear to her.

After her honeymoon Roberta constantly lamented that she had become 'nothing but a patient' and could not be 'my daughter' any more. Her hatred and anger towards me increased steadily during the last 15 months of treatment. She had finally realised that the overall effect of therapy was to make her feel increasingly ordinary, when she had intended that it would make her feel increasingly special. She was appalled that I had appeared to offer her both a psychotherapy training and an exclusive intimate relationship, but instead had relegated her to the mere rank of patient. She suspected that I took pleasure in destroying her grandiosity, and felt that I would rejoice to hear that she was overcome with humiliation when she realised for the first time, on boarding a bus, that she was as ordinary as everyone else on board. She also finally realised that I did not dress for her and accepted that I did not necessarily feel the same as she did about everything she told me. These disillusionments made her feel that 'all the shine' had gone out of our relationship and that I had made her feel perpetually 'scratchy and itchy'. These adjectives suggested that we were now experienced as separate but still touching, in a hostile way.

Now that Roberta was convinced that I had lured her into therapy on false pretences, she assumed that after seducing her I would abandon her as her mother had done. If we were entirely separate then rejection must surely follow. She threatened to leave first, but then resorted to another ploy in her attempt to re-establish the illusion of intimacy to which she was still partly addicted. She took a job which necessitated appointments after work. It emerged that she was sure that I would meet this need by seeing her in my home where she felt sure I must have a consulting room. A dream revealed that she intended moving into my bed, just as she had done between her parents. However, in order to meet her demands for new times I reduced her sessions temporarily to twice a week. Roberta threatened to terminate immediately, but she reluctantly decided to continue for another six months. Although so furious she felt terrified of managing without me.

Throughout the remaining period of therapy Roberta recurrently insisted that she was leaving me because I would not see her in my home; it was clearly up to me to accommodate her if I wanted to keep her. Although Roberta's demands for intimacy within the transference had seemed like the need of a deprived child for a period of indulgence, Roberta's demands for the intimacy of my home became a most intrusive imposition and an example of the malignant use of regression that Balint described. Roberta herself recognised these demands as a sign of her own intrusiveness, insatiability and addiction to exclusive relationships. Perhaps they can also be seen as her means of stage-managing her move to freedom by giving herself sufficient reason to hate me.

After she found that I would not see her in my home, Roberta made no further attempts to re-establish her narcissistic illusions. She was surprised to discover that it was possible to sustain moments of what she called 'authentic intimacy' in which she experienced close rapport while yet acknowledging herself to be a patient among other patients. However, such moments were rare, for her anger with me predominated. Termination was experienced as a mutual rejection and as a sign of our mutual hatred. She accused me of having seduced her and masturbated her but never having loved her. Leaving was a way of protecting me from her murderous hatred, but also a way of depriving me of the satisfaction of having a long-term patient. She experienced her termination as abortion and knew that she wished to destroy my work and to triumph over me. At last her sexual rivalry was flagrantly displayed.

The positive function of this phase of destructive attack on the analyst has been described by Winnicott (1969). He believed that it was the patient's destructiveness, combined with the analyst's capacity to survive it, which enabled the patient to relinquish the analyst as a transitional object and to use him constructively as a separate person in shared reality. The changes which she made do indicate that she had achieved this.

In spite of her hatred, destructiveness and despair, Roberta continued to retain a positive picture of what had been achieved. She had believed it to be impossible to feel both happy and ordinary, but now, both in her marriage and at work, she found that this was so. She became able to tolerate being separate from Tony, was much less dominating towards him and sometimes allowed him to take control in intercourse. More important, she had lost her perpetual sense of dissatisfaction. This, as she said, was nothing to do with sexual fulfilment, but with the capacity to be separate, to tolerate being alone and to feel free from the pressure to create idealised relationships. The depression, which had dogged her whenever idealisation failed, had gone. In spite of all her fury and disappointment, I was surprised to find that Roberta continued to feel grateful for what I had helped her to achieve.

Roberta opened her last session with a gift of flowers and ended it with a wish to vomit to ruin my room for other patients. Her farewell openly displayed the intense ambivalence from which her narcissism had protected her. She had relinquished her initial need of me as a transitional object and had allowed a genuine encounter which had enabled her to recognise and accept her separate existence, to sustain it outside the context of our immediate relationship and so to achieve the possibility of feeling satisfied.

CONCLUSION

The course of Roberta's treatment bears out the belief of both Kleinians and Winnicottians that narcissistic illusions serve as a defence against ambivalence; as Roberta's illusions diminished so her ambivalence in the transference increased. Naturally, it is impossible to know whether a Kleinian technique, involving immediate interpretation of the narcissistic transference, would have been therapeutically more effective. I have simply aimed to illustrate the value of Winnicott's approach. It seems to have been important to allow the narcissistic transference to flourish long enough to begin its own spontaneous dissolution since this approach provided time in which to explore the source of the transference in family relationships and to utilise its optimism to revitalise development. Immediate interpretation of its defensive aspects would have spared Roberta the repetition of the experience of seduction at the cost of failing to understand her apparent initial seduction by her parents and the role which her attachment to them as internal representations still played in perpetuating the need for her illusions. Perhaps Roberta's impressive capacity to use therapy may also have been in part a repetition: the repetition of relationships with certain nannies whom Roberta at first discounted (as her parents had done) but whom she acknowledged had enabled her to recognise some of her parents' failings and had shown a respect for reality which her parents appear to have lacked.

References

Ainsworth, M. (1983) 'Patterns of infant–mother attachment as related to maternal care'. In D. Magnusson and V. Allen (eds.), *Human Development: An Interactional Perspective*. New York: Academic Press, pp. 35–55

Alvarez, A. (1992) *Live Company*. London/New York: Tavistock/Routledge

Balint, M. (1968) *The Basic Fault: Therapeutic Aspects of Regression*. London: Tavistock Publications

Bollas, C. (1987) *The Shadow of the Object: Psychoanalysis of the Unthought Known*. London: Free Association Books

Main, M. and Hesse, E. (1990) 'Parents' unresolved traumatic experiences are related to infant disorganised attachment status: is frightened and/or frightening parental behaviour the linking mechanism?' In M. T. Greenberg, D. Cicchetti and E. M. Cummings (eds.), *Attachment in the Preschool Years*. Chicago: University of Chicago Press, pp. 161–82

Main, M. (1995) 'Recent studies in attachment'. In S. Goldberg, R. Muir and J. Kerr (eds.), *Attachment Theory: Social, Developmental and Clinical Perspectives*. Hillsdale, NJ: Analytic Press

Milner, M. (1955) 'The role of illusion in symbol formation', Chapter 5 in M. Klein *et al.* (eds.), *New Directions in Psycho-analysis*. London: Tavistock Publications

Searles, H. (1956) 'The psychodynamics of vengefulness'. In Searles, *Collected Papers on Schizophrenia and Related Subjects*. New York: International Universities Press, pp. 171–91

Steiner, J. (1993) *Psychic Retreats*. The New Library of Psychoanalysis 19. London and New York: Routledge

Winnicott, D. W. (1951) 'Transitional objects and transitional phenomena'. In Winnicott (1958), *Collected Papers: Paediatrics to Psychoanalysis*. London: Tavistock Publications, pp. 229–42

Winnicott, D. W. (1952) 'Psychoses and childcare'. In Winnicott, *Collected Papers*

Winnicott, D. W. (1954) 'Metapsychological and clinical aspects of regression within the psychoanalytic set-up'. In Winnicott, *Collected Papers*

Winnicott, D. W. (1969) 'The use of an object and relating through identification' *International Journal of Psychoanalysis* 50, Part 4: 711–16

11 There is no such thing as an adolescent

Teresa Bailey

INTRODUCTION

It is perhaps rather clichéd to adapt Donald Winnicott's statement that 'There is no such thing as an infant', but it is an important idea to keep in mind when working with children. They do not exist in isolation, separate and independent. They come with parents, carers, significant adult figures and siblings. We should add that there is no such thing as a toddler, a child, or an adolescent, as their parents are always present in our work, even if we are working alone with the child.

Most child psychotherapists today would not consider working individually with a child unless the child's parents or carers were being worked with in parallel. This has not always been the case, but is the norm now. The aims are to support the child's individual therapy; to help parents/carers see the vital role they have in the child's treatment; to help them think about what is going on for them as they are excluded from the process going on between their child and the psychotherapist. In the past, psychiatric social workers would have done this skilled and important work. Now, we rely on our child psychotherapy colleagues, if we have them, or on other members of the multi-disciplinary team.

Parents are not born parents, they are made into them by having children and some adults find the roles thrust upon them become increasingly demanding as their children grow up. They cannot remain fixed as parents of, say, a 2-year-old, when their daughter is 16. Parents have to redefine their ideas, their identity as parents, as their children develop, just as their adolescents have to as they negotiate their way into adulthood.

The move from puberty into adolescence is a normal, natural process that does not need to be turbulent or traumatic. However, the work I will be presenting here will examine how and where things can go awry, sometimes badly.

Families are not always prepared for the pain of separation, of having to re-negotiate what was a familiar relationship and adjust their positions within the family. Sadness, nostalgia, loss may be turned into aggression and anger, attempts to hold on to something that has to be let go. It can feel unfair that the things of childhood have to be given up both by parents and their children. Perhaps little thought is given to the parents of young adolescents. It is as if they were silent and helpless observers of the drama of puberty and the teenage years. Yet, this stage of their children's lives can be painful and wrenching.

Some parents underestimate the need their children still have of them in the teenage years, expecting them to separate quickly and easily, and can be resentful of still being needed. In my work with the parents of adolescents, it is striking how vivid their own teenage years become as their children grow up and how difficult it can be to allow their children to live free from the shadow their own adolescence casts over the family at this time. Those parents who have depended on their relationship with their child may feel very rejected at this time, become depressed and/or wish to retaliate. Couples who have had a common interest in their children but not much else may find themselves facing unresolved relationship difficulties when the child removes himself/herself from the triangle.

Most work undertaken with parents in Child and Adolescent Mental Health Services (CAMHS) involves a therapist seeing parents and children together as a family group, or one clinician seeing the parents while another works with the child. The latter is usually in order to support and maintain the child's therapy. Parents might be seen in order to help them understand difficult and demanding behaviour in their child and find strategies for managing this and their responses to it. It is unusual for the child not to be seen by a clinician separately or at the same time.

A common way of working with the parents of babies and toddlers is through parent–infant psychotherapy, where parent/s and child sit and play in the presence of the therapist who helps them try to understand the experience of what is happening for adults and child and draws attention to the responses of each to the other. Video feedback is also a way of working with parents to let them have some thinking space within their often emotion-laden interactions with the child, where thought can be stampeded by impulses to act and react.

Much of this work is undertaken with the parents of babies, toddlers, and latency-aged children. Work with teenagers, on the other hand, tends to leave the parents aside, as it seems more appropriate, developmentally, to work with the adolescent on his/her own. However, if the teenager who is causing concern refuses to engage in any form of treatment, yet is clearly in difficulties, working with the parents alone may be a possible way of helping the young person. For the parents, it can be a useful way of having support in managing their anxiety, hostility, resentment and distress.

This chapter looks at work with three sets of parents: a lone mother, a lone father, and a separated parental couple. In two of the cases there was a high level of disturbance in the young person. One of the teenagers was receiving treatment separately elsewhere.

For all three sets of parents, their children's adolescence had stirred up unmanageable emotions in them, reawakening many unresolved feelings they still carried from their own adolescence. A common theme in all three cases was intense, uncontainable hostility and impotence engendered in the face of their children's developmentally appropriate ambivalence and anxiety about the move to adulthood.

When both parents and teenagers are going through the same process at the same time, it can be explosive.

WORKING WITH PARENTS OF TEENAGERS

The work that I am going to describe is not like the parent consultation work normally done in clinics, where the parents are seen in order to support the child's therapy. It more resembles parent–infant work.

This is work that involves keeping in mind not just the adolescent, but the adults as parents, and as a parental couple, with their own adolescent histories well to the fore during their children's teenage years. This is similar to Fraiberg *et al.*'s (1980) 'Ghosts in the nursery' but with the adolescent process in mind. Adolescents tend to provoke their parents' superegos and parents are then fearful of others' superegos, especially those of professionals they have contact with. Their own parental objects may be very fierce. The therapist can provide ego support to parents, an ego auxiliary to be alongside when things are difficult, not to advise and reassure but to be present and point out strengths, experience, skills, capacities that can get lost among fears of incompetence and inadequacy.

This type of work requires the therapist to establish and maintain a stance in the consulting room that allows thinking about the parent who is present, the absent parent, the parental couple, and the teenager whose presence is represented powerfully in the parents' minds and filtered through to the therapist via their own anxieties and defences. The room can become very crowded, with echoes of the parents' own histories. The therapist's task is to help unpick tangles, make links, separate out adult and teenage emotions and desires that have become fused into a single mass. She has to try to withstand the onslaught of projections and transference, using counter-transference as a guide to what is going on in the midst of what can be very disturbing work, full of despair.

It is interesting how quickly a triangular space (Britton 1989) can be recreated, even if there is just the therapist and one parent in the room. The existence of the third is always present: the therapist's mind, the adolescent, the absent parent. The therapist's task is to be part of that process but able to observe it too and help the parents step back and observe it as well, without fearing its collapse if they do, or worrying that stepping out of it will exclude them.

A transitional space can be created, a safe platform from which to view the process together. This allows neutrality, the time and room for the introjection of a thinking object, which can lead to ideas about the possibility of change:

> A third position then comes into existence from which object relationships can be observed. Given this, we can also envisage being observed. This provides us with a capacity for seeing ourselves in interaction with others and for entertaining another point of view whilst retaining our own, for reflecting on ourselves whilst being ourselves.
>
> (Britton 1989)

The therapist also has to be aware of and work with the envy of the parent towards her, as the parent imagines the therapist to be a much better parent herself, full of the right ideas, but withholding them from the parent. I have found that parents often expect to be criticised or given advice and can experience the lack of these elements as keeping something from them and secretly condemning them. This is why an alliance between therapist and parent is so essential but if the therapist identifies too much with the parent or the adolescent, the work will stall. It can be an overwhelming positive experience for parents too, not to feel criticised, but understood, and have an experience of a benign (grand) parental object.

Case 1: Ms A and Eve

Ms A was a lone parent who came to the service because she had tried to strangle her teenage daughter. She was horrified that she had got to such a point of desperation. She and her partner had divorced some years earlier but kept in regular contact by phone. Eve, Ms A's daughter, saw her father during the school holidays. Mother and daughter had been very close until Eve reached 15. Ms A said she then realised she was beginning to lose her role as her daughter's ideal companion.

Greenberg (1975) describes adolescence as a phase in which 'the aching void created by the dethronement of the objects is filled by a variety of surrogates'. The fear, too, of the loss of self can be very powerful at this time when 'There is not yet a capacity to identify with parent figures without loss of personal identity' (Winnicott 1963: 244).

Ms A was shocked at her daughter's change in attitude towards her, the challenges to what she had previously accepted without question. Ms A felt pushed aside by Eve's peers and the feelings of rejection that this aroused in her were almost unbearable.

Eve appeared to her mother to be too nonchalant about her schoolwork, obsessed with the Internet. Ms A was baffled and angry that her daughter would sit in her room doing homework while listening to music, texting friends and chatting on the Internet. Ms A feared Eve would fail at her studies and end up destitute. She began to sink into a state of despair and fury, dreading some unavoidable catastrophe ahead of them. This seemed to be far beyond the usual parental anxiety about a child's academic performance. It was only by exploring with Ms A her own experience of adolescence that light could be shed on the fear that consumed her at the prospect of her daughter's separation from her.

Ms A had only recently begun to experience uncontrollable aggressive impulses towards her daughter. These terrified both of them. Yet she clearly loved her daughter and wanted her to be happy – but it was as if she became unable to regulate her emotions towards her daughter. She would be extremely punitive and totally *laissez-faire* by turns. If she felt she had let her daughter get away with something, she wanted to impose an unfeasibly harsh punishment on her for what she felt was Eve's exploitation of her mother's weakness. The level of aggression she felt towards Eve at this time meant that any form of limit setting was felt by Ms A to be an act of sadism. She was unable to disentangle her aggression from her parental right to regulate her child's behaviour, so she swung between harshness and impotence. It was an interesting mirroring of the 'all or nothingness' that is such a feature of adolescence. There is something in the re-working of earlier experiences by the teenager that can provoke within the network and the family around the adolescent primitive defence mechanisms, which cause enormous distress and destructiveness unless they are openly acknowledged and dealt with – not unlike what happens in networks around offenders where the primitive functioning becomes enacted in the network (Davies 1996).

Ms A was an intelligent, articulate, no-nonsense businesswoman, who told me in a matter-of-fact way that she 'knew' she was a bad mother because she hated her daughter. As with the other parents I am presenting in this chapter, she was only too aware of her hostility towards the child who was growing up and learning to separate. It was the loving feelings she had once felt that seemed to have gone for ever, along with her little girl. Ms A sometimes could not bear to be in the same room as Eve. She told me she wanted her to leave home. In fact, she often ordered her out of the house. Ms A was convinced Eve would fail all her GCSEs and end up with nothing. She talked with contempt of her daughter's friends, her musical taste, and her clothes.

When I explored with Ms A what her life had been like when she was a teenager, she told me she had been separated from her parents at the age of 13 and sent to boarding school in another country. This happened because her father died, leaving money for a private education. Her mother sent her away to an exclusive boarding school. I asked about her relationship with her father. Ms A said they used to have fierce rows and that her father had thrown her out of the family home on several occasions and at times would not allow her back in for days on end. When I pointed out to Ms A what she had told me about wanting to throw Eve out of the house, it was a shock to her, but at the same time something of a relief.

Ms A succeeded brilliantly at boarding school. Education proved to be her salvation from loneliness, fear and depression. She threw herself into her work, making it impossible for her to think about the series of losses she had been forced to undergo. Without it, she believed, she would have disintegrated, perhaps taken her own life. Ms A could not believe that Eve would survive if she failed her exams. She envied and resented what she saw as her daughter's casual attitude towards education, her teachers and her homework.

It took some months of work to help Ms A disentangle Eve's life from hers when she was 15. Initially we worked on her acceptance that her daughter's way of studying was different from hers then, gradually, that their lives as teenagers were different. We talked explicitly about the fact that for Eve, becoming a teenager would not mean abandonment, leaving her mother and surviving alone, as it had for Ms A.

As Ms A began to be able to tolerate very painful memories, pressure seemed to lift from her relationship with Eve. Eve did well in her school exams, and won first prize in a maths competition, much to her mother's surprise. Ms A was tearful with pride as she told me of her daughter's success, and said she realised she was not, after all, the terrible mother she thought she was. Their separation, she came to see, did not have to be sudden, final and catastrophic. It was painful for her, as it often is for many parents, but she could still have a good relationship with her daughter, even if it was going to be different from the one they had shared for so many years previously.

For Ms A, adolescence had been a time of death, loss, depression, separation and loneliness. Eve's burgeoning independence struck terror into Ms A, resonating painfully with her own experience of forced separation and premature independence. In an attempt to pre-empt the oncoming disaster, as she saw it, she had tried, unsuccessfully, to eject her daughter from her life. Her envy of her daughter's freedom from responsibility and anxiety, Eve's apparent lack of awareness of her good fortune, as her mother saw it, overwhelmed Ms A, sometimes filling her with feelings of guilt. Her envy, arousing feelings of loss and vulnerability in her own adolescence turned swiftly into anger in an attempt to fend them off. She projected massively onto her daughter and then wanted to destroy what she perceived in her.

With the projections named and understood, Ms A could take them back and gradually Ms A's adolescence receded into the past where it belonged. At the same time, Eve seemed to become more alive in the work. I began to see a clever young girl who was witty, fun, and who loved and looked up to her mother. What Ms A came to realise through the work we did together was how much she loved her daughter, and what a good mother she was and had always been.

Peter Wilson (1991) describes adolescence as a time of 'widely fluctuating moods, inconsistencies in manner, attitude and beliefs and a general unpredictability . . . a pressing desire to plunge into activity in order to find out and feel real. The readiness to reflect on experience is not complete: and the capacity for self-observation only partially developed.' When parents become caught up in this whirlwind, it is hard for them to find a way out of it so that they can think and not themselves become forced into action. Time alone, away from the child, sitting with a therapist who does not advise on actions they 'should' or 'should not' take, but who can listen and make observations and connections, can be a real source of support when parents feel totally powerless.

IN THE CONSULTING ROOM WITH PARENTS

Work with parents of troubled adolescents is not always given the central role it deserves. Clinicians work extensively with the parents of toddlers and infants and child psychotherapists will usually ask colleagues to work with the parents of a child in individual psychotherapy. Yet this is an area of great importance, particularly given the level of difficulties young people experience at this time.

Anna Freud (1966) described adolescence as producing 'its own symptomatology which, in the more severe cases, is of a quasi-dissocial, quasi-psychotic, borderline order'. Reassuringly, she adds, 'This pathology also disappears when adolescence has run its course.' Geoffrey Baruch (2001) conveys adolescence as a time when psychosocial disorders increase in frequency: offending behaviour, suicidal and self-harming behaviour, depression, eating disorders and drug and alcohol use and abuse. Of course, this does not apply to all adolescents by any means. Yet they do have to deal with a world which is more dangerous and frightening, where consumerism rules, and perhaps some are at more risk at times from their peers than from the adults around them. Their need to be 'street-wise', and their capacity to be so can be shocking for parents whose own teenage years were not so risky outside the home.

The work itself is not easy or comfortable. I frequently experienced an intense feeling of despair and lack of skill at the end of initial sessions with parents of troubled teenagers. They were the sessions I dreaded, as I knew I would be confronted with overwhelming anxiety, fear, hatred, loss of hope and an insistence on advice and help to solve the problem quickly. I came to recognise the despair in me as a necessary prerequisite for the work. I needed to be open to receiving the parental projections, which included a powerful sense of failure, before the work even began. This was always the most difficult part for me, managing my own fear of my limitations and ineffectiveness, unable to meet the expectations of the parents sitting in front of me. Yet, the acknowledgement of their anger and disappointment at my inability to provide a quick fix provided the basis of setting up the alliance for working together. I would have to disillusion them by not being able to provide the answers they sought. This may be similar to the disillusion adolescents experience as they realise that their parents are not the all-powerful, all-knowing adults they once believed them to be.

The disillusion has been present before, of course, throughout the latency period. Parents have already had to learn that the child's teacher knows best, that other mums cook much nicer food and that their friends' dads tell funnier jokes than their own dads do.

The adolescent will need to locate his own uncertainty and powerlessness in the parents, distancing himself from their own vulnerability. The fragile sense of self, however, can leave adolescents at risk from an often impoverished capacity to cope with the vicissitudes of life.

Case 2: Mr and Mrs B and Andrew

Mrs B came to the service in complete desperation. She said she was at the end of the road but was prepared to have one last chance before giving up completely. My heart sank as I felt the burden of her expectations.

Mrs B was a weary-looking, articulate woman, separated from her husband, with two sons. She had been involved with mental health services for many years, both for herself and for her elder son, Andrew. At the beginning of the first session she told me she had 'been there, done that, got the tee-shirt'. She had had her own psychotherapy for two years, been in family therapy, couple therapy, counselling, groups.

My heart sank even further. The depressingly clichéd jargon tripped off her tongue: 'boundaries', 'low self-esteem', 'issues', 'inner child', 'transference', 'projection', 'internal world'. I decided very quickly to avoid any of these words and phrases at all costs. They were devoid of meaning, and I believed were there for Mrs B to protect herself from her very raw and painful feelings towards her son. They were also there to fend me off, disarm me and denigrate my thinking, and to keep me at bay. My mind, my thoughts, were experienced by Mrs B, in my opinion, as an unwanted third presence in the work. This discovery informed my work with Mrs B throughout.

I also had the sense that Mrs B had been successful in keeping professionals at a distance by being aggressive. When her words were aggressive towards me, my counter-transference told me that something else was going on because I did not feel intimidated, I felt sad and hopeless.

Mrs B told me she was taking anti-depressants and drinking quite heavily in order to cope with her distress and anger towards her son. Andrew was 14 and had recently left a residential school where he had stayed for five years. He was now living at home with Mrs B and her other son, Michael, who was 8 years old. Andrew had a history of verbal aggression and violence towards his mother and brother. He was a child who had never been able to sit still at school, would hurl chairs and equipment around the classroom and was abusive to his teachers and his peers. Andrew had recently started attending individual psychotherapy sessions at another centre.

Mrs B and her husband had separated two years previously but saw each other regularly when Mr B visited Michael. Mrs B said her husband had no time for Andrew: they had fought physically in the past. Andrew remembered his father throwing him down the stairs and could not forgive him for this.

Mrs B had grown up in a physically abusive home, beaten by both her parents. Despite this, she said that she loved her mother very much and that they had been very close. When Mrs B's father died, her mother became involved with another man, with whom Mrs B then became involved. Mrs B insisted that she had wanted the relationship with this much older man and, when I raised my eyebrows, insisted that it was not abusive. I wondered if her belief that she was in control of this relationship made her feel less vulnerable. It could also mean that she did not have to think about her mother's role in allowing the abuse or about her rivalry with her own mother.

In the first few weeks of our work together, I was baffled by Mrs B's relationship with her older son. It was clear that she loved and hated him with equal passion. It was a violent, unpredictable relationship. She wanted him to leave the house for good, but she felt she could not manage her feelings of guilt if she were to force him out. He was continuing to be violent with her, punching and kicking her, smashing windows and doors in the house, stealing money from her. He was also bullying Michael. It sounded unbearably frightening, but I had to keep in mind Andrew's experience of his mother and father, his having to leave home because he had been unmanageable, his father's rejection of him, and his desperate wish to stay at home with his mother – a wish that came across in her description of him.

Aware of Mrs B's aggression, I asked about her part in what was happening. She told me she was hitting Andrew and in fact they had physical fights with each other. At one point, she said, she had only just stopped herself from smashing a chair over his head during one very violent argument.

One of the challenges of working with the parent of a young person without the young person in the room is that a complex transference builds up. I felt I was being drawn in to identify with Mrs B and I struggled to keep this young man in mind as a 14-year-old child, and not a violent adult thug, despite the picture being painted for me. When I succeeded in doing this, I realised again that Mrs B found it difficult to share my mind with a third person, and I began to think about her difficulties generally in dealing with couples and her intense rivalrous feelings when excluded from something intimate between others. I had asked about Mr B coming to these sessions right from the start, but now I began to press a little more about his absence.

I remembered what she had said about her relationship with her mother's boyfriend. I thought about her wish to establish us as a couple, apart from all the other therapists, counsellors, professionals. I knew I would have to take up these issues in the transference with Mrs B if we were going to get anywhere. This is not something I would normally do in this type of work, but I was aware that she might build up a powerful positive, even erotic, transference that could easily be punctured by any perceived rejection on my part. For this reason, I prepared her for (and dreaded) the first break in our work. Our relationship was a robust and challenging one, and I feared it would become unmanageably confrontational, like her relationships with others in her life.

I asked about Andrew's birth and the time around it, in order to get a sense of how Mr and Mrs B had coped with becoming a threesome. They had been very much in love, she said. The birth of their first child snapped something in this relationship and the baby seemed to sit between them like an obstacle, keeping them apart. Mrs B looked after the baby but felt resentful of his interference in her relationship with her husband. Mr B was angry too and wanted little to do with the child. He felt he had 'lost the love of his life' (his own words).

Andrew was thus born into a situation that rendered him an unwanted, disruptive presence. This is what he continued to be as he grew up. Mrs B described him as a baby who cried a lot and demanded a lot of attention. She depicted the first year of Andrew's life as exhausting and lonely and said she was 'held hostage' by her baby.

It was clear how important Mr B was to Mrs B and to the children, even to Andrew. I spent many weeks trying to persuade Mrs B to bring her husband to the sessions. She would bear back the message that he had had enough of 'that psychology therapy bollocks'.

At the end of the last session before the first break, smiling and tearful, Mrs B said she understood I had to have a holiday. I was wary of this depressive presentation, as I had a feeling that its counterpart would be back with a vengeance after the break. I was right. When we started again, she launched into a verbal attack, which I struggled hard to withstand.

I spoke to her about her fantasies about what I had been doing and with whom, and that she had experienced the break as a cruel abandonment of her on my part. I linked this with the experiences she had told me about in the past where she had found it unbearable to be excluded by a couple. She found this idea rather curious but was prepared to think about it with me.

I wondered if she was having difficulty coping with having Mr B and Andrew around at the same time, because she could only deal with one at a time. The fights always seemed worse when they were together, and either Andrew or Mr B would have to leave the house. She said that, actually, she had always found it hard to have both of the boys together and would often separate them so that she could be with one or the other. Her feelings of guilt about having excluded Andrew from her relationship with his father by sending him away to a residential school had turned her wish to compensate for this into an unbearable burden, like a millstone around her neck.

Once he was back at home, Andrew would bully and verbally abuse her, following her into every room in the house, provoking her until she

could bear it no more and she would hit back. She had often told him
she would make him leave the family home and she described him
sneering at her in contempt and saying, 'You would never be able to,
you haven't got it in you.'

It seemed to me that having Mr B in the consulting room would help Mrs B
with the problem of accommodating more than one person in her mind at a
time. Fortunately Mr B, she said, had noticed a slight change in her; she
seemed calmer, he thought, easier to talk to. He was becoming curious
about what was happening and wanted to give it a try. I wrote to him
inviting him to join us, even if it were just for a one-off session. He agreed,
and came with Mrs B to our next session.

Mrs B was happy and nervous, almost as if she were bringing a new
boyfriend home to meet her mother. Mr B was very nervous too. I asked
him to tell me his view of how things were with Andrew. Each time he
spoke, Mrs B would interrupt him to add something, correct something
or dismiss what he had said. When I pointed this out to her, she was
embarrassed, but laughed and said she was not used to having to listen
to him. I had to make a space for his thoughts and words, and he was
initially shy and reluctant to speak. I asked him why that was. Mr B
said he thought he had nothing useful to contribute in actions or words
and he knew he was a terrible father and that Mrs B had had to cope
all on her own. He would often sink into the chair, looking small and
depressed.

He told me he had been beaten frequently by his father and was
convinced that this meant he had no capacity to be a good parent. I
challenged this view by asking why he had come to this session if he
thought he was hopeless. He became rather tearful, as did Mrs B. I
asked him if he was prepared to have a go and attend the sessions with
Mrs B. He said he would try. He went on to tell me how he wanted to
go back home but could not while Andrew was there and wanted him
out before he went back. He felt excluded by Mrs B's relationship with
their son.

Mr B and Mrs B attended every subsequent session together until the
work ended.

The work with Mr and Mrs B went on for over a year, in weekly sessions.
I came to admire this couple who had struggled with so much and had had

to overcome beliefs about themselves as parents that they had held for such a long time. They came together each time and, gradually, Mrs B was able to let Mr B have his own views on what was happening in the family, between him and the boys and between them as a couple. Even Mr B's slouched posture changed as he became more confident about saying what he felt and where he thought he could help. As for Mrs B, she was able to allow Mr B to help and be virile and competent, be her partner.

An interesting event occurred where Mr B was clearly able to do this. Andrew came home one night with a gun, which he said was loaded. He had been up to a housing estate and said a Yardie had given it to him to look after and had warned him not to lose it. Andrew threatened his mum not to say anything about the gun, but then became frightened and upset. She rang Mr B who came round immediately and locked the gun in a strong box and then in a cupboard.

The parents came to their session and reported this to me. I asked what they planned to do about it. They were both paralysed with indecision. Mr B wanted to get the police involved, as there was no way he was having a weapon in the house. Mrs B wanted to get rid of the gun somehow and protect her son. They could not agree. I stepped in. I said that if they did not report it to the police then I would have to. Mr B said he would do it himself. He looked at his wife, expecting her to be angry but she nodded her agreement. When they came the following week, they were both relaxed and smiling. Mr B told me he had sorted it all out. He had spoken to the police who said it was a BiBi gun (air pistol). To Mr B's aston-ishment, Andrew had thanked him over and over for what he had done, saying he had been really scared. Mrs B was clearly very pleased with her husband's actions. Mr B said he felt like a real father for the first time in his life.

Mr B slowly began to stamp his authority on the home situation, despite not living there. He put locks on the doors and windows that Andrew used in order to get out at night to go wandering around the housing estates. He barred him from entering his mother's bedroom without permission. He set rules down for his behaviour. Eventually, the couple decided that Mr B should move back into the family home. They feared Andrew's reaction as he had threatened to burn the house down if his dad ever came back to live with them, but when it happened, he was pleased.

Mr and Mrs B were able to discuss strategies for managing Andrew's behaviour. They agreed ways of helping each other when things became difficult. Mr B said he would 'lose it' if Andrew started having a go at his mum, or at him, so he would have to leave the house for a while to 'cool off'. I asked why they could not respond as a couple when this happened. They decided they would walk away from Andrew if he started shouting and would retreat to their bedroom and lock the door. This proved very effective with Andrew, not least because of its shock value, as he had expected a fight, and then a split between his parents. They agreed not to shout at each other in front of him, and to support each other in his presence even if they disagreed. They had their fights away from him.

Mr and Mrs B continued to talk and develop strategies to curb Andrew's violence and abusive behaviour. Mr B decided Andrew should stay at home after all and not be forced to leave. He felt they could live together as long as there were clear rules in place. They knew, however, that he would need to leave when he was a bit older and could get supported housing. They began to apply for it knowing it would be some time before it came to fruition.

Andrew continued to have violent outbursts but they were fewer and lasted a shorter time. Mrs B continued to take anti-depressants but was able to cut down on her drinking. Mr B was happy to be back at home and no longer felt impotent either as a husband or a father. Mr and Mrs B were very worried about our work finishing, fearing they would not be able to manage alone. I pointed out to them that they had each other to turn to, and also that they were coming to realise what good parents they could be together. The final session was difficult because it was sad and I sensed there was also the risk of some aggression towards me from Mrs B, because loss could make her feel vulnerable, and this could lead to a need to defend herself. Impressively, she managed her anger, and I saw that it was hard for her.

I told Mr and Mrs B to contact me if they had worries about Andrew in the future, but a year on, I had heard nothing. I hoped that was a good sign for these extraordinary parents who showed such commitment and courage in the face of appalling difficulties.

Andrew continued in his therapy.

Case 3: Mr C and Sam

A widower, Mr C, came to talk about his 17-year-old son who had been violent at home for some time. He had kicked down doors, smashed widows, broken pieces of furniture, punched holes in doors and woken neighbours with his shouting and swearing. Mr C had spent large sums of money repairing the damage Sam had caused in the home. Sam was smoking cannabis heavily, and Mr C suspected he was involved in petty crime. Mr C also had a daughter, aged 13, who was also prone to temper outbursts but was much less aggressive than her brother.

He felt isolated and rejected by his neighbours because of his son's behaviour. People stared at him, he said, and watched his every move, condemning his inability to keep his son under control. He spoke about Sam with contempt, even hatred, and blamed him for ruining his life. They had been fighting physically.

Mr C told me he had been seeing a counsellor for depression but he was only able to have six sessions and he wanted more. I explained the nature of the parenting service I could offer him and said I could not help him in the way he had perhaps hoped I would, as I would be looking with him at his parenting of his son. I acknowledged that it might be hard to spend time thinking about Sam, given his clear resentment towards him. However, Mr C said he needed to find a way of tolerating his son as he was on the verge of kicking him out of the family home but did not think he was ready to manage on his own outside the family.

Mr C was taking anti-depressants and said he felt like a failure for having to resort to them. He was also drinking quite heavily in order to 'numb my senses'. As Sam was using a lot of cannabis himself, I suggested that both he and his son needed to self medicate.

Once again, I felt confronted with a hopeless task, a relationship between a father and son that seemed to have deteriorated beyond repair. However, as Mr C was willing to give it a try, I decided we should go ahead.

Mr C was one of three children but had no contact with his siblings as they had all fallen out after their mother's death. Mr C had been the youngest child and the closest to his mother. There had been considerable domestic violence from his father towards his mother and Mr C said he had often wanted to run downstairs and protect her. He had done this once or twice, placing himself between her and his father. He spoke of his terror and abhorrence of violence. Mr C said his father had been deeply disappointed in him as he was not able to follow a career in the civil service as his father had expected of him. Instead, he became a designer, which angered his father. Mr C said his mother was indulgent with him and his world 'collapsed' when she died.

A seemingly well-educated, confident man, Mr C presented as articulate with a capacity to reflect in a somewhat intellectual way. He seemed distant and yet very vulnerable. At the end of each session, I was filled with an enormous sense of sorrow and once or twice I found myself in tears when he had left.

I asked about Sam's mother. Mr C had met and fallen in love with her very quickly. She was Asian, 'beautiful, sexy, intelligent, creative and effervescent'. Not long after they married, she became pregnant and had Sam. Three years later, they had another baby boy, Thomas. Thomas was found dead in his cot when he was four months old. The suspicion that someone could have done something to the baby to cause his death took root in Mr C and poisoned his relationship with his family. Mr C's daughter, Katy was born soon after Thomas' death. Sam began displaying behavioural problems and he was sent to a boarding school nearby when he was 5 years old. He would come home at weekends. Mrs C suddenly developed cancer of the liver and died within the year. While she was ill Mr C discovered she had been having an affair with a man at work for several years. He was devastated.

Shortly after his wife's death, Mr C was diagnosed with cancer and was told he had 10 years to live. He had to have one of his legs amputated at the knee and had a prosthetic limb fitted. I wondered what effect this had had on his relationship with the children. He said he wanted them to be independent, cope without him and he did not think they would miss him much. He often said he wanted to run away from the family home and never go back. On one occasion he had stayed out overnight and the children were frantic with worry. This was a surprise to him. I pointed out that he had done something normally associated with an adolescent.

The children had grown up knowing little of their mother as Mr C was unable to talk about her because he was so distressed at losing her but also because he was filled with a raging jealousy. He expressed his intense disappointment that neither of the children seemed interested in the 'other side of their culture' but given his exclusion of them from their mother's memory, I wondered if they worried he would not allow them to become interested. Somehow, it was as if they would be intruding upon something private that was his alone. We discussed how he could start talking to the children about their mother and encourage them to visit her grave, which was some way away from their present home. He had not realised that his children might have felt excluded from mourning their mother's death, as if it only belonged to him. I wondered if he could perhaps look through some of his wife's possessions and photos with the children. When he did this, his daughter said she had been making a secret shrine to her mum in her room. Mr C said she could put it in the sitting room if she wanted to. She and Sam asked if they could go to the cemetery together to see their mother's grave.

Much of this phase of the work with Mr C was spent untangling his feelings about his wife, her betrayal, her death and his feelings about his mother, who he was also still mourning. She had died of cancer some years earlier. We also discussed his relationship with his disappointed father and what he was bringing from that into his relationship with Sam. I put the case for Sam, what he might be experiencing. Mr C had never considered that any of Sam's behaviour could be linked to depression and loss.

It was at this stage that I asked Mr C to tell me what Sam was like when he was not destroying the house, what he loved about his son. He told me that he was funny, clever, artistic and musical. He broke down as he spoke. We began to explore what the loss of their mother had meant to each of the children and Sam in particular. I asked if his own feelings about the death of his mother made it very painful for him to imagine Sam's feelings about his mother's death.

I also asked Mr C if he thought Sam's mother's death had triggered any feelings about his dead brother. Mr C was astonished to think that there could possibly be any sort of connection in his son's mind. Mr C explained that he had never been able to think much beyond his own grief as he had found it all too overwhelming to bear. I mentioned Thomas' death and his suspicion that someone in the family had had something to do with it. He denied Sam would have known this, but I said he might not have needed to be told; it may have been clear from the reaction of the adults around him that they thought he had caused something catastrophic. He was, after all, sent away from the family home shortly afterwards.

The work proved to be slow and painful for Mr C as we explored his sense of failure as father. He became more depressed the more aware he was of Sam's upset. Then, out of the blue, things seemed to change.

Mr C arrived one day to tell me that Sam had repaired his bedroom door. He had kicked it in some weeks previously and Mr C had refused to do anything himself about it. Sam had made quite a good job of it, he said. I asked him if he had told Sam this. He said he would know he had done a good job and anyway, he would not care what his dad thought. I disagreed and suggested he say something positive to Sam without commenting on the bits of the door he had not managed to paint evenly. Mr C was sceptical but said he would try.

When Mr C came back the following week, he said he had commented on how well Sam had done and Sam then said he would paint his room. It had been black and looked 'disgusting' to Mr C. Mr C was surprised and cynical about whether Sam would get around to doing it. I linked Mr C's reaction to his son's efforts to do something on his own with his own father's responses to Mr C's attempts to do things. He went on to make many links of his own and said he realised why he was so scared of his son. it was the violence that petrified him, evoking feelings in him of a helpless enraged child. He gradually gained the capacity to believe that frightening things could be thought about and did not have to be enacted.

It emerged that Mr C's social isolation mirrored his isolation from his children. He saw himself as an outsider in society and in his family. Judging by his son's reaction to the attention he had received, I said Mr C might enjoy doing something with his son. He said he was too frightened to ask in case Sam laughed at him and rejected him. We talked about ways in which he could approach his son. Eventually he invited Sam to go and see a film with him. (It was made in the country of his mother's birth.) Sam said yes. Mr C wept as he told me how proud he had been walking along the road with his tall son, who had combed his hair and put on clean shoes to go out with him. In the cinema, Sam said his seat was too narrow for him and had leaned on his father's shoulder throughout the film. Mr C was immensely moved at this.

What Mr C had needed help with was retrieving and reviving the love he had felt for his son, which he feared had gone for ever. He blamed himself for being a 'bad' parent, and had come to hate his growing child, in whom he recognised himself. Much of the work centred on separation, loss, envy, resentment and raw sadness. Mr C's troubled adolescence and the violence in his parents' relationship haunted his own marriage and cast a shadow over his relationship with his adolescent son.

CONCLUSION

Work with parents has long been fundamental to working with children.

Winnicott provided support and consultation to parents through his radio broadcasts (1964), writing and virtuoso interventions (1971) in an impressively charismatic and compassionate fashion. The Anna Freud Centre and the Tavistock Centre have provided parent work within projects based in the clinics.

There are some parallels, I think, between the work I have described here and that undertaken by clinicians working through parent–infant psychotherapy: Dilys Daws (1989), Juliet Hopkins (1992) and Daniel Stern (1995). However, the major difference is that the adolescents were never physically present in the room and I never met them. Nevertheless, they did prove to be 'a material, live prop' (Cramer 2000) for the projections of the parents.

In my work with the parents of teenagers, I have always struggled hard to represent the adolescent in the consulting room without being their advocate. I was acutely aware of the danger that I could be placed in the position of the one who 'knew' how to parent these adults' children, knew better than they did. I always made it clear that they were the experts on their own children and we could examine together the awful feeling of humiliation of being a parent who 'cannot cope', as if parents of adolescents should have all the answers after 13 or more years.

I hope that I was able to be an ally for these parents in exploring something painful and frustrating, looking for meaning and understanding together. I was explicit about what I could offer, and what they could bring to the work. Their disappointment in my not being able to give answers and solutions was a good starting point for addressing feelings of failure and disillusion after much hope.

Ending the work with these parents was always immensely difficult for them and me. They feared they would not be able to manage without the sessions, but, as I had made clear from the start, I was only a small part of what they had managed to accomplish. I always missed the intense nature of the working relationship we had forged together.

Ms A and I worked together for about three months. Ms A got a new job and her daughter did well in her mock examinations. Mr and Mrs B and I spent 15 months in weekly sessions. Mr B moved back into the family home and Andrew stayed on. Mr C attended for just over a year. He asked to be referred for psychotherapy and encouraged his son to have psychotherapy too, which Sam went on to do.

Erikson (1995) writes:

> In their search for a new sense of continuity and sameness, adolescents have to re-fight many of the battles of earlier years, even though to do so they must artificially appoint perfectly well-meaning people to play the roles of adversaries.

The same might be said for the parents of adolescents.

References

Baruch, G. (ed.) (2001) *Community-Based Psychotherapy with Young People: Evidence and Innovation in Practice.* Hove, UK: Brunner-Routledge

Britton, R. (1989) 'The Missing Link: parental sexuality in the Oedipus complex'. In R. Britton, M. Fieldman and E. O'Shaughnessy (eds.), *The Oedipus Complex Today: Clinical Implications.* London: Karnac Books

Cramer, B. (2000) 'Helping children through treatment of parenting: the model of mother/infant psychotherapy.' In J. Tsiantis *et al.* (eds.), *Work with Parents: Psychoanalytic Psychotherapy with Children and Adolescents.* London: Karnac Books

Davies, R. (1996) 'The interdisciplinary network and the internal world of the offender'. In C. Cordess and M. Cox (eds.), *Forensic Psychotherapy: Crime, Psychodynamics and the Offender Patient,* vol.XI, *Mainly Practice.* London: Jessica Kingsley

Daws, D. (1989) *Through the Night: Helping Parents and Sleepless Infants.* London: Free Association Books

Erikson, E. (1995) *Childhood and Society.* London: Vintage

Fraiberg, S., Adelson, E. and Shapiro, V. (1980) 'Ghosts in the nursery: a psycho-analytic approach to the problems of impaired infant–mother relationships'. In S. Fraiberg and L. Fraiberg (eds.), *Clinical Studies in Infant Mental Health.* London: Tavistock

Freud, A. (1966) *Normality and Pathology in Childhood.* London: Hogarth Press

Greenberg, H. (1975) 'The widening gyre: transformations of the omnipotent quest during adolescence' *The International Review of Psychoanalysis* 2: 231–44

Hopkins, J. (1992) 'Infant–parent psychotherapy' *Journal of Child Psychotherapy* 18: 5–19

Stern, D. (1995) *The Motherhood Constellation: A Unified View of Parent-Infant Psychotherapy.* New York: Basic Books

Wilson, P. (1991) 'Psychotherapy with adolescents'. In J. Holmes (ed.), *Textbook of Psychotherapy in Psychiatric Practice.* London: Churchill Livingstone

Winnicott, D. W. (1963) 'Hospital care supplementing intensive psychotherapy in adolescence'. In Winnicott (1965), *The Maturational Processes and the Facilitating Environment.* London: Hogarth Press

Winnicott, D. W. (1964) *The Child, the Family and the Outside World.* Harmondsworth, UK: Penguin

Winnicott, D. W. (1971) *Therapeutic Consultations in Child Psychiatry.* London: Hogarth Press

Part III
Taking the broader view

12 Doing 'something else'

The value of therapeutic communication when offering consultations and brief psychotherapy[1]

Monica Lanyado

Analysis for analysis' sake has no meaning for me. I do analysis because that is what the patient needs to have done and to have done with. If the patient does not need analysis then I do something else.

(Winnicott 1962: 170)

The influence of Winnicott on many of the contributors to this book is very evident, possibly particularly in this chapter which draws heavily on his interest and willingness to do 'something else' with patients who, for a variety of reasons, cannot be offered more traditional forms of psycho-analytic treatment. His professional development from paediatrician to child and adult psychiatrist to psychoanalyst provided him with rich opportunities to observe and work with people, in many differing environments, in sickness and in health, throughout the life cycle. Winnicott's writings contain numerous rich accounts of his varied therapeutic encounters with children. In addition, his adult psychoanalytic practice provided the opportunity to reflect on and hypothesise about the kinds of childhood experiences and inner worlds that his patients had had.

Winnicott's analytic technique and approach to treatment are distinctive, but, in the deliberate absence of a purely Winnicottian analytic group and training school, those wishing to learn from and develop his work with children must abstract from his writings the essence of his way of psycho-analysing and communicating with children. This non-didactic, creative use of his work may be what he had hoped would happen if his work stood the test of time. He did not wish to encourage a new analytic group which might have risked eventually becoming perceived as the font of some kind of Winnicottian orthodoxy of thought. The idea of orthodoxy of any kind runs counter to Winnicott's views on creativity and the ways in which he hoped his ideas would seed further ideas which would grow in others' minds.

Somewhat unfortunately, this position possibly also resulted in Winnicott's work not being as widely studied and valued, particularly by child and adolescent psychotherapists, as it might otherwise have been. In many respects, as the chapters in this book indicate, his ideas and ways of thinking about the work have been very much alive and germinating within the Independent child psychotherapy tradition, and are now busy bearing fruit. Child psychotherapists today increasingly appreciate and utilise many different approaches to the child because of the sheer diversity and demands of the work. The previous clear boundaries between different psycho-analytic training traditions are dissolving and a new ground which can encompass different theoretical approaches, as and when appropriate to different patients, is emerging.

THE CLINICAL NEED TO 'DO SOMETHING ELSE'

It can feel like something of an anomaly, having completed a psychoana-lytic training in which intensive three to five times weekly psychotherapy is at the core, for the therapist to spend more clinical time post-qualification applying and drawing on the therapeutic skills developed during this pro-cess rather than continuing to see patients intensively in clinical practice. This chapter focuses on some of these 'applications', which are rooted in the core training in intensive psychoanalytic psychotherapy, and offers thoughts about the ways in which Winnicott's ideas about the holding environment and therapeutic communication can provide a theoretical and technical framework for understanding the clinical processes involved. This is about psychotherapists doing 'something else', which is a valuable way of working with a much larger and wider group of children and their families than is practical through psychoanalytic psychotherapy alone. This is not a watered-down form of psychoanalytic treatment, and for many referrals it can be the treatment of choice. I am enthusiastic about working in this flexible and free-flowing way and hope to enthuse others so that they also become able to enjoy this way of working.

I want to emphasise that I do not approach this kind of consultation work or brief therapy from the point of view of thinking that scarce resources mean that it is 'only possible' to do brief work. On the contrary, I feel that brief work or timely consultations can be the best way forward for many children and families who come to us for help (see Lanyado 1999). I have found that it is helpful to be able to offer this kind of work as soon as possible after referral, on the principle that 'a stitch in time saves nine', as spacing out consultations after the first contact can then be more tolerable for the family. Whilst advocating this work, I do not want to give the impression that I am naïve about the very stretched clinical resources that are available to those in need, within the public as well as the private sector. This is simply a way of trying to meet that need in as creative and positive a way as possible.

Before moving on to my clinical examples, I want to place this way of thinking and working within the context of Winnicottian thought.

THE HOLDING ENVIRONMENT AND THERAPEUTIC COMMUNICATION

It is possible to read Winnicott's works and feel peculiarly as if meeting the man. Here is a psychoanalyst working in the 1940s, 50s and 60s, who sits on the floor and plays with his young patients in an apparently unsophisticated and ordinary way, and who communicates enthusiastically by phone and letter with parents. There are times when, to me, he appears a bit obscure in his comments and where he blurs the usual analytic boundaries, but this is accompanied by a sense that in the main he was probably able to act in this way and not cause insurmountable difficulties in the transference relationship by virtue of his long therapeutic experience and because what he was relating on paper was a highly condensed and rather enigmatic version of what took place in the treatment.

Above all, it is clear that he is very much his own person in the consulting-room. Because of this, his clinical accounts can more sensibly be understood as encouraging therapists to be true to themselves in relating to their patients, as opposed to encouraging others to imitate him at his most enigmatic or anarchic. Looking at his work in this light enables the reader to preserve the gems of his wisdom without incorporating the idiosyncrasies of his personal style.

When Winnicott interprets unconscious material the reader gains the impression that interpretations are offered much as the spatula is offered in his classic paper 'The observation of infants in a set situation' (1941) – that is in a manner which seems to say, 'Here is something, an idea to play with and if you find it interesting, we can play with it together.' But, of course, for Winnicott, this way of playing had a very serious purpose which was at the heart of his analytic work, while simultaneously being valued as a potentially enjoyable and healthy experience in its own right. Open enjoyment of the work and of the children he worked with is always present in Winnicott's writings as is his playfulness with the many different kinds of audiences he addressed – including the general public who greatly appreciated his BBC radio broadcasts in the 1950s. It seems that he went out of his way to communicate with, and entertain, his audience by throwing in many mischievous and at times deliberately amusing and surprising comments.

This performing style seems to have been present whether he was addressing a non-analytic audience or the British Psycho-Analytic Society. Typically, he starts his brief, but in clinical terms important, paper 'The aims of psychoanalytic treatment' with

In doing psychoanalysis I aim at:

> Keeping alive
> Keeping well
> Keeping awake

I aim at being myself and behaving myself.
Having begun an analysis I expect to continue with it, to survive it, and to end it.

I enjoy myself doing analysis and I always look forward to the end of each analysis. Analysis for analysis' sake has no meaning for me. I do analysis because that is what the patient needs to have done and to have done with. If the patient does not need analysis then I do something else.

In analysis one asks: how *much* can one be allowed to do? And, by contrast, in my clinic the motto is: how *little* need be done? (Winnicott 1962: 166)

Winnicott concludes this same paper by saying: 'If our aim continues to be to verbalize the nascent conscious in terms of the transference, then we are practising analysis: if not, we are analysts practising something else that we deem appropriate to the occasion. And why not?' (1962: 170).

These thoughts from the 1960s feel all the more relevant today. There are many times when analytically trained child psychotherapists find themselves 'practising something else' that they deem appropriate to the occasion. They may have to restrain a child physically, attend case conferences and write court reports about a child patient. At times they may need to be very present within the professional network to try to improve communication between professionals about the child, and to be alert to the tendency for these complex external networks to re-enact the child's internal conflicts. Within the psychotherapy session the therapist may have to behave more like a nursemaid or cleaner, or may feel like a stern teacher or policeman whose primary task is to establish and maintain boundaries.

Winnicott's argument would be that this is all part of what is appropriate to maintaining the facilitating environment for that particular patient. Indeed, without undertaking these aspects of the work, therapy can all too often break down and the child is left without the help that he or she needs. Psychoanalytic understanding provides the explanation for taking these aspects of the work so seriously and, although this at times may feel far removed from 'verbalizing the nascent conscious in terms of the transference', it is essential in providing the possibility that this form of analytic work may eventually be able to take place. Psychotherapists wisely practising 'something else' are carrying out important psychotherapeutic tasks in the child's best interests.

The best examples of Winnicott doing 'something else' can be found in *Therapeutic Consultations in Child Psychiatry* (1971a) which describes series of spaced consultations with 20 children aged from 21 months to 16 years. The types of referral look typical of any busy child and family clinic before physical and sexual abuse became a major part of the caseload. Some of the children clearly needed much more intensive work than Winnicott was able to offer or indeed to find elsewhere for them. However, a significant number of other children were able to make good use of very limited therapeutic time. For child and adolescent psychotherapists, there are important clinical issues raised by this work in terms of how to conceptualise initial consultations (which is the way I prefer to think about what are often called 'assessment sessions'), brief work and the development of each individually tailored psychotherapy treatment plan.

In his introduction to *Therapeutic Consultations*, Winnicott makes it clear that he sees this work as being essentially about *enabling therapeutic communication* to take place between the patient and therapist. I would add to this the importance of therapeutic communication taking place during this process, between the therapist and the child's parents and/or closest carers. For me, Winnicott's clearest exposition of what he felt actually happened in the consulting-room in terms of communication between patient and therapist can be found in 'Playing: a theoretical statement', a chapter from *Playing and Reality* (1971b). Other contributors to this book have their own favourites (see Horne, Chapter 13). Typically, this definitive statement on this matter is a densely packed condensation of his theories of human development, growth and creativity, incorporating his thinking on transitional phenomena and the central importance of play as a medium of self-expression. At the risk of being repetitive – as I have also used this quote in Chapter 8 – Winnicott says:

> Psychotherapy takes place in the overlap of two areas of playing, that of the patient and that of the therapist. Psychotherapy has to do with two people playing together. The corollary of this is that where playing is not possible, then the work done by the therapist is directed towards bringing the patient from a state of not being able to play to a state of being able to play.
>
> (Winnicott 1971b: 44)

This way of thinking implies an informal, creative attitude on the part of the therapist – a therapist who is encouraged to be in a frame of mind that can play with ideas and be playfully available to a child. It requires the therapist to be able to be playfully 'present' for the patient – an aspect of the therapist's use of Self that I have written about in more detail elsewhere (Lanyado 2004). This way-of-being is not the same as the therapist simply having fun with a child, it is 'play with a serious purpose'. A consultation or session with a child in these terms can be viewed as an opportunity for the process of a child's ability to communicate through play, *in its own right*, to be examined and thought about, not only for its content but also for how free or inhibited it is. Being playfully present does not mean that the therapist's own agenda is allowed to intrude into the process. But it does mean that, for *authentic* communication to take place between therapist and child, the therapist's 'area of play' and the child's should overlap, creating a transitional play space that can then potentially provide the therapeutic surprises that Winnicott felt were so important. It is in this overlap that ordinary creativity and growth can be seeded and find expression.

It is important to bear in mind that the emphasis on the importance of play and everyday creativity that is so evident in Winnicott's work emerges from his theoretical views about ordinary emotional development. These views were the result of a rich combination of his clinical experiences as a paediatrician in an ordinary 'well-baby' clinic, and his work as a psychoanalyst with emotionally troubled children, adolescents and adults. His theories contain an implicit trust in the existence of an innate capacity for personal growth throughout life. The therapist's role is re-cast into one which is essentially concerned with establishing and maintaining an environment in which the individual could potentially start to grow again or indeed develop for the first time. From a Winnicottian perspective, emotional disturbance is seen as the result of blockages in or divergences from the path of the individual's potential for self-realisation – what Winnicott thinks of as capacity for each one of us to become our 'true self'. It is the therapist's task to help patients to become free of these impingements on the path of their personal growth, free of blockages in their individual and natural developmental path. Therapy is very much about helping patients to move closer to what feels like their true Self.

Winnicott emphasised the similarities of this to the good-enough mother–baby relationship, these parallels of holding and communication being central to this way of thinking about the psychotherapeutic task (Winnicott 1960). Phillips makes this point succinctly when he says:

> Whereas for Freud psychoanalysis was essentially a 'talking cure' dependent on two people talking to each other, for Winnicott the mother–infant relationship, in which the communication was relatively non-verbal, had become the paradigm for the analytic process, and this changed the role of interpretation in psychoanalytic treatment. For the neurotic and the psychotic patient, for the child and adult, interpretation was a sophisticated extension of infant care, albeit a crucial part of the analyst's primary aim in the treatment which was to establish and maintain an environment conducive to growth.
>
> (Phillips 1988: 138)

In clinical practice, these concepts led to a different way-of-being with the (child) patient. What was implied was an attentiveness to the setting of the treatment which went beyond what is, I think, generally meant by containment. For Winnicott, the provision of maternal care, or the provision of a therapeutic setting, resulted in a tailor-made, active adaptation of the carer's or therapist's mind to the needs of the individual infant or patient. This adaptation needed to evolve from the minutiae of what was being communicated between the baby and mother, patient and therapist. In infant care, this was seen in the attention to detail that the mother gave her infant – in the way that she held, fed, soothed and protected her baby from unnecessary interruptions in his or her state of being. By implication, the setting, and the establishment of any piece of clinical work, therefore was aimed at providing a similarly attentive environment within which significant growth and communication could safely be explored and experienced. In other words, the therapist was required actively to adapt his or her mind, the setting and form of psychoanalytic treatment to the patient, rather than the patient being required to adapt to the classical psychoanalytic model.

To illustrate and develop these Winnicottian concepts of holding and communication as well as the importance of playing in Winnicott's sense within the therapeutic process, I am going to give two examples. In each case, particularly at the start of treatment, interpretation was used sparingly for reasons that will be illustrated and discussed. As I understand it, interpretation within the holding environment, in a Winnicottian sense, is not the same as the mutative interpretation (Strachey 1934). The emphasis is changed from seeing interpretation as a powerful therapeutic tool used by the therapist to elucidate unconscious processes, to seeing it as being a verbal crystallisation of shared experiences in the therapy, arising from communication (verbal and non-verbal) within the holding environment of the therapeutic space. Importantly, while the analytic work in the transference relationship and its interpretation may differ depending on the frequency of therapy, the other major Winnicottian components of the therapeutic process – holding, communication and playing – can be thought of as 'constants' across all varieties of psychoanalytic therapy and can thus provide a framework for thinking about brief and non-intensive work.

Both of my examples deal with the impact of trauma on the patient, which Winnicott saw as being massive impingements on the individual's sense of 'going-on-being'. Part of the task of therapy could be described as helping the patients to rediscover developmental and creative paths in their lives, having been swept off course by the overwhelming events they had experienced (Lanyado 2004, ch. 1). The first example describes work with a family who were developing well before the youngest child tragically was killed in an accident. The second example describes time-limited work with a sexually abused and abusing 16-year-old boy. As it is difficult to strike a balance between preserving patients' confidentiality while conveying the essential features of their trauma, only material that bears directly on the subject of this chapter will be presented.

A GRIEVING AND ANGRY FAMILY

Mrs X consulted me nine months after the death of her 2-year-old daughter in an accident. She was suffering greatly and in an undiminished way over time, and was worried about the impact of the little girl's death on her husband and two young sons. The older son 'Billy' had responded to the traumatic loss by becoming overly responsible for his parents and very serious in mood, and the younger son 'Johnny' was very aggressive and demanding, causing lots of arguments and fights at home. Mr X was somatising his distress in a rather alarming way.

Mrs X had consulted various other sources for help but seemed to have found that, in her extremely fragile and sensitive state, she was only able to tolerate a very small amount of what felt to her like 'not being understood', before the pain she was trying to cope with became overwhelming. From the very start I was therefore highly aware that I would need to make every effort to adapt maximally to her and her family's needs if I were to be able to hold them in therapy and to help them. With hindsight it is possible to see how very much this is like the maximal adaptation of a mother to her newborn infant, or to an ill child. In the ordinary course of events, this kind of hyper-adaptation eases off as the child becomes more integrated and able to cope with pain and frustration, when the process of disillusionment sets in and separateness is more tolerable (Winnicott 1960). In therapy, this process of disillusionment plays a key part in helping the therapist to find a wise balance between 'holding' an anxiety for some while for patients who cannot bear it or recognise it as their own, and becoming able to talk about and interpret the nature of the anxiety itself.

In the first two months of treatment, I met with Mr and Mrs X once weekly, but not with the boys. There was a pressing need to help the parents to approach the first anniversary of their daughter's death and start to regain their ability to be good-enough parents to their sons. My initial approach was essentially supportive and non-interpretative, simply helping them to survive and to begin to be able to think about their living children again as opposed to being constantly full of pain about their dead daughter. My awareness of Mrs X's barely contained pain made me very conscious of the need to hold her gently in the transference without appearing to make any emotional demands on her – which was what transference interpretation might have felt like at that time. In my counter-transference fantasy, I felt very like a mother nursing a fragile child who might not survive, waiting until she was stronger before hoping for any more robust response to the therapy. Mrs X was so immersed in her grief that, for a long while, she was unaware of how therapy held her, and took her relationship with me very much for granted. She was simply very needy, and I responded to this.

It was a sign of Mr and Mrs X's gradually renewed thoughtfulness and resilience when, two months into treatment, they pressed me to see the boys for a consultation. The boys had not been securely held within their parents' hearts and minds since the shock of their sister's death. There was increasing mayhem at home which was possibly an outcome of the boys' sense of their parents regaining some resilience and being more able to face their sons' angry and uncontrolled behaviour. I had not met the boys before this because the parents' needs had taken priority. I had also hoped to help the parents to appreciate how much they themselves were able to help their sons, particularly when they were feeling so guilty about not having been able to protect or save their daughter.

Meeting with the boys confirmed the view that I had gathered from the parents' account, that they were emotionally healthy but very upset. They were friendly, expressing themselves freely through play, but struggling to cope with their anger about the death of their sister and the emotional unavailability of their previously attentive and good-enough parents. They had taken to reading their parents' faces carefully, to gauge how preoccupied they were at any time with thoughts of their sister. We decided that for a little while, as long as seemed helpful, I would see the boys together weekly as well as continuing to see the parents weekly. What I was trying to convey to the parents was a sense that we would need to work together in different ways at different times in the therapy, according to the family's needs. This sense of fluidity in the treatment plan was helpful as an antidote to the family's sense of being stuck in their ability to mourn the loss of their daughter and sister. In the counter-transference I started to feel like a maternal grandmother who needed to help care for all her daughter's family because her daughter was unwell and overwhelmed. Daws draws attention to this aspect of the therapist's relationship to parents in brief parent–infant psychotherapy (Daws 1989).

Four weeks into the boys' treatment, in the first session after the anniversary of the sister's death (which had not proved as re-traumatising as the parents had feared), the younger boy started to play with a large wooden fire engine and large wooden boat. He connected them with sticky tape and said 'It's rough', meaning that the sea was rough and the fire engine was somehow helping the boat. Although I still felt at this point that it was too soon to use transference interpretation with the parents, the boys' interest and curiosity about me suggested that they were ready for this kind of communication. I spoke to them about the boat being rather like their family which was going through a very rough time, and needing the help of the fire engine, me, to help them through it. This was the first interpretation I had made to the boys. The older more defended boy, Billy, initially took this literally but the younger child was immediately affected by what I had said, and started to look at me in a very direct and curious way.

I tried to explain to the older boy that I was meaning that his family, or more specifically his parents, were *like* a boat, not that they really were a boat and, as I explained this, the younger child came to stand right in front of me, commanding my attention. He said with some urgency and insistently, 'Mummy and Daddy and Billy and me were in a boat and it sank.' He said this twice looking searchingly at me and expecting some sort of answer from me. Billy denied that this had happened and I said that I understood this, but it was as if Johnny was telling me about something that was a bit like a dream. This made sense to Billy and both he and Johnny continued to play as they had been before, however with an idea in their minds that had been set in motion for both of them by Johnny's intense communication and my response.

They continued to play with this idea for the rest of the session. Billy mused about how storms at sea can seem to come from nowhere, and Johnny talked about sand-castles which get knocked down by the sea, however strong you try to make them. I talked about the power of the sea, but also about how ships can and do sail the sea despite this. I then interpreted how their family had been sailing along in the sea, in an ordinary everyday sort of way, when the sudden storm of their sister's death felt as if it had sunk them all. I talked more specifically of the boat being like Mummy and Daddy who usually kept them safe at sea, but that now it felt to them as if the boat was no longer safe to sail in. Billy developed this idea, talking about ships sinking because they were too overloaded or even because they were shot at by cannons. I said that what he said was important because he seemed to feel that his family and the mummy–daddy ship had been attacked. He agreed. Meanwhile his little brother listened attentively and elaborated with ideas of sharks and other dangers in the water.

The readiness with which the boys responded to interpretation and were able to develop it illustrates what was to be a turning point in their therapy from which they were able to grow some new ideas and understand more about their inner worlds. This arose from the mutual and intense play with ideas that led up to the interpretation, and that in turn enabled the boys to carry the ideas further in their response to it. The material about the mummy–daddy boat expressed and confirmed what I was able to see so clearly in my work with the parents. I needed to help the parents to become buoyant again before being able to help them, through interpretation, to find their way through life without their daughter. I will discuss the technical balance between holding and interpretation later in this chapter.

The interpretative process within the transference with the parents started six months into treatment, following Mr and Mrs X's first expressions of intense anger towards me, the previously highly 'adaptive' mother, when I made a comment which they felt was out of touch with their sorrow (and indeed, possibly in a rather mild way, actually was). By this point, I was meeting with the parents on a more intermittent basis – roughly every three or four weeks, and seeing the boys fortnightly. It was important to be therapeutically very economical with the frequency of the sessions, and offer no more than was really necessary, as this was essentially a healthy family, who were in danger of pathologising a terrible life event. Following my comment, Mrs X directly expressed her anger towards me. Up until this point in the therapy, she had simply felt held in a way that she could take for granted. The lack of adaptation implied by my comment started the process of Mrs X's disillusionment with me, a process which she could only just tolerate, but within which I could start to interpret her feelings towards me in the transference. This insight prompted thought in her about where our work together was leading and the need for her to rediscover the thread of her inner life, and who she was, following the terrible blow of her daughter's death. This was a profound change of emphasis in the way she thought about her work with me.

The family's treatment went through further changes in its form. At one point, Mr X became extremely depressed and needed help in his own right from a colleague of mine. There were also a few sessions when I worked with the boys individually, after it had become clearer how very differently they had personally experienced and tried to understand the traumatic loss of their sister. All of the sessions were spaced out in time according to the family's need and my other clinical commitments. As with much of this type of consultation work, the treatment programme was very individually tailored to meet the family's needs.

I have not seen any other family in quite the same treatment programme – but the fluidity with which we responded to their changing needs, particularly as their process of mourning stopped being so impeded, is a principle behind all the therapeutic consultations that I undertake. This is one of many things that I learnt from reading Winnicott's *Therapeutic Consultations* – how vital it is to be prepared to play with many treatment options in my mind and discuss these openly with parents and their child or teenager before deciding how to proceed after the initial consultations.

Before discussing this brief account of what I now think of as a 'therapeutically economical' way of working with a family, I want to describe another way in which a brief time-limited series of consultations can result in some much needed deeper therapeutic work.

BRIEF WORK WITH AN UNWILLING ADOLESCENT BOY

This example raises similar questions about holding and communication to the first, but in a very different treatment context.

The introduction to *Therapeutic Consultations* is packed with clinical wisdom about 'making sense of psychoanalysis in economic terms' (Winnicott 1971a). In the context of this chapter, it is important to note that Winnicott emphasised that his aim in writing about the consultations was not to report symptomatic results, but to illustrate examples of *communication with children*. These communications were therapeutic because of the increased self-knowledge that grew from them. In addition, Winnicott discussed the importance of communication with the parents in order to understand further and help the child. Underlying the work is his conviction that, for the therapist successfully to make use of the therapeutic consultation, 'one must have in one's bones a theory of *emotional development* of the child and of the relationship of the child to environmental factors' (Winnicott 1971a).

The particular theory of emotional development that a child psychotherapist has in their bones will naturally vary from person to person and grows from a combination of personal preferences and training, clinical and life experience. It is also a theoretical underpinning, personal to each therapist, which needs to be constantly updated and adjusted as new patients challenge and expand existing ideas. In brief work, not only does the therapist have to work harder to reach out to the patient because of the time limitations – that is to be more present as I have discussed elsewhere (Lanyado 2004) – but the therapist's theory of emotional development will also be much more present, affecting which aspects of the clinical material to respond to, and which to leave alone. This is another of the questions of technique that this book is raising.

The brief work with 'Don' that I shall now describe was part of a hypothesis-generating research project on sexually abused and/or abusing adolescent boys, which is more fully referenced at the end of this chapter. Twelve psychotherapy consultations (which followed between four and six psychological and psychiatric assessment sessions) were offered to boys as an opportunity to talk and think about their difficult lives. Qualitative research data were gathered in the process. This very unpromising treatment group provided a number of therapeutic surprises, as these extracts from Don's therapy illustrate. He was 16 years old at the time of these consultations. Fuller details of the study are described elsewhere (Hodges, Lanyado and Andreou 1994).[2]

Considerable efforts were made to ensure that the research programme offered a reliable and safe place in which the boy would get individual attention albeit at times to aspects of himself that often he did not consciously feel he wanted to think about. The unusualness of these efforts and attention to detail may have encouraged some curious anticipation of what would take place, and even some hope in the boys, as they progressed through the various stages of the research project and then started their psychotherapy consultations. As with a surprising number of other boys on the project, Don was able to use the sessions in the manner of Winnicott's therapeutic consultations – that is he became interested and drawn into the process. This is reminiscent of something interesting being offered to the infant (the spatula again?) which he or she may in time be able to play with.

From the start of his sessions, Don clearly linked the sexual abuse he had suffered from his stepfather with his own sexual abuse of his sister. He was in no doubt about this and said that he had 'done to her what he done to me'. But he also repeatedly stated throughout the time that we met, 'I have no idea why I did it.' He found it extremely difficult to think about what he had done and at times went into blank, dissociative states. It was never clear whether he deliberately 'cut off' when he did this, or whether this was an unconscious defence mechanism. He was depressed and despairing because he missed his family and was still attached to, but very angry with, his stepfather (who was in prison) of whom he said, 'I hate him for what he did to me', 'He's ruined my life', 'He didn't teach me right and wrong', but also, very poignantly, 'He was the best dad I ever had.'

During the course of Don's sessions, I observed that, whenever Don's complicated current family was worrying him, he was prone to becoming extremely manic in defence and would often turn to drink, at times becoming seriously drunk and disorderly. As the oldest boy in a large family, with many of his siblings in and out of care and his stepfather in prison, he felt responsible for his mother and his brothers and sisters. This was despite the fact that it was also very clear to him that he was in reality unable to help them, having actually abused his position of trust, and that it was impossible for them all to live together again following his abuse of his sister. In addition, in sadly realistic moments, he was able to admit that even if they could all live together again, it would 'do my head in'. It was important that the everyday realities of his life were firmly in my mind during his sessions, otherwise I could not hope to understand what was going on within him. The following sequence of extracts from the last six of his sessions illustrates the flow of the material and the interweaving of my active response to his external environment, in order to provide a holding environment for therapy, and my attempts to understand his internal world.

Don, a rather deliberately 'laid-back' character, became angry with me for the first time when he felt I had kept him waiting for his session for a long while because of the other children I saw. In fact he had arrived very early for his session. I had not seen this belligerent and aggressive side of him before. Within the transference I felt that I had suddenly become for him just like his mother, who was so busy with all her other children that he always had to wait for her. In the week following this session, I thought a lot about how his laid-back defence had led me mistakenly to believe that therapy was not that important to him. I was determined to pay much more careful attention to him and, as a result, was completely thrown when he arrived for his next session in a noisy, manic and aggressively 'high' state in which he was totally unreachable.

I wondered if he had been drinking or had taken some drugs before the session but could observe no obvious evidence of this. His behaviour was so extreme that it made me wonder whether he had an incipient manic-depressive disorder. I was relieved when he left the session early and I phoned his children's home to try to make sense of what was happening. My phone call confirmed the anxieties that this very supportive children's home had had about him over the preceding week or two. The staff's view was that Don was very worried about his mother who, he had recently heard, had 'gone to pieces' following a number of brief relationships. This had resulted in all his brothers and sisters being split up and taken into care. In addition, he had not seen his mother for many weeks and missed her a great deal.

The staff were glad that I had contacted them as this confirmed their feeling that they needed to be particularly vigilant in their care of Don to ensure that he did not run away from the home to find his mother, or go on a terrifying drinking spree as he had in the past to deaden his pain. They could see that his increasingly aggressive and argumentative behaviour in the home was leading up to this and were able to respond sensibly and sensitively to this boy, to whom they felt very committed and attached.

When I next saw Don, he was calmer and I was able to refer to the way he had been the week before. When I tried to encourage him to talk about why he might have been this way, he was evasive, as he also was when I tried to enquire about his family. However, he was busily using his charm and blarney to side-track and amuse me, and stop me taking seriously his behaviour and mood in the last two sessions. I eventually commented that I felt that if he didn't laugh, he'd cry. He asked me to explain this, and from this point on in the session he sobered and for the first time started to talk more seriously about himself.

He shyly told me about much deeper stirrings within himself of an almost philosophical nature, and then he told me about his poetry. This astounded me as what he started to share was lyrical and touching and clearly very private. Towards the end of the session he started to be able to think about taking up the offer of individual once-weekly work with a colleague of mine, closer to his home, at the end of the research project – but only if he could stay firmly in charge of it and stop when-ever he liked.

Unfortunately, sessions nine and ten that followed this breakthrough were highly defensive again, leaving me despondent about his future. As a part of the research protocol, these sessions needed to address the question of the sexual risk that he presented to children. He con-tinued to minimise this and to deny that he really needed treatment. The defensiveness was reinforced by his feelings about the sessions coming to an end (which was another focus of the research protocol of the last few sessions), something that he found himself feeling more affected by than he had expected. However, this was followed by a more hopeful session eleven and he was able again to contemplate the possibility that he might need to go for regular therapy. This was reflected in the poems he shared with me during the session, that he had written in a special book which he kept at the children's home, and that he wrote down again for me to keep in the therapy room.

The poems, while being very simple in structure, dwelt on elemental subjects – rain, sun, snow and wind. There were tears in the rain which would never end, and the danger of burning rather than the gift of life from the sun; but there was some hope expressed in the children he described playing in the snow. The final poem of the group – about the wind – was given the importance of a page to itself. It conveyed the desolate persecuting image of a windy street scene; but the last line said, 'The wind is here *nearly* every day' (my italics), expressing an important glimmer of relief in this otherwise depressing internal landscape.

Don opened his final session by saying that he had thought about it a lot and realised that he did need help about his sexual behaviour. He would like to be referred to my colleague, for once-weekly treatment. He continued reliably in this treatment for another six months before starting work, when it became more difficult to arrange session times. His therapist felt that he had made good use of this time, and hoped to maintain contact with him over the years.

SOME HELPFUL GUIDELINES WHEN OFFERING THERAPEUTIC CONSULTATIONS

This discussion will focus on five main points:

- the parallels between ordinary parental care and the therapeutic process

- the value of working directly with the adults in the child's holding environment
- the balance between holding and interpretation
- the importance of 'playing' in Winnicott's definition of psychotherapy, and finally
- the significance of 'small but important change' in therapy.

The description of the therapeutic environment and function as having parallels with the ordinary tasks that parents fulfil in caring for their children is, of course, a metaphor, but one which can help to give direction and structure to the therapeutic process. The vast expansion of research in developmental psychology, particularly about the first year of life with 'ordinary' infants, vividly demonstrates the incredible attention to detail that mothers offer to their babies. This is particularly important at the start of life, and we now 'know' (in research terms) that the first few weeks of life, a period within which many researchers in the past thought little of interest happened, is actually a period which is teeming with incredibly fine and delicately tuned communications between parents and children.

For those who have observed babies for training purposes this comes as no surprise, but what the research importantly draws attention to is the intense effort made by parents at this time to understand what goes on in their baby's mind. This is one of the reasons why a mother of a newborn baby can at times feel so exhausted from caring for her baby, even though, to the outside eye, she has actually 'done' very little all day. It is possible that this intensity of effort is also characteristic of the start of therapy, intensive as well as non-intensive, and is particularly important when the contact is brief or once weekly. In this respect, these ways of working place great demands on the therapist. This results from the need for the therapist to hold the patient in mind over longer gaps in time in once-weekly or less frequent open-ended therapy, and the need to reach out more actively to the patient from within the therapist's 'area of play' (as referred to in Winnicott's definition of psychotherapy) in time-limited therapy.

In addition, it should be noted that the metaphor that Winnicott presents barely mentions the father's role in child care and this is an area which is receiving much more attention today. We are now more aware of the problems of role stereotyping which bedevil psychoanalytic terminology than we were in the past. Parent–infant observation offers clear examples of fathers providing a very similar kind of holding, care and play to the way that mothers do – indeed, it is quite common to observe that fathers may have more time to play with their growing children than mothers do. This is an area that goes beyond the realms of this chapter but that is of great importance when thinking about the more 'male' function of setting boundaries as well as holding, and in terms of male identity as expressed through the father's playfulness with his child. The father's state of mind when preoccupied with his children, and the ways in which this is similar to or differs from the mother's state of mind, warrants careful study. 'Primary paternal preoccupation' may prove to be a valuable area of observation, and indeed a fascinating start has been made in this direction by Tracey and her colleagues (Tracey *et al.* 1996).

The active adaptation of the therapist to the patient's needs, in terms of open contact with parents and other carers, raises important issues relating to the interface of internal and external relationships and internal and external reality. It is possible to argue from my clinical examples that being too cautious about communications with the child's carers may have risked difficulties in, and the possible breakdown of, the external holding environment. Mr and Mrs X could have withdrawn their children from treatment, thus exacerbating the family's problems. There were many times when they only just managed to cope with their day-to-day lives, only in part because of their grief-stricken, sleepless nights. Don could have gone on an alcoholic and delinquent binge, running away from the children's home, as he had in the past.

It was also helpful for me to know about external issues in the children's lives, such as the disintegration of Don's family and the lack of contact with his mother, in order to understand and make connections with his inner world – connections which were not being made elsewhere due to the impact of his destructive behaviour on the hard-pressed staff in his children's home. While there are major implications regarding the meaning of confidentiality in this context (which is possibly more helpfully thought of in terms of protecting the essential privacy of the patient, as opposed to creating an atmosphere of secrecy), the benefits of creating a therapeutic alliance with the parents/carers far outweigh the difficulties of struggling to deal wisely with issues of confidentiality, for all involved with the child.

In addition, the therapist's readiness to communicate with the adults/carers helps to facilitate and encourage well-informed external responses by these carers to a child's behaviour, which is thus made more comprehensible. While in many cases it may well be preferable to have a colleague working with the adults, this is often not possible in practice. In addition, there are a significant number of cases, such as with Mr and Mrs X, where this may even not be advisable. There are times when only direct contact between the child's therapist and their adult carers will suffice, and indeed Anna Freudian colleagues have long advocated this approach with certain patients, particularly children under 5. This working alliance of adults around the child, such as my work with Mr and Mrs X and my contact with the staff at Don's children's home, needs to have as its aim the creation of a parental couple or network constructively 'holding', thinking about and working to help the child (Lanyado 1991). Where working relationships surrounding a troubled child struggle to avoid splitting and polarisation, the result for the child is a very positive experience of being, and feeling, emotionally held in the minds of the key adults in their lives. This is in contrast to working relationships in which inadequate communication within the system leads to conflict, confirming the child's persecutory anxieties about such contacts, or the child's fears of their own destructiveness.

As already indicated, interpretation in this Winnicottian view becomes one of the many therapeutic interventions, albeit frequently a pivotal one. I would now add to this the therapeutic significance of what Stern and his colleagues call 'moments-of-meeting' that I have written about elsewhere (Lanyado 2004, ch. 1; Stern *et al.* 1998). Both clinical examples illustrate how the carefully adapted therapeutic setting provided the space within which play and/or playful thought could take place. While this is not very surprising for the young brothers, it should be noted that their behaviour at home was very difficult and one of their parents' main concerns was that they were unable to play together without fights rapidly breaking out. This had not been the case before their sister's death.

Working with young adolescents is notoriously difficult because of the developmental thrust away from intimacy with adults which makes working in the transference anathema for so many of them. In addition, there is a problem for young people of finding the right words to express deeper feelings, as well as the common adolescent approach to life which is in the main more inclined towards action than introspection. As a result, many therapists find that a more conversational manner in the sessions holds these patients in treatment better than the traditionally more reserved manner that they may feel more familiar with (see Horne, Chapter 13). This leads to an uncomfortable sense that the therapist is behaving non-analytically. I would argue that this is not so. As a result of this more active and playful role, the therapist is able to get closer to the adolescent process and occasionally interpret in a light but subtle way, which the teenager can respond to. My comment to Don that if he didn't laugh he would cry was this kind of playful interpretation. It arose from our relationship which allowed for humour, both as a means of very necessary defence for Don and as a form of playfulness which was enjoyable in its own right for Don and myself. This provided a safe base from which he could dare to become more serious and surprisingly introspective. I discuss the value of humour and playful interpretation in more detail in Chapter 8.

An additional question arises: why isn't interpretation alone sufficient, for example, in Mr and Mrs X and their sons' case, to help to 'mend the (parental) boat'? Why do we need to provide a 'holding' experience as well? Part of the answer may lie in the belief that this kind of healing can only be done by the patient for themselves, within the holding environment of the therapy. This is a view often expressed by Winnicott, most powerfully in his paper 'The capacity to be alone' (1958) and expanded further by Balint in *The Basic Fault* (Balint 1968). However, as I have described elsewhere, the 'presence' of the therapist in these circumstances has a profound impact in enabling patients to persevere with their efforts within the therapeutic process, possibly particularly where there has been serious traumatic experience (Lanyado 2004).

Further parallels between the therapeutic process and the parent–infant relationship lie in the ebb and flow of integrated and unintegrated states within the infant, which Winnicott describes as developing into a more integrated whole as a result of the experience of being held in the mother's attentive mind, and responded to by her maximally adaptive behaviour during infancy and times of stress. The experience of being held in the mind of the therapist when these unintegrated states arise in therapy can in time be introjected by the patient, resulting in a sense of feeling stronger and more able to bear emotional pain, even when this pain remains undiminished in intensity. From this point of view, interpretation given prematurely, while the patient is in a deeply unintegrated state, risks interrupting the natural process of growth and recovery which the patient needs to discover within themselves, rather than within the awareness of an external relationship (Balint 1968). The holding relationship provided by the therapist and taken for granted by the patient in these deeply regressed states helps the patient to reach this healing process. This was part of the early therapeutic process for Mr and Mrs X. When the patient is in more integrated states, and more aware of the therapist's separateness, interpretation crystallises meaning from the clinical material. The important issue of when to interpret to the patient, and when the interpretation needs to stay within the therapist's mind, goes beyond the realms of this chapter but is discussed fully with regard to adult patients by Balint.

It is also interesting to note that, in the above examples, as a result of the attentive and playful milieu of the therapy before the interpretations were given, the younger brother and Don were both actively interested in what I was saying and seemed eager to hear more, indeed to risk more self-exposure because of this interest. The strength of this wish to reach and understand the nature of the True Self is an important motivator in enabling patients, and individuals in everyday life, to keep exploring the inner world, even when this is painful and difficult.

Thus the clinical material demonstrates how playing, which is one of the most important mediums of therapeutic communication between therapist and patient (particularly child and adolescent patients), can be seen as being a crucial factor in the work that surrounds interpretation. Winnicott's definition of psychotherapy places play at its heart – as already quoted above, 'Psychotherapy has to do with two people playing together.'

Finally, the outcome of what could be described as 'small but important change' within brief therapy challenges the assertion that brief work in particular cannot achieve much. A turning point towards a healthier direction, from a very convoluted developmental path, can in the course of time lead to a very different place in emotional life. This was demonstrated by Don. I think that it is unlikely that Don would have started to communicate authentically with me within the more usual four-session initial consultation period. However, the safety of twelve sessions with some clear structure within them, and a clear end in sight, while initially approached with great caution, became an opportunity for him to get involved with the process while knowing that he had a way out of it if it became too frightening. This was so for a surprising number of the boys in the research study. The small change that Don made resulted in him acknowledging his problems, regularly attending weekly therapy and wanting to keep in touch with his therapist after he had started work. Therapy for Mr and Mrs X and the young boys was made up of many such small changes which constituted new and healthy emotional development.

There are implications in terms of the way clinical assessments are seen in the light of all this. As stated at the beginning of this chapter, I prefer to think of them as therapeutic consultations in which important small changes can take place, irrespective of whether ongoing therapy is an outcome. In this respect the experience of a short series of therapeutic consultations can be of benefit to the patient, not only as a means of developing a particular treatment plan, but as an experience in which something small but important happens, and through which the patient knows him- or herself slightly better as an immediate outcome. It is a valuable therapeutic experience in its own right.

Non-intensive, 'brief' psychoanalytic work, and therapeutic consultations can be of value to many patients, and should not be viewed as 'diluted' intensive work but as a therapeutic discipline in its own right. As intensive psychoanalytic psychotherapy is likely to remain very much less common or available than these 'applications' of the work, an open mind towards the broad range of psychoanalytic treatments that are actually practised, and the theories that underlie them, is much needed.

Therapeutic communication can take place in many settings if the person/s seeking help is/are listened to and given the kind of attention that is at the heart of psychoanalytic treatment. It is this ability that is being used by the therapist in the forms of treatments discussed in this chapter, and it is from these abilities that the children and their families who seek our help are able to benefit.

Notes

1 An earlier version of this paper was published in 1996 in the *Journal of Child Psychotherapy* 22(3): 423–43 as 'Winnicott's children: the holding environment and therapeutic communication in brief and non-intensive work'. The paper has been revised and updated for inclusion in this book.

2 The research team consisted of Dr Arnon Bentovim (Consultant Child Psychiatrist), Dr Jill Hodges (Consultant Child and Adolescent Psychotherapist), Professor David Skuse (Professor of Behavioural Sciences), Monica Lanyado (Consultant Child and Adolescent Psychotherapist), Chriso Andreou (Senior Child and Adolescent Psychotherapist), Jim Stevenson (Senior Lecturer in Psychology), Dr Bryn Williams (Research Psychologist) and Dr Michelle New (Clinical Psychologist).

I would like to thank Julia Fabricius and Judith Edwards for their helpful and thoughtful comments on this chapter when it was originally published.

References

Balint, M. (1968) *The Basic Fault*. London: Tavistock

Daws, D. (1989) *Through the Night. Helping Parents and Sleepless Infants*. London: Free Association Books

Hodges, J., Lanyado, M. and Andreou, C. (1994) 'Sexuality and violence: preliminary clinical hypotheses from psychotherapeutic assessments in a research programme on young sexual offenders'. *Journal of Child Psychotherapy* 20(3): 283–308

Lanyado, M. (1991) 'On creating a psychotherapeutic space'. *Journal of Social Work Practice* 5(1): 31–40

Lanyado, M. (1999) 'Brief psychotherapy and therapeutic consultations: how much therapy is 'good-enough'. In M. Lanyado and A. Horne (eds.), *The Handbook of Child and Adolescent Psychotherapy: Psychoanalytic Approaches*. London: Routledge

Lanyado, M. (2004) *The Presence of the Therapist: Treating Childhood Trauma*. Hove, UK: Brunner-Routledge

Phillips, A. (1988) *Winnicott*. Fontana Modern Masters, ed. Frank Kermode. London: Fontana

Stern, D., Sander, L. W., Nahum, J. P., Harrison, A. M., Lyons-Ruth, K., Morgan, A. C., Bruschweiler-Stern, N. and Tronick, E. Z. (1998) 'Non-interpretive mechanisms in psychoanalytic therapy: the "something more" than interpretation' *International Journal of Psycho-Analysis* 79: 903–21

Strachey, J. (1934) 'The nature of the therapeutic action in psychoanalysis' *International Journal of Psycho-Analysis* 1(5): 127–59

Tracey, N., Blake, P., Warren, B., Hardy, H., Enfield, S. and Shein, P. (1996) 'Will I be to my son as my father was to me?' *Journal of Child Psychotherapy* 22(2): 168–94

Winnicott, D. W. (1941) 'The observation of infants in a set situation'. In Winnicott (1958) *Collected Papers: Through Paediatrics to Psycho-Analysis*. London: Tavistock Publications

Winnicott, D. W. (1958) 'The capacity to be alone'. In Winnicott (1965), *The Maturational Processes and the Facilitating Environment*. London: Hogarth and the Institute of Psycho-Analysis

Winnicott, D. W. (1960) 'The theory of the parent–infant relationship'. In Winnicott, *The Maturational Processes and the Facilitating Environment*

Winnicott, D. W. (1962) 'The aims of psychoanalytic treatment'. In *The Maturational Processes and the Facilitating Environment*

Winnicott, D. W. (1971a) *Therapeutic Consultations in Child Psychiatry*. London: Hogarth and the Institute of Psycho-Analysis

Winnicott, D. W (1971b) *Playing and Reality*. London: Tavistock Publications; Harmondsworth, UK: Penguin, 1980

13 Interesting things to say – and why[1]

Ann Horne

The general principle seems to me to be valid that *psychotherapy is done in the overlap of the two play areas, that of the patient and that of the therapist. If the therapist cannot play, then he is not suitable for the work*. If the patient cannot play, then something needs to be done to enable the patient to become able to play, after which psychotherapy may begin. The reason why playing is essential is that it is in playing that the patient is being creative.

(Winnicott 1971: 63)

Modifications of technique are departures from the 'normal' range of techniques applicable to neurotic children. There is no absolute psychoanalytic technique for use with children, but rather a set of analytic principles which have to be adapted to specific cases. Variations in technique represent appropriate specific adaptations of the basic set of analytic principles rather than deviations from standard technique.

(Sandler, Kennedy and Tyson 1980: 199)

PROLOGUE

James's father was waiting in the hallway of the clinic. 'James is in the car but he won't come in. I wondered if *you* could get him to come in – I can't. He has been bullied at school but the bullies are all taking their national exams [i.e. they are four years older than James] so James has been asked to stay off until they are punished after their exams. I think it's affecting him. I think it's very unfair – as if he is the one to be punished. Oh, and he's wearing a skirt.'

I said that I would not go out to persuade him to come in but I would say hello to him as he had made the very long journey (1½ hours by car) to get here. As I approached, James (age 12) shuffled his belongings across the back seat to make space and I asked if he were inviting me in. He nodded. His father sat a little distance away on a low wall. Inside, I said that it seemed a shame to have come so far and for us not to say hello. He nodded and smiled. I wondered if he found it hard to talk of what was so much on his mind? 'I'll come in!' – firmly and clearly. He pulled his trainers on to his bare feet: they were quite large and black and seemed very incongruous with the brief denim skirt he sported and which he tugged modestly down. Then he rummaged behind him, found a pair of sports shorts, and pulled these on *under* his skirt. I looked at this. 'Having things both ways today?' James grinned and nodded. 'Ready?' Nod. I tried to open the back door. The child safety locks were on. . . . We were trapped like two children together. James found this hilarious.

Was it 'right' to go out to the car to see James?
Was it 'right' to go into the car?
Was it 'right' to laugh with him about our predicament?
Is psychotherapy sometimes allowed to be playful?

INTRODUCTION

It takes time in work with young people to gain confidence not only in making interpretations to them but in making decisions about what one should or should not do as a therapist. Over one's shoulder there lurks a superego figure of a kind, 'The Great Child Psychotherapist in the Sky' as I call it, whom one assumes would do it all

a correctly (an interesting concept)
b calmly and
c in a brief sentence, gathering all aspects of the child's problems and behaviour into one succinct mutative interpretation – the all-encompassing comment that changes the way the child makes sense of himself.

Moreover, it would all probably be done from the therapist's seat in the therapy room, obviating the need occasionally to be under tables, or running downstairs after agile latency-aged boys, to be jumping to save goals – or to find oneself in the back seat of a Ford estate car, locked in, with a 12-year-old boy wearing a skirt.

Aspects of such a harsh professional superego are clearly destined to be taken to one's own analyst or therapist where one hopes a slightly less punitive conscience can be fostered! However, there does remain the central technical issue of *how* one addresses children and young people and the troubled parts they bring with them, and how one simply *is* with them. This emerges constantly in supervision. It is remarkably easy, when one is working as a supervisor, to think of what might have been said: it is the time of calm reflection after the event, after all, and time to think is something that many children do not grant us in the passion of the therapeutic encounter.

This chapter, therefore, is offered as one way of thinking *before* the event – and it may enable trainees to see their wise old bats of supervisors as less than magical, as occasionally flummoxed themselves and as just having more experiences from which to have worked things out! It also keeps a promise to my supervisees that *someone* has to write the paper on 'Interesting things to say to children'. . . .

The experience of supervising, of being a supervisor, involves in itself the creation of a 'transitional space', an 'intermediate area of experience' (Winnicott 1951/1971) in which the child *qua* child, the child as perceived and experienced by the trainee, and the child as perceived by the supervisor all come together. Casement describes the progress of supervision as leading to a dialogue between the external supervisor, the internalised supervisor and the 'internal supervisor' that becomes established in all of us and that, with time and experience, is available to be called upon when we need space for thought in a session (Casement 1985: 32). This 'internal supervisor', however, needs to be able to operate with playfulness if it is not to re-enact harsher aspects of our own or our patients' superegos. I would also argue for playfulness between supervisor and supervisee. If, as Strachey first outlined (later developed by Loewald 1960), during an analysis the analyst as 'new object' is introjected into the patient's superego, modifying its harshness (Strachey 1934), so the process is parallel with the supervisor in supervision.

We fear 'acting in' – normally an expression used when the patient acts out part of their psychopathology within the session, but I would also like to think about it in relation to psychotherapists who fear they may act (rather than reflect) when in the presence of a particular child and the material that the child brings. This can be true especially when we feel the force of our counter-transference, when our own feelings become hard to manage – feelings of being overwhelmed and paralysed, of great sympathy and compassion, or of rage and an internal urge to be angry with the patient or to retaliate sadistically. Space for thinking is vital. It is also equally vital when we think of challenging our professional superegos and doing something different with a child. It is always in the unexpected place in therapy (unexpected to the child) that we consciously do not act in accordance with the child's internal objects and psychic structure – e.g. we are careful not to give interpretations that mirror the child's superego if this superego is punitive. Indeed, 'tempering . . . (the) superego' is part of the patient–therapist relationship whereby 'the patient internalises affective attitudes from the therapist' (Gabbard and Westen 2003). Such care is usual and can have a huge impact on child or adult. It is also in the unexpected place in the therapy that we may consciously do something more playful. Such interventions must arise from a clear understanding of the child's psychopathology, the nature of the treatment alliance and our clinical knowledge and framework. To say to James, 'Having it both ways today?' was fine but may well have been contraindicated with another child.

DEFENCES: RESPECTING AND ENGAGING WITH CURIOSITY

We were approaching a holiday break. Pamela had been a hard child to work with, resistant even to the articulation of feelings, never mind being miles away from gaining insight. When I told her of the approaching break she shouted, 'Good!' I smiled at her (she had expected something punitive from this outburst). 'Well, you wouldn't want to miss therapy too much!' She roared with laughter – it somehow spoke to the bizarre in assuming she might miss me when in sessions she constantly muttered darkly how she would like to stop coming, but it also addressed her attachment and wish for the therapy to continue. We had captured something and she felt recognised in her ambivalence and in her reversal – if I were discarding her for the summer she would most certainly discard me verbally. I wished that I had been more playful with her earlier. Anne Alvarez has talked of a similar approach: to the child who hurls, 'I hate you!' at her, she may well say, 'Well, you wouldn't want to like me *too* much', similarly reaching the defence and ambivalence but in a non-persecuting way.

Timothy was 13 and invariably late for sessions. The Child Guidance Unit in which I then worked had closed by the time he was due for his appointment; there was no one in the reception area, and I would go to the waiting area at the time of his session. If he was not there, I returned to my room, leaving the door open for him to enter. About 15 minutes into his session time, I would hear in the distance a faint tuneful whistling – the *Monty Python's Flying Circus* song 'Always look on the bright side of life'. It grew gradually louder and behind it arrived a defensively smiling Tim. Looking on the bright side of life was not easy for him, trapped in a sado-masochistic relationship with a single parent mother who beat him and intruded into his sexuality. He felt compelled to exclude major adults in his life (he spent his maths lessons reading novels and in this manner silently winding up his maths teacher) as contact so easily felt like impingement and intrusion to him. It was hard to hope that a therapist would not also be sadistic.

I struggled for several weeks with how to address this (this was a three-times-weekly therapy, an important post-qualification experience of more intense work, so it meant a *lot* of sessions where Tim missed time). Eventually I said that I thought he really needed to be in control of when our sessions began – so many things felt out of his control and it was essential to take charge of what he could. It was a pity, however, that taking control in *this* way also cost him 15 minutes of *his* time. I sympathised with his dilemma and wondered if he might reflect on it himself. Tim began to come on time. It fitted into a general theme in the therapy about control and what I called his tendency to shoot himself in the foot – by his need for one particular defence (e.g. to keep any intrusion out), or by repeating the anxieties of his childhood as he did in maths, silently goading his teacher into retribution and so setting himself up masochistically for punishment, he would often end up in trouble in school. It was a good day when he reported that he had met with the deputy head (a benign man, confused by Tim but willing to help him) and in this meeting told him, 'Ann says I shoot myself in the foot.' Now Tim was being proactive in enabling the environment to respond appropriately – and the phrase seemed to have developed real resonance for him. Such phrasing allows one to ally oneself with the child – not with the defence – and to return the projections for thought.

During my own training I was fortunate – very fortunate – in my teachers. It seems invidious to single out one when I learned from so many. However, Anne Alvarez in clinical seminars introduced me to the phrase 'It seems difficult to hope that . . .' This phrase draws heavily upon Anna Freud's understanding of the defences as necessary – possibly inappropriate, but the only solution to be found by the child at that point – and so to be respected (Freud 1936). It does not deny, collude with or attack the defence as it is being used; rather, it addresses the issues underlying the need for that defence and also includes the possibility of change, of things being differently perceived or experienced. It remains one of the most helpful 'interesting things' to say to a child when one is being creative about the defensive structure. George gives a good example of when this phrase can be used:

George had expressed a strong wish to be a girl, leading to his referral at the age of 9. A 'replacement child', conceived after the death, at birth, of a much-wanted girl, and ill at his own birth, he was for his parents both blessing and bane – his survival was celebrated, his masculinity not. He attended for once-weekly therapy for two years. A talented child, he gained a sense of self from his singing, acting and dancing skills and performances. During his therapy he would from time to time use the couch – spread out on it in seeming relief – and was able to talk or be quiet, as he felt the need. One day he managed to talk of how angry he was at his sister's death; angry with the hospital and also just angry. There was a painful pause. I commented quietly that he was rightly very angry with all the grown-ups and sometimes he found it very hard to hope that they wanted him just to be George. After a few moments he swung his feet off the couch and stood up. 'I wondered what kind of singing voice I'll have when my voice breaks?' 'Can we hope for a George voice?', I offered. 'A George voice!' – he smiled.

ANXIETY

It has long been a feature in psychoanalytic work with children to take issues up in the displacement, especially when the child's anxiety is too great to enable a transference interpretation to be made or when words have for the child a concrete reality. Talking of murderous rage can be heard as accusing the child of actually killing the objects. Displacement is especially effective with younger children where anthropomorphism – of animals and even bricks – allows high emotion to be explored in a safe, removed arena. It can lead to some extremely bizarre conversations, as it did for me with a 20-year-old who sidled up to relationships via his love of Thomas the Tank Engine. 'How would Thomas feel about..' was useful and could open up fantasy in the displacement of Thomas and his favourite female engine, Lady. But one had to concentrate on not feeling foolish – possible if one is absolutely certain as to the value of such displaced, parallel conversations.

> Anna Freud has pointed out that the procedure of giving interpretations about a person or figure onto whom the child has externalised aspects of his own self, thus accepting the externalisation for the time being, is not necessarily collusion but, rather, a way of approaching threatening mental content gradually.
>
> (Sandler, Kennedy and Tyson 1980: 165)

For the abused child, indeed, it is often through such displacements that affects can begin to be recognised and given the symbolism of words for the first time.

Maria had suffered extreme sexual abuse at the hands of her drug addict mother's partner, and severe emotional and physical neglect. She tended to deal with her world by dissociation, inhabiting a realm of wild animals, which seemed to her to be more honourable in their interactions with each other than untrustworthy humans. For several months, conversation between therapist and child concerned these animals – rapacious only when necessary, at the mercy of humans, strong yet vulnerable. Only once extremes of affect could gradually be recognised and named in the animals could Maria begin to tolerate their resonance with parts of herself and their relevance to the transference relationship. In this way she slowly, in Miss Freud's words, 'came near the defended content' (Sandler *et al.* 169). We may be more inclined to think of such a technique when we have the child's shame in mind – e.g. shame about murderous feelings towards siblings – or narcissistic pain, where too direct an approach may reinforce and strengthen inappropriate defences (Parsons 2003). We also need to be able to use it when affect, if reawakened too quickly, may overwhelm and drive the child to more desperate defences.

'Me-to-choose time' arose in work with an abused and abusing adolescent boy:

For the first few months Wayne found the process of attending for fifty-minute sessions desperately persecutory. Arriving felt like being locked away by his father, when anything could happen; leaving – no matter how carefully the therapist tried to prepare and warn him – was a repetition of abandonment. After much thought, his therapist gave him control of the last ten minutes of the session: he could choose at what point he left within this ten minute space, although she would always remain in the room for his full time and he would wait in the waiting room with his escort until she emerged to say goodbye. He rarely used this control, although he occasionally drew attention to the fact that it was now 'me to choose time'. Much later in his therapy he reflected on this and on the impotence he had felt as a child. He could now recognise states of anxiety and think rather than act. (Horne 1999)

Anne Hurry in a lovely paper describes the work of assessing troubled adolescents (Hurry 1986). Following a helpful passage in which she describes the use of neutral words – 'strange' feelings rather than fearful or shameful ones – she has pertinent comments to make on hope and despair, recognising this axis and the capacity of the adolescent to cling to one, denying the other:

> it is necessary to bear in mind the adolescent's potential ambivalence towards change, and to bear in mind that for many young people despair can be less painful than hope which places them in what is felt as a much more vulnerable position. . . . Technically then, it is important to be prepared to take up whichever aspect of his ambivalence the adolescent is least conscious of. When the adolescent despairs it is possible to interpret the hope which he is inviting the interviewer to carry for him, and to note the evidence for this hope in the very fact that he has come. When the adolescent is only enthusiastic about treatment, it may be necessary to take up his need to deny his doubts and fears, or even the way in which he is seeking in his choice of therapy to perpetuate the childhood state wherein he does not bear responsibility for himself.
>
> (Hurry 1986: 41–2)

PUBLIC SITUATIONS AND THERAPIST HUMILIATION

I have lastingly embarrassing memories of trying, not long after I had qualified, to assess a seriously abused and emotionally neglected child who stormed and raged, kept the therapy room door open, and made noisy excursions to the waiting room where her mother sat, glad of the break from her daughter and patently enjoying my only too evident struggles. 'The Great Child Psychotherapist in the Sky' loomed large in my mind at this time.

> At one point Kelly attacked me viciously, kicking, punching and spitting. I told her that if she continued, I would have to hold her flailing arms, thinking that the usual tack of having to end the session would probably not work as the boundaries of the session had become so permeable anyway. I tried to grapple in my mind with her seeming sadism and my humiliation. She attacked again. Telling her what I was doing, I held her arms. At the top of her voice she yelled, 'She's sexually abusing me! Help!' I let her go with a sense of despair; she ran out to the waiting room in triumph.

The work continued with Kelly, her mother and her baby sister together. I think this was right but have often wondered what a comment on the lines of 'It seems difficult to hope that I will not be a grown-up who abuses you' might have done. At that point, I was too caught up with my superego and my counter-transference to be able to think. It was a useful, if salutary, lesson. Now, I think, I would not continue the individual assessment sessions as they were too fearful for Kelly, and be explicit about this, but move speedily to seeing the three together – but I have had a very long number of years to reflect on it!

The vignette of James, stuck in the back of the car despite having made a very long journey to the clinic, shows how one can begin to think about the private and public boundaries of therapy and the therapeutic relationship. His history is important.

> James is the second of his parents' three children. He has a brother who is two years older than he is and a sister who is three years younger. Referred by his doctor for gender dysphoria – it was said in the referral letter that he dressed often as a girl, his close friends were girls and that he displayed effeminacy but it was uncertain whether he was aware of this – he had been referred on to me by a specialist Gender Identity Development Service to see if he might be engaged in psychotherapy, while my Gender Service colleagues continued to work with his parents. Despite his not being around to be brought to the first appointment – he was eventually found hiding in the boot of his father's

car – at the next appointment when he and his father met me with the specialist child psychiatrist, he separated surprisingly easily to spend time on his own with me. The child psychiatrist had judged the timing of this meeting and separation exceptionally well.

At our first encounter, James ignored all the toys in the room and curled up in an easy chair, his thumb in his mouth. He spoke so softly I could barely hear him. He kept his eyes on my face – unusually not exploring, even visually, the room in which he now found himself. I did not feel an object of curiosity in this, however, rather an object to be kept in sight in case it did something unpredictable. The regressive pose said a lot about what felt safe for him in relation to a new object – being a regressed baby was preferable to risking being a pre-pubertal boy. James smiled a lot – especially when I could not hear him and had to ask him to repeat things. There was control here, too.

I did not make this a long meeting. James surprisingly asked to return to meet again at the earliest time I could give him. In subsequent sessions he often played an aggressive and violent mother. At one point he stated, 'Mums like girls, Dads like boys. So girls get off with every-thing with their Mums.' A less evident theme was the equation of any sense of male potency and agency as delinquent and to be discouraged. I heard that his mother helped him choose which of her old clothes – including her underwear – he might play with and be given by her to wear. James also told me clearly that he was a boy, not a girl, and had no wish to be a girl. We came to a form of words about 'playing with ideas of boy and girl' that he agreed with. I had thought that fortnightly sessions might be all the intimacy he could manage but both he and his father, after a term of fortnightly therapy, agreed to weekly work.

James is brought by his father, a large, obese man who suffers from diabetes and a heart condition. His work is sedentary. His vulnerability is not put into words but is, I think, in his son's mind. James's mother has an Asperger-ish quality about her and finds it too easy to be cruelly castrating of James: their times of intimacy seem to centre round his fetish.

What I feel I can say to James is underpinned by my understanding of him: a boy whose development verges on puberty and the questions of sexuality and identity that raises, whose masculinity is attacked by a mother who supports his cross-dressing, who cannot bear any energy, dissension, or sense of masculine potency from him, and who complains bitterly about such behaviour. Misbehaviour in James's case is developmentally very appropriate – the only way to separate physically and sexually from such an ambivalent object. Yet identifications with a fragile-seeming father are also difficult and James has not yet been able to engage with any male influences in school.

It was important not to fall into the trap of becoming 'the expert' who would winkle James out of the car – this would have been doomed to failure and is a situation that we are often put into by families. It would also have undermined his father's role. It was, however, important not to replicate the castrating or distant mother, hence my trip out to the car, beyond the boundary of waiting room and therapy room, and my engagement with James. His pulling on his shorts *under* his skirt was fascinating as it enabled him to maintain the feminine outside but with a male covering (boy's shorts) of the male organs: thus I commented on the need for both. Playfulness is really quite a serious and informed business!

ACTING OUT

The 'nice neurotic child' of the early days of psychoanalysis may have been a little bit of a myth – or a feature of private practice. Today in public service work, we are more likely to have referred to us children whom others struggle to understand and contain. Where thought is generally absent, it becomes important to create an arena where it might become a possibility. In doing this, we have to wonder constantly abut the nature of the anxiety that the child struggles with, that necessitates the only discoverable response of mindless activity. Being able as therapists to seek a space for thinking is essential.

There is an interesting piece of 'Portman lore' – ideas refined over the years by the psychotherapists and psychoanalysts who work at the Portman Clinic in London with a patient group who are always difficult and often dangerous – that helps us think about the concepts of 'activity' and 'danger'. If a therapist is working with a violent patient, the tendency in other therapeutic settings is for the therapist to sit in the chair nearest to the door: if the situation feels unsafe, there is a quick exit for the therapist. Seemingly paradoxically, but actually faithful in psychoanalytic terms, Portman lore says that the psychotherapist should allow the patient the seat nearest to the exit. For most violent patients, the anxiety aroused by a suddenly perceived threat to the ego leads to a violent reaction in the service of protecting the ego (Glasser 1998). Having an exit available thus frees the patient *not* to have to attack, but to preserve the ego (self) by escape.

In such a brief description one can see how the therapist has to do three things:

a   there has to be awareness of the risk of danger – after all, that is probably why the patient was referred;
b   there has to be a clear understanding of the meaning of the violent act and why violence might occur;

c   there has to be considerable trust in the psychoanalytic knowledge base
     and the therapeutic process.

It is also important that we think about the context of the therapy – in
terms of the clinical space but also with young people in terms of the
supportive network that allows therapy to become a treatment of choice.
Too often I have heard of therapists who engage with children when the
environment is neither supportive nor able to withstand the impact of the
therapy, and the therapy is stopped when the children act out. This is
abusive and thoughtless.

With adolescents in particular one has to be careful to avoid humiliating
them with one's interpretations – or using the interpretation as a weapon
with which to hit back. Splitting off the adolescent's more infantile part
from the adult, thinking part can help the young person and engage them
with the mature part of the self that can reflect on the activity-based
defences of the infantile part. Addressing this with curiosity – joining with
the thinking part – is also useful: with the risk-taking delinquent one can
comment on the little part of them that wished it could run or escape the
past traumatic experiences, and how this part still repeats the feelings of
risk, fear and high adrenalin surge, hoping this time to be in control of
them. One can then be curious about why this still happens – and space for
thought is created.

In a similar way, for the child or young person who acts out with the
body, who might be viewed as functioning at a level of what I think of as
'body-based defensive manoeuvres', one can address the body itself as a
separate entity that cannot itself think but which does operate as a source
of memories and at times acts on these.

> Genevieve had been abused from the age of 3 by her half-brother who
> had himself been abused sexually by his mother (who still cared for
> Genevieve and her younger siblings). She had begun to act out sexually
> at the age of 6, with peers in school and with her little brother. This was
> impossible for her to talk of – indeed, when I met her at age 7, words for
> Genevieve were concrete entities where to speak them made their
> content real. Eventually, after her mother had accosted me in the
> waiting room with a gruff, 'She's doin' it again – you know – these dirty
> things – with her brother', Genevieve and I managed a brief conver-
> sation about her body and the interesting way it remembered things that
> had happened to it. When it felt compelled to do things to her brother, it
> was remembering what had happened to it. It made sense. Genevieve's
> eyes shone – she was overwhelmed that there might be a reason and
> that it did not mean that she was simply 'bad'.

It is not merely with bodily acting out, however, that one can use such a deliberately created split. Anna Freud describes how, in engaging with

> a seven-year-old neurotically naughty little girl. . . . I suddenly separated off all her naughtiness and personified it for her, giving it a name of its own and confronting her with it, and eventually succeeded in so far that she began to complain of the person thus newly created by me, and obtained an insight into the amount of suffering she had endured from it. The 'analysability' of the child came hand in hand with the insight into the malady established in this way.
>
> (Freud 1927: 12)

The word 'interesting' is one I tend to overwork . . . Partly, the phrase 'Now that's very interesting' gives one a tiny space for thinking, even while one is fleetingly wondering what the Great Child Psychotherapist in the Sky would do this time. More importantly, it gives one a form of words for engaging with the thinking part of the child in relation to the infantile part, and sets up a climate of curiosity. To the child who has acted in the session one can say, 'Now that was really interesting' – and the unexpected phrase challenges superego and defence, addresses the ego, and enables thought. I learned this from my own supervision: as I brought my intensely passionate but often Houdini-like adolescent training case to Anne Hurry, she would say, 'Now why did you do that? That was interesting.' It opened up supervision as an exercise in curiosity and learning. I use this still.

THE STRUGGLE FOR THOUGHT AND THINKING SPACE

Lucy Alexander, a BAP trainee, was working in three-times-weekly psychotherapy with a bright, passionate 5-year-old, dislocated from her native Italy and brought, together with her two brothers and half-brother, to a small English city by her Italian mother and English father. Ariadne would regularly become a whirlwind in sessions, both with her body and in her words and feelings. This prevented thought on the part of her therapist and on Ariadne's part, too. After some reflection in supervision, we decided that Lucy would introduce the concept of 'thinking time' towards the end of each session – a 10-minute period for thinking about that day's session. Sometimes this works, sometimes 'thinking' is too scary a concept for a child. Ariadne took to it with great delight. Occasionally, she would include the toy elephants who, she said, also needed to think – especially if they had been playing out difficulties in their elephant family, oedipal rivalries and sibling wars, and uncertainties about the place of girls. Always, in this 'thinking time', she bravely brought the theme back to her own anxieties. Between them, Lucy and Ariadne went on to create their own special containment during the session – 'the slowing down place', Ariadne's idea, a corner of the room where Ariadne went of her own accord when her feelings became tumultuous. This was such an imaginative invention and was possible because of the nature of their therapeutic relationship and because the therapist was available to meet the creativity of the child. It was a real 'Winnicottian' creation. It did not arise from supervision: it occurred in the 'overlap of the two play areas' (Winnicott 1971), that of the therapist and that of the child.

It can be interesting (again a useful word!) in the early stages of trainees' work to see that they worry about enjoying sessions with children. Could this really be psychoanalytic psychotherapy when it is also, from time to time, fun? As they gain experience and near the end of training, they can allow themselves to enjoy the process of work and the progress made, and recognise that 'fun' accomplishes huge internal and developmental shifts. 'Play is work', as a child once reputedly told Winnicott with great seriousness.

WHEN PLAY IS NOT POSSIBLE

> First you have to build the house before you can throw anyone out of it.
> (Anna Freud, quoted in Sandler, Kennedy and Tyson 1980)

I agree with Winnicott that 'if the therapist cannot play, then he is not suitable for the work', absolute though the statement may seem (Winnicott 1971). For the *child* who cannot play or be playful, for whom Winnicott urges 'something needs to be done to enable the patient to become able to play, after which psychotherapy may begin', there is still the psychoanalytic solution of 'developmental therapy' and the therapist as 'developmental object' (Hurry 1998). We do not often enough value Anna Freud's great contributions of the analysis of the ego and the superego, as well as the unconscious id (Edgcumbe 2000); Hurry's book also reminds us of the Hampstead Clinic's work on developmental deficit and help.

Failures in the early environment inhibit 'the evolving mental process itself, which is a more generalised, primitive defence' (Fonagy *et al.* 1993). The capacities for thought, curiosity, feeling and emotion may be stunted as in the case of Maria (above) and as in the cases of many of the children we see today when there has been early, especially pre-verbal, trauma. As Anne Hurry reminds us, whether this be due to conflict (and thus a primitive defence) or deficit, 'the analyst's task is to engage inhibited or undeveloped processes within the analytic encounter' (Hurry 1998: 67). Thus work on noting affect, naming it and giving it legitimacy is necessary before the child is able to gain mastery, predict emotional actions and reactions, and regulate that affect. Spontaneity is the key, as Hurry and her colleagues describe, but crucially the interventions arise from that transitional space, the play area that the therapist reminds the child lies between them.

This ego structuring matters if the child is to be able to come to use therapy. Moreover 'it is also important that the analyst be prepared to move between the developmental/relational stance and the interpretative, as Anna Freud described. . . . Both developmental relating and understanding are necessary; each can potentiate and reinforce the effects of the other' (Hurry 1998: 71–2).

CONCLUSION

Perhaps we can now see that ideas of 'right' or 'wrong' – my questions about James at the start of this chapter – fit uneasily into a perspective that takes the relationship as primary and where curiosity and engendering curiosity (about child, about therapist, about the process between them) is a key tool in what we do in the analytic encounter.

It can be very helpful in work with children and young people to use the unexpected or surprising in our comments to them: it enables us to become 'subjective objects' and 'new objects' for their engagement and use. We need to be clear about the children we see, to have a flexible formulation as to their difficulties in mind. We need to be firm in our trust in the psycho-analytic method and its usefulness. Then we can begin to play – with perceptions, with ideas and above all with possibilities.

Note

1 I should like to thank all the trainees and colleagues – from the British Association of Psychotherapists, the Anna Freud Centre, the Scottish Institute for Human Relations and the Czech Society for Psychoanalytic Psychotherapy in Prague – who have allowed me to engage with them in thinking together about children and young people in therapy.

References

Casement, P. (1985) *On Learning from the Patient*. London and New York: Tavistock Publications

Edgcumbe, R. (2000) *Anna Freud: A View of Development, Disturbance and Therapeutic Techniques*. London and Philadelphia: Routledge

Fonagy, P., Moran, G., Edgcumbe, R., Kennedy, H. and Target, M. (1993) 'The roles of mental representations and mental processes in therapeutic action' *Psychoanalytic Study of the Child* 48: 9–48

Freud, A. (1927) *The Psycho-Analytical Treatment of Children: Technical Lectures and Essays*. London: Imago Publishing Co. Ltd

Freud, A. (1936/1968) *The Ego and the Mechanisms of Defence*. London: Hogarth Press

Gabbard, G. O. and Westen, D. (2003) 'Rethinking therapeutic action' *International Journal of Psychoanalysis* 84: 823–41

Glasser, M. (1998) 'On violence: a preliminary communication' *International Journal of Psychoanalysis* 79(5): 887–902

Horne, A. (1999) 'Sexual abuse and sexual abusing in childhood and adolescence'. In M. Lanyado and A. Horne (eds.), *The Handbook of Child and Adolescent Psychotherapy: Psychoanalytic Approaches*. London: Routledge

Hurry, A. (1986) 'Walk-in work with adolescents' *Journal of Child Psychotherapy* 12(1): 33–45

Hurry, A. (ed.) (1998) *Psychoanalysis and Developmental Therapy*. London: Karnac Books

Loewald, H. W. (1960) 'On the therapeutic action of psychoanalysis' *International Journal of Psycho-Analysis* 41: 16–33

Parsons, M. (2003) personal communication

Sandler, J., Kennedy, H. and Tyson, R. (1980) *The Technique of Child Psychoanalysis: Discussions with Anna Freud*. London: Hogarth Press and the Institute of Psycho-Analysis

Strachey, J. (1934) 'The nature of the therapeutic action in psychoanalysis' *International Journal of Psycho-Analysis* 15: 127–59

Winnicott, D. W. (1951/1971) 'Transitional objects and transitional phenomena'. In Winnicott, *Playing and Reality*. London: Tavistock Publications. Reprinted Harmondsworth, UK: Penguin Educational, 1980

Winnicott, D. W. (1971) 'Playing: creative activity and the search for the self'. In Winnicott, *Playing and Reality*

14 Conclusion

Where Independent minds meet

Monica Lanyado and Ann Horne

Within any tradition that calls itself 'independent' there must arise a spectrum of theoretical and technical possibilities. The absence of 'orthodoxy' is in itself a liberation, allowing us to test theory in the clinical laboratory and, where we find it wanting, to feel free to say so. Further to this, it offers space – transitional and potentially transformational – to *adapt to* the patient, to be in this sense genuinely 'maintaining not only intellectual but affective contact in the analytic situation' (Rycroft 1958: 83). As Bollas has commented, every Freudian needs to be also a Kohutian, a Kleinian, a Lacanian and a Winnicottian at times (quoted in Rayner 1991: 294).

The development of orthodoxies, conceivably essential in the early consolidation and affirmation of any theory as it grows up, was perhaps even more pressing in the case of psychoanalysis: a remarkably unscientific science, it sought 'theory' as a defence against accusations of illogicality. Yet in its 'apparently illogical method of enquiry', non-scientific but rational in its approach, dependent on free association, psychoanalysis equally requires a rigour of thought and appraisal to be brought to its findings – and orthodoxies can militate against such evaluation. It is not at all surprising that those who lie between Freud and Klein also find important creativity, transitional space and phenomena, the active presence of the therapist, and a therapeutic process that keeps in mind the early infant–mother relationship. The focus is on the process – and the affect within it.

When we add the research evidence (as in Chapter 3) that theoretical predilection, personal bias and one's own experience of supervision will all lead to a fairly individualistic outcome – that with experience we may well come to 'do' what we do not preach – the question of how we come to learn to do what we do becomes an interesting one. Moreover, how does anyone learn to 'do' psychotherapy, when the therapist's actual moment-to-moment behaviour in the room cannot be prescribed in more than broad ethical and professional principles because of the constantly changing interpersonal relationship that is at the heart of all psychotherapy? The experience that unfolds in the consulting room during every session is highly unpredictable and non-linear, which is why a step-by-step manualised kind of approach would act like a straitjacket to the essential spontaneity of each therapeutic encounter.

Whilst 'technique' can be copied – as any behaviour may be learned – it does not become useful, safe or grounded in the whole approach of the therapist without a great deal of learning from experience. This kind of learning involves at times having to take therapeutic risks, indeed at times making mistakes – but then learning from them (Rayner 1991: 8; Casement 2002). The therapeutic risk can then become a therapeutic opportunity, but it cannot take place if the therapist is unable to experience an openness of mind that allows for variation from what may be felt to be the 'norm' in technical terms. We have stressed that the so-called norm is frequently a fantasy on the therapist's part and, in practice, therapists are actually behaving in very different ways with their patients because they have found that these ways work. These differing responses are neither spoken nor written about enough. We have tried to redress this a little in this book.

Process recordings of sessions, which are discussed with a supervisor during training and afterwards, not only capture the step-by-step process of how one thing leads to another in the session, they also capture deeper assumptions held by the supervisee. These need to be examined as a personal contribution to the totality of the counter-transference – in the way that Heimann (1960, 1965), Rycroft (1956) and King (1978) *inter alia* have written. Maybe the whole question of how a therapist develops 'technique' could more accurately be described as an apprenticeship, in which as well as directly benefiting from the intellectual insights and understandings of her or his teachers and personal analysis, the 'apprentice' also actively identifies (consciously and unconsciously) with good as well as not-so-good aspects of the teacher's and analyst's technique and whole demeanour and attitude towards the patient. This is a highly individual process, intrinsically related to the therapist's ever developing skills in listening to, attending to and understanding the patient, as well being an outcome of the therapist's own personal journey through life.

Deviating from an assumed technical 'norm' is therefore highly loaded, because it may also involve a separateness of thinking from these highly personalised identifications with teachers who are also still greatly respected. This is an intergenerational process and one that we should all get used to – it is, after all, how children grow up! To respect a teacher does not mean that he or she should be seen as omniscient. Whilst it's very flattering to the teacher's ego, it is very bad for the profession and the growth of psychotherapeutic knowledge. For the profession to be alive, new ideas need to be welcomed and explored. This is not heresy, it is creative growth.

One of the rationales for producing this book has been a 'wish to engage in discussion about what actually happens in the consulting room, as opposed to what it is felt "ought" to be happening' (p. 2). When we originally met as a group of potential contributors, we realised that discovering where Independent minds meet was going to be interesting – if not challenging – because our very independence of mind led to many different ways of working. We knew we had the same theoretical roots and were keen to see how each of us conceptualised how we had grown clinically and technically from these roots. As noted in our introduction, what emerged much more strongly than we had originally realised was how much each of us had taken aspects of Winnicottian theory and used and grown them in the 'culture' of our own consulting room experience.

Sternberg's theoretical chapter in many ways reminds us of the 'story so far' in terms of historical differences about technique as well as the contemporary developments. Reflecting on the book as it has emerged, her chapter sets the scene for what we feel are further technical developments, which have been well tested in the consulting room. The contributors' clinical accounts, and their ideas about their technical and theoretical implications, are in the well-established tradition of psychoanalytic research emerging from experiences in the consulting room, and provide thought-provoking findings, particularly when viewed as a whole.

Together with an Independent mindset, an empiricism characterised by Rayner (1991: 4) as 'a natural leaning towards experiment and trial and error', there are a number of Winnicottian concepts and theories which greatly influence what Independent clinicians working with children and young people currently do in the therapeutic encounter. They seem to group naturally around the following:

- that the individual's emotional life and development are inseparable from the environment in which it takes place – making the interaction of the internal world and external world a central concern in all therapeutic work, in the development of theory and in the creativity of practice;
- the implications of the Winnicottian connection between 'playing', 'therapeutic communication' and the therapeutic process;
- the idea that therapeutic work takes place in a transitional area which is effectively co-created by the therapist and the patient, unique in each patient–therapist dyad;
- the developmental achievement inherent in enabling patients to experience 'the capacity to be alone' in the presence of the therapist in a manner which brings a reflective quality to the transitional area of experience;
- the necessity of working with defences against anxiety in a way which gradually unfreezes, detoxifies, or neutralises them within the holding therapeutic relationship, allowing the patient to let them go when he or she no longer needs them.

It has become evident that the contributors to this volume think about the child's emotional well-being as inseparable from the environmental provision he or she is currently experiencing, as well as what he or she has experienced in the past. This is particularly evident in the chapters by

Bailey, Dowling, Gibbs and Hamilton, but is implicit in all the clinical work presented here. The continual interaction of the child's internal and external worlds requires that the therapist be prepared to engage thoughtfully with both. The difficulties that this raises in terms of confidentiality are felt to be outweighed by the advantages of the improved therapeutic communication that emerges in the consulting room as well as with the parents, carers and professionals who play such key roles in child and adolescent patients' lives.

The significance of the connection between playing and the therapeutic process is a key concept that, we realised early on in this process, greatly influences our work. Winnicott writes about 'playing' in an evocative and at times elusive way. This is both a strength and weakness in his writing. He is not definitive about what he means, but the more one reads his work, the more the idea takes root. In this volume, we have thoughts about the value of the playful presence of the therapist, the therapist's ability to allow herself to see the funny side of some of the clinical situations she finds herself in – and how this can be therapeutic and lead to change within the therapeutic process. We do not see this playful responsiveness in the therapist as technically 'incorrect', but as facilitating the whole creative process of therapy. It combines the Independent understanding that it is not possible to be utterly 'neutral' (so better to understand and use this) with the 'serious play' of analysis that takes place in the me–not me space (Bollas 1987).

Winnicott's ideas about playing are intrinsically linked to his interest in the rich potential of transitional experiences, and the environmental provision that enables these experiences to take place. A good deal of the initial phase of a child or young person's therapy can be conceptualised as the gradual adaptation of the therapist to the patient's need for a particular kind of therapeutic environmental provision. Through the therapist's growing ability to 'hold' the patient in mind in a manner that is unique to each patient–therapist dyad, a transitional space can be conceptualised within which free and spontaneous playing can occur. The patient starts to have new ideas. This space is transitional, because it lies in-between the internal and external world in a way that can tolerate the paradoxes this presents (Winnicott 1971). Hopkins uses this idea in thinking about what she sees as the 'transitional relationship' between herself and her deeply regressed patient. Bailey writes about the transitional space that she arrives at when working with the parents of adolescents, in which all the internal and external issues surrounding the adolescent can co-exist, in all their messiness and contradictions, and be held in mind by the therapist. It is this technical skill of the therapist that she sees as paving the way to some creative resolution of the *impasse* they have all reached.

The difficulty of working with very damaged patients, who have erected what may have been life-protecting defences in order to cope with terrifying and overwhelming internal and external events, has long been a rather contentious psychoanalytic issue. The contributors to this volume use many different approaches, which seem to be underpinned by reaching towards ways of communicating helpfully and therapeutically with the patient in whatever ways seem to work. Hopkins describes her decision to work with the positive regressive state that her patient could reach at times, and sees this as 'unfreezing' or 'de-constructing' the defence and the underlying anxiety. The editors share her experience that the therapist's ability to be playfully present is another path towards 'antidoting' or 'detoxifying' the emotional issues that are locked up behind extreme defensiveness. Hamilton views the symptom that the mother–infant couple bring to her as the 'best solution' they have been able to find, before seeking therapeutic help – a very Winnicottian and Anna Freudian view of how defences come to be structured. The mother, due to her early life experiences and feelings of severe rejection, was unable to cope with ordinary separateness and separation and the ordinary process of mourning as a part of positive developmental progression. Interpreting the symptom to the mother in this more positive light is an example of therapeutic communication that could be heard by the mother as it eased its way behind her vulnerability to feeling that she was criticised and a bad mother.

Dowling sees the provision of a therapeutic experience, in which the often very psychologically damaged parents she is working with can feel 'alone in the presence of someone', as enabling them in turn to provide this valuable experience to their children. This is another way of communicating with highly defensive patients. Additionally, this Winnicottian concept of the value of the 'capacity to be alone' connects to ideas about the need gradually to grow or enlarge the capacity for reflective thought in the patient. The transitional space within the therapeutic relationship is then also a space within which it becomes possible for reflective thought to take place.

The influence of Winnicott and post-Winnicottian thinkers has been evident. The applications described in this volume demonstrate that the empirical creativity of the Independent and independent mind is still alive and well in psychoanalytic child and adolescent psychotherapy. Lomas comes to mind:

> An independence of mind is absolutely necessary if Freud's work is not to be permitted to stagnate. Scientists must be allowed to have ideas that depart from accepted thinking, and artists need to be free to paint what they are inspired to paint. Psychotherapy is no different. . . . Unfortunately, practitioners do, in fact, tend towards a 'special clique' and to think and feel in terms of the clique. Those of independent mind who wish to break out into a wider world inevitably face intellectual and professional conflicts. . . . If psychoanalysis is to grow and flourish, it needs to be taught, practised and discussed in a way that reduces this cost. The greatest potential for psychoanalysis, to my mind, lies in bringing the discipline out into a wider world in which ordinary language, morality and ways of being are central to the endeavour.
>
> (Lomas 2002: 92–3)

References

Bollas, C. (1987) *The Shadow of the Object: Psychoanalysis of the Unthought Known*. London: Free Association Books

Casement, P. (2002) *Learning from our Mistakes*. Hove, UK: Brunner-Routledge

Heimann, P. (1960) 'Counter-transference'. Reprinted in *About Children and Children-No-Longer: Collected Papers 1942–1980*, ed. M. Tonnesmann. London: Routledge, 1989

Heimann, P. (1965) 'Comment on Dr Kernberg's paper on "Structural derivatives of object relationships"'. Reprinted in *About Children and Children-No-Longer*, ed. Tonnesmann

King, P. (1978) 'Affective responses of the analyst to the patient's communication' *International Journal of Psychoanalysis* 59: 329–34

Lomas, P. (2004) 'The question of independence in psychotherapy'. In J. Pearson (ed.), *Analyst of the Imagination: The Life and Work of Charles Rycroft*. London: Karnac

Rayner, E. (1991) *The Independent Mind in British Psychoanalysis*. London: Free Association Books

Rycroft, C. (1956) 'The nature and function of the analyst's communication to the patient'. Reprinted in Rycroft, *Imagination and Reality*. New York: International Universities Press, 1968

Rycroft, C. (1958) 'An enquiry into the function of words in the psycho-analytical situation'. Reprinted in *Imagination and Reality*

Index